Louis and Clara Lewin, circa 1890

Across the USA and Canada in 1887

A German Scientist Experiences North America

by
Dr. Louis Lewin

Translated into
English from the German original
by
Herta Jaffe and Daniel Sachs

iUniverse, Inc.
Bloomington

Across the USA and Canada in 1887
A German Scientist Experiences North America

Originally published in German by Bo Holmstedt and Karl-Heinz Lohs (Berlin: Akademie Verlag, 1985) (2d ed. 1990), ISBN 3-540-52518-1.

iUniverse books may be ordered through booksellers or by contacting:

iUniverse
1663 Liberty Drive
Bloomington, IN 47403
www.iuniverse.com
1-800-Authors (1-800-288-4677)

ISBN: 978-1-4620-1952-6 (sc)
ISBN: 978-1-4620-1953-3 (ebk)

Printed in the United States of America

iUniverse rev. date: 08/23/2011

Dedication

This English-language translation is dedicated to the memory of all those who have gone before and upon whose shoulders we stand, and in particular to

- Louis Lewin, my greatgrandfather, born Tuchel, West Prussia 1850, died Berlin 1929.

- Clara Lewin, his wife, born Osnabrück, Germany 1858, perished in 1943 at Theresienstadt concentration camp, Czechoslovakia.

- Their daughter, Gertrud Lewin Marcuse Landsberg, born Berlin 1884, perished in 1944 at Theresienstadt concentration camp, Czechoslovakia.

- Their daughter, Herta Lewin Jaffe, born Berlin 1886, died Yifat, Israel, 1988.

- Their daughter, Irene Lewin Sachs, born Berlin 1888, died New York, 1985.

"May the memory of the saintly be a blessing."

Daniel Sachs
Bethesda, Maryland, USA
March 2011

Acknowledgments

I recognize and honor the vital contributions of those who played a role in bringing these letters to the English-speaking public:

- to Louis Lewin, the author of these letters;

- to his wife, Clara, who saved them for decades and gave them to her daughters for safekeeping;

- to their youngest daughter, Irene Lewin Sachs, who preserved the letters for further decades and turned them over for publication in the German original;

- to their middle daughter, Herta Lewin Jaffe, who translated the letters into English;

- to Professor Bo Holmstedt of the Karolinska Institute in Stockholm and Professor Karl-Heinz Lohs of the University of Leipzig, whose respect for Louis Lewin caused them to have his letters published in German in 1985 by the Akademie Verlag, Berlin;

- to Hilla Giladi, Herta Jaffe's grandniece, who preserved the typewritten manuscript in the English translation and provided it to me;

- and to my wife, Ruth; my brother, Benjamin; and my children, Julia Loeb, George Sachs and Noah Sachs. Each of them gave generously of their talents in the editing and revision of the Introduction and in the production of this book.

Daniel Sachs

Table of Contents

Introduction

This travel diary, the journal of the travels of Dr. Louis Lewin through Canada and the United States in the summer of 1887, is an important addition in two genres: the literature of the history of medicine and the literature of the European scientist of the nineteenth century assessing the progress of the United States, a booming nation soon to take its place among the Great Powers.

Louis Lewin: Professor, Scientist, Author, Advocate

Louis Lewin was eminently qualified to undertake his seven-week journey in 1887 to North America and to play the part of the careful observer. As a scientist, he could objectively evaluate the state of medical education in the United States and Canada and collect material for further research. Moreover, as a scientist, he had a keen eye for detail, and for assembling those little details into a harmonious whole. As a Jew, an outsider, he could understand the plight of those less fortunate than he, and could appreciate the contributions that they were making, and would continue to make, in the industrialization of the continent. Perhaps also because of his modest upbringing and subsequent transformation into an educated German, he had a keen eye and ear for what was authentic and what was phony, for cant and for humbug.

Particularly in the fast-moving world of science and technology, we are so caught up in the newest and latest that we often forget the contributions made by earlier scientists, those who laid the foundations for the discoveries and inventions of more recent generations. These scientists did not have at their disposal the electron microscopes, Hubble telescopes and other tools that researchers use today. Nor did they have a pool of volunteers willing to subject themselves to research and experimentation, as is now the norm. When research subjects were needed, the scientists exposed themselves, often at great personal risk, to the substance which they were studying. Louis Lewin was of that school, ingesting hallucinogenic drugs and carefully noting their effects on him. He deserves to be remembered today, eighty years after his death, as one of those men who laid the foundations of his discipline, psychopharmacology.

It gives me great pleasure to bring to an English-reading audience this journal of Lewin's seven-week journey across the United States and Canada. There is much to learn from these letters about the man, his strengths and his foibles, and about his impressions of the North America of 1887.

Louis Lewin was born on November 9, 1850, in the town of Tuchel, at that time part of West Prussia and now, renamed Tuchola, part of Poland. His father, Hirsch Apfelbaum, was born and spent his early years in Suwalki. Today, that town lies in northeastern Poland but at various times in its history it has also been under the control of Lithuania, Russia, and Prussia. Hirsch Apfelbaum, later Lewin, had fled westward from Suwalki to escape anti-Jewish pogroms.

Louis Lewin had been born on the family's westward journey. In 1856, Hirsch and his wife, with Louis and their two daughters, settled illegally in Berlin, a city which at that time was growing from a sleepy provincial capital into a booming world-class metropolis. At some point in their journey westward they changed their family name from Apfelbaum to Lewin, a name still distinctly Jewish, but less identifiable as *Ostjüdisch* (Eastern Jewish). Having settled the family in Berlin, Hirsch, a traditional Orthodox Jew with a minimal formal education, made a bare-sustenance living for his family as a shoe-repairer.

In those days, Jewish immigrants from the East were concentrated in a neighborhood in Berlin's *Mitte*, or core, known as the *Scheunenviertel* (the "Barn-Quarter"). That's where the Orthodox Jewish synagogues were concentrated, as were the *mikvahs* (ritual baths), the kosher butchers and the other establishments which met the ritual needs of an Orthodox Jewish family, and that's where the Yiddish dialect was spoken that Hirsch Lewin and his family brought with them on their flight westward. The main thoroughfare in the *Scheunenviertel*, the place where Jewish businesses and institutions were concentrated, was the *Grenadierstrasse*, and it was to the *Grenadierstrasse* that Hirsch Lewin brought his wife and their three children when they arrived in Berlin. The *Scheunenviertel* of Louis Lewin's childhood was a deplorable urban slum: living conditions were harsh, sanitation rudimentary, education minimal and malnutrition and social pathology rampant. Withal, it was also a vibrant center of social and cultural life and dissent of all kinds, from the far-right to the far-left.

Louis Lewin's childhood was by no means an easy one. As a boy, he attended a Jewish day school, a *cheder*. The urge to learn must have been awakened early in him, and his strong interest and aptitude in the sciences brought him to the attention of the teachers at the *cheder*. They told his parents that the traditional Jewish education could not bring out the best in a boy so obviously talented in the sciences, and that they, the boy's parents, would be acting in his best interest if he were enrolled in a secular secondary school, the *Friedrich Werdersche Gymnasium*.[2] This was the same Gymnasium that the famous German-Jewish poet Heinrich Heine and other illustrious Germans had attended.

His father wanted no part of the change in his son's schooling; the limited education that had been good enough for him would serve young Louis as well. Perhaps he feared also that a secular education would spur his son to put his Orthodox Jewish upbringing behind him. But Lewin's mother, Rachel, saw the wisdom in what her son's teachers were proposing, and prevailed on her husband to consent to the proposed move. Of course, another hurdle remained: the Gymnasium was not tuition-free, and for the Lewin family the payment of their son's tuition was out of the question. Providence intervened: a full tuition scholarship opened the door for Louis into this new world.

Still, there were other obstacles to overcome. The process of acculturation, from the narrow world of the *Scheunenviertel* to the wider world of modernism, was not an easy one. When he first entered Gymnasium, Lewin could not yet speak fluent German; at home, he and his family spoke a mixture of Yiddish and German. This marked him as an outsider to his classmates, the target of much teasing and humiliation. He would remember those childhood humiliations for the rest of his life; they must have contributed to his prickly disposition, his alertness to slights both real and perceived.

Among those who taught Lewin at the Gymnasium, one man was to have an enormous influence on him: Paul Anton de Lagarde,[3] later to become Professor of Oriental Languages at Göttingen University and one of the most learned men of his time. De Lagarde encouraged Lewin to obtain a University-level education, advocated on his behalf for Lewin's admission to the Friedrich Wilhelm University,[4] and, during his years there, helped him financially. Ironically, de Lagarde in his later years became an outspoken anti-Semite. He regarded the Jews as a cancer, and went so far as to urge that they be exterminated. Amazingly, the friendship between these two men, Lewin, the Jew, and de Lagarde, the anti-Semite, continued unabated until the latter's death in 1891, notwithstanding the ideological gulf between them.

After graduating from Gymnasium, Lewin began his medical studies at the University. There he acquired a working knowledge of French, as well as Greek, Latin and Hebrew. After writing a prize-winning doctoral dissertation entitled, "Experimental Researches on the Effect of Aconitines[5] on the Heart," he graduated in 1875 with a medical degree.

It was probably at this time in his life that Lewin shed the orthodox

Jewish coloration of the *Grenadierstrasse* and took on a Western style of thinking and acting. One can well imagine that this created a powerful internal tension in his thinking and conduct between the "old" Lewin and the new one, and perhaps an external conflict with his parents and former friends as well. He did not, however, cut his ties with his Jewish faith, as so many other acculturated Jews of his generation did. Even though he now assumed the aura of the "Western man of science," responsive to the new ideas that were exploding in the Europe of the 1870's and 1880's, he remained an observant Jew in many respects. He continued to observe the Sabbath, walking on Saturdays the considerable distance from his elegant home in the Tiergarten section of the city back to the *Scheunenviertel* to pay his respects to his parents. On departing from his parents' home, he took care to leave with them a 20-Mark gold piece, to try to ease their financial burdens.

At the same time, there were elements of his former life that he firmly turned his back on. Foremost of these was the *Ostjüdische* culture of the *Scheunenviertel*. It was a rule at the family dinnertable that Yiddish was not to be spoken there. His children were not permitted to use even the familiar Yiddish expressions that were then (and today) used even by otherwise assimilated Jews.

After completing the compulsory one year of military service, Lewin worked for a time in Munich under Pettenkofer[6] and Voit.[7] Through his work with Pettenkofer, he became aware of the public-health dimensions of the social problems which were all too familiar to him from his childhood; he was later to use this scientifically-oriented approach in dealing with the industrial hygiene issues submitted to him for his expert opinion.

On returning to Berlin, Lewin became an assistant to Liebreich[8] and gained his habilitation[9] from the Friedrich Wilhelm University as an instructor in Pharmacology, Toxicology and Hygiene.

In 1883 Lewin married Clara Bernhardine Wolff, whom he had met during a brief stay in Hamburg. The daughter of Benjamin Wolff, a *melamed*, or private tutor in Jewish subjects, she was born in Osnabrück, in Westphalia, and had been raised in Hamburg. Louis and Clara Lewin were to have three daughters: Gertrud, born in 1884, Herta, born in 1886, and Irene, born in 1888.

In 1893 Lewin gained the title of Professor (it appears that, in the Germany of that day, one could have the right to that title without being formally attached to a University faculty). Only in 1919, when he was 69, was he named Honorarprofessor in the Technical High School in Charlottenburg and, soon thereafter, Adjunct Professor at the Friedrich Wilhelm University. However, he never attained the tenure which his academic achievements surely entitled him to, because the price of tenure was conversion to Christianity, and this was a price that he was unwilling to pay.

In an appreciation which appeared in the *Frankfurter Allgemeine Zeitung* on January 24, 1930, after Lewin's death, Dr. Richard Koch[10] wrote that, "Until his last breath," Lewin "enjoyed a comforting pride in adhering to the beliefs of his ancestors." Perhaps it was that "comforting pride" that prevented Lewin from succumbing to what Dr. Koch referred to as "that corrosive bitterness that other men were subject to, at finding their career path obstructed by obstacles having nothing to do with their professional abilities."

On his return to Berlin from Munich in 1878, the University did not offer him a teaching position, despite the brilliant record that he had compiled there as a medical student. Consequently, he opened his renowned lecture hall in rented quarters at Ziegelstrasse 3, establishing himself there as a *Privatdozent*, an academic who did not have formal faculty status at the University. Fortunately, Lewin's scientific talents and his skill in presenting them to students were such that they were willing to pay at the door to hear his lectures, even though his course was not part of the university curriculum and his students could have met the requirements for graduation without paying extra to hear his lectures.

One of his students, Siegfried Loewe,[11] recalled that

> Lewin's lectures were always meticulously prepared. I don't remember a single instance when an experiment which he had set up and was demonstrating to his rapt audience didn't work out as it was supposed to. The outlines of his lectures were always written out on the blackboard without a single erasure. Lewin spiced up his presentations by throwing out questions at his audience. His private lecture-room was as crowded at the end of the semester as at the beginning. . . . All in all, Louis Lewin's course was my favorite recollection from my student days. He was, it is fair to say, a man who— as a scientist, as teacher, and as a man—was held in the highest esteem, a man who sought, and found, the hearts of his students.

Lewin's talents extended beyond the purely academic. He had a sophisticated appreciation for the arts, especially for sculpture, and was a skilled sculptor in bronze, who enjoyed making three-dimensional copies of classical Greco-Roman figures. One of his students, W. Rosenstein, wrote in his memoirs (1930) that characteristic of his multifaceted talents were his deep insights into the fine arts. In him were united a deep understanding for the masterpieces of old with a completely unusual skill in handicrafts. In the intervals between two lectures one could often see him, in a small room off of the auditorium, artfully chiseling away at a bronze sculpture.

Rosenstein recalled that Lewin had an acute intellectual honesty and required it in no lesser degree of his colleagues.

> His assessments of other scientists could be cutting, sometimes even scathing, but even so, those who were on the receiving end of his criticisms understood that he was animated by only one desire: the discovery of the truth. If and when his position stood in contradiction to that of the prevailing scientific opinion, neither the number nor the prominence of those who opposed his position could divert him from what he saw as the correct view.

This somewhat harsh judgment of Lewin is echoed by R. K. Müller, who wrote in Lewin's *Festschrift*[12] that

> It is certainly true that, at times, Lewin failed to recognize the limits of his knowledge and was reluctant to admit error even when he was shown to have been wrong. To accept this weakness on his part one must still grant that, more often than not, he was right; still, it was a failing of his. But who among us would keep a reckoning, that a man as brilliant and with such a universality of spirit as Lewin's would still show weaknesses? On the contrary, they shield us from the tendency to make heroes out of mere historical constructs, which we should guard against in our depiction of men of flesh and blood.

Whether because of professional jealousy or anti-Semitism on the part of his colleagues or, on his part, his prickly disposition or the stubbornness with which he clung to his scientific theories and refused to surrender his religious convictions, relations were not good between the eccentric and independent-minded Lewin and the medical-school faculty of Berlin University. A cartoon from the 1920's [*see page xv*], shows Lewin's isolated position clearly, even though he was one of the most distinguished academics of his time. It shows the renowned faculty of the Berlin University School of Medicine dragging a wagon up a steep hill toward its peak, the peak having on it a signpost labeled, in Latin, "To the Greater Glory of Medicine." Marching with his colleagues is the pathologist Otto Lubarsch,[13] dean of the medical school faculty at that time. Lubarsch, a Jew, was later to become an apostate and a vocal supporter of the Hitler regime, but his apostasy and vocal anti-Semitism didn't protect him: during the Nazi regime he was removed from his post as dean. The only faculty member who is not marching up the hill in the van of the wagon, or seated atop it, is Lewin; he is shown seated on a step at the rear of the cart, holding a vial of poison, his back turned to his colleagues.

Berlin University Medical School Faculty, 1920's

Politically, Lewin was a radical, opposed to the ruling Prussian regime, and a strong advocate for Germany's underclass. He was an associate of August Bebel[14] and corresponded with Karl Liebknecht[15] on worker-health protection issues and industrial hygiene. He also served on the governing body of the organization that administered the local homeless shelter, serving in that capacity with Bebel and Rosa Luxemburg.[16] When the Weimar Republic first came into power in 1918, Lewin welcomed it, but his enthusiasm later changed to disillusionment. Whether he was ever a member of a political party is not known, although he was certainly aligned in his political beliefs with the Social Democrats.

His strong sympathies with the working class undoubtedly originated in his poverty-stricken days as a boy in the *Scheunenviertel*. Given those sympathies with the downtrodden, it is not surprising that he turned his knowledge of chemistry and toxicology to good use in advocating strongly for protective labor legislation and industrial hygiene. He wrote in the 1922 *Deutsche Revue* that

> Whoever among civilized men owns property which may be dangerous to others has a duty to do his utmost to abate those dangers or to shut them down altogether. The duty is owed not only on legal grounds, but by all those who benefit from wage labor of any kind, whether physical or intellectual.

Lewin repeatedly emphasized this position in his writings, seeking always to protect industrial workers from poisons and other injuries. So it was a logical consequence of Lewin's thinking on this subject that, in his book, *Die Gifte in die Weltgeschichte* (Poisons in History,[17] in the chapter dealing with the military uses of poison gases, he wrote clearly and unequivocally that

> Among men the ugliest of weapons is poison [*gas*], which reappeared in Europe as a weapon that can wreak destruction from afar, after it had disappeared from Europe for centuries out of reluctance [*to use it*] on moral grounds.

Lewin went on to say that military necessity can never justify or excuse the use of poison gas. He expressed this point even more precisely a few years later in the fourth edition of his *Textbook of Toxicology*:

> Poisons are disloyal weapons, and whoever uses them, with the intention of inflicting grave harm upon the enemy, is an outlaw power which places itself outside the norms of the law of nations. If ever men in leadership would quietly and dispassionately heed their noblest feelings—which is, unfortunately, inconceivable—then they would be gripped by a sense of shame about all that is perpetrated in the name of what is most hateful in war, and the first and foremost of these is that infamous weapon, poison gas.

Early in 1929, Lewin spoke out at a conference of the Women's League for Peace and Freedom[18] against poison-gas warfare. Despite the illness which was to cause his death some ten months later, Lewin could not pass up the opportunity to participate in this event, to speak clearly and distinctly against the use of poisons for military purposes. His appearance at this conference, in his last year of life, demonstrates Lewin's combative spirit: he called situations and persons fearlessly as he saw them. Another student, Wolfgang Heubner, said of Lewin that "wasn't content to be numbered among the satisfied ones [or *"appeasers"*]," that he had to be engaged in the daily tumult of life.

Lewin's earliest books dealt with the effects of alcohol and morphine. He was one of the first scientists to study the medical and biological effects of morphine. Cocaine also interested him. In describing this drug in 1885, he came into conflict with Sigmund Freud, an advocate of the use of morphine and cocaine.[19] Lewin was among the first to show that the use of the two drugs in combination was dangerous. Lewin and Freud had other differences as well, relating to the latter's pioneering work in psychoanalysis. Lewin never understood Dr. Freud, referring to him sarcastically as "Joseph the Dream-Interpreter."

His two books, *The Side-Effects of Medications* (1st ed. 1881, 3d ed. 1899) and his *Textbook of Toxicology)* (1885, 4th ed., under the title *Poisons and Poisonings*, Georg Stilke 1929) demonstrate Lewin's amazing knowledge of medications and poisons. In 1905, he was a co-author, with H. Guillery, of *Die Wirkungen von Arzneimittel und Gifte auf der Auge* [*The Effects of Medications and Poisons on the Eye*]. Later came books on blood poisoning, on the detection of the smallest traces of arsenic in the blood and on carbon monoxide poisoning. In the last decade of his life, he presented his wide audience with two especially handsome books: in 1920, *Poisons in World History* (Berlin, J. Springer), and, in two printings, *Phantastica, The Tranquilizing and Excitant Drugs* (1924 and 1927),[20] the latter a book that tells, in artful language, the story of poisons and their effects on the workings of the mind. These two books were made available again in reprints after World War II.

For many years, Lewin had a particular interest in the effect on the blood of toxins such as hydroxylamine, phenyl-hydroxylamine, phenylhydrazine, and nitrobenzene. Using a spectroscope, he was able to identify the changes in the blood resulting from these toxins, having earlier in his life conducted his own research in this area (published as *The Spectroscopy of Blood*, 1897).

As a scholar-expert, Lewin enjoyed the highest reputation. He was much sought-after for expert opinions in that branch of forensic sciences that deals with toxins, and published a volume of his opinions on that subject (Leipzig 1912). These opinions were often thought to be controversial, but were motivated by a strong desire to protect workers in the workplace. He was predisposed to use his intellect on behalf of the oppressed, for those working with poisonous metals and chemicals, and for those caught up unjustly in the toils of the justice system.

Lewin continued to be productive until the end of his days. In the late 1920's there was a renewed interest in psycho-pharmacology in Germany and elsewhere. Lewin and others became interested in the properties of the South American beverage extract, *Banisteria Caapi*,[21] lecturing on this subject before the Berlin Medical Society on February 13, 1929. Lewin was already old and sick by that time, but he managed despite his infirmities to complete his monograph, entitled *Banisteria Caapi, a New Narcotic Drug and Pharmaceutical*.

In 1926, Lewin suffered a stroke from which he never fully recovered. Three years later, in 1929, Lewin developed sepsis, evidently the result of leukemia. He continued to lecture for a while, but eventually had to be admitted to the clinic on *Ziegelstrasse*—next door to his laboratory. He died there on December 1, 1929, at the age of 79.

Commemorating the 50th anniversary of Lewin's death, the German-Swiss medical historian Erwin H. Ackerknecht (1906-1988) wrote in an appreciation of his life these bitter words:

> [W]hoever knew Lewin, honored him, loved him, finds a certain feeling of relief that it was granted to one of the greatest of the great Jews in German medical history to die before 1933.

It is true that he died four years before Hitler ascended to power as Chancellor as a result of the 1932 elections, but in his eight decades of life Lewin had seen in Germany, and had personally experienced, anti-Semitism in its many forms. Particularly in his last decade of life, having witnessed, or read about, assaults on Jews everywhere in Germany by members of the nascent National Socialist Party (the Nazis), he, with his usual prescience, was warning his family that Germany was no place for Jews. It may well be that it was because of his origins as an outsider, an *Ostjude*, that he saw clearly what native-born German Jews did not see and refused to see.

Dr. Richard Koch wrote of Lewin that

> In our times there are people who tap their potential in life in their own unique way and who by their stature and through their abundant accomplishments set themselves apart from others. Such men have become increasingly rare. Their disappearance makes the world poorer. Only after they are no longer among us do we realize who they were . . . Even though [*Lewin*] had a long and fulfilling life, he died with still more to give. Had he been given more time, he would undoubtedly have disclosed to us even more of the

competence with which nature had abundantly endowed him.

Assessing Lewin's life and his legacy, Dr. Koch wrote that

> The fundamental inspiration of his body of work came to him from that place where all exact research ends: from a religio-ethical predisposition and point of view that permitted no compromise, no trimming or deal-making. His warm humanity shines through from his hundreds of writings . . . and illuminates every course of lectures that he gave, and in the expert opinions that he wrote for the courts, in which he cut through the dry language of legal rights to the loftier terrain of human rights. And therein lies his true greatness.

Nothing remains to be said except to express the hope that the life and works of Louis Lewin have found their well-deserved enduring place in the history of medicine.[22]

Louis Lewin's Travel Journal

The reader of Louis Lewin's travel diary may be able to form his own direct impression of this extraordinary teacher-personality and of this truly endearing, although sometimes slightly cranky, man with a big heart and keen intellect. This travel diary also represents an interesting piece of cultural history in its description of a trip across the Atlantic in the early days of tourism. Readers of our own era, when travel by jet is commonplace and a trip across the Atlantic takes eight hours instead of nine days, as in Lewin's time, may find these impressions especially charming, giving them cause to meditate on the need for occasional "creative pauses" in their busy lives.

The Letters—an Introduction

Over a period of seven weeks, from August 1 to September 19, 1887, Louis Lewin and his uncle-by-marriage, John Rudolph Warburg,[23] traveled westward across Canada, returning across the United States, using trans-Atlantic ships, riverboats, coastal steamers and trains. Nowadays, a seven-week trip with the same itinerary might require a total of perhaps seven days of travel time, flying by airplane from point to point. Not so in 1887: of those 50 days of travel time, almost half of them were spent en route. Of course, there were compensations: Lewin was able to see at ground level much of the United States and Canada which we who fly over that same terrain by airplane cannot see, and form impressions of the landscape and of his fellow human beings and their works that we who speed aloft from point to point by airplane cannot develop.

We do not know what spurred Lewin to travel to North America. It may well be that Warburg initiated the idea and that Lewin was invited along as a travel-companion. Be that as it may, we may infer that Lewin had several purposes in mind in initiating or agreeing to undertake this journey. The first was, undoubtedly, to experience firsthand the continent that he was increasingly becoming aware of through his readings of scholarly research in medical journals. His visits to the Smithsonian Institution in Washington, D.C. and to the Parke Davis & Co. offices in Detroit fall under this heading. He also took the opportunity to inform himself of the state of medical education in this country, visiting, with mixed impressions, the medical schools of McGill University, Johns Hopkins University, the University of Pennsylvania and Harvard University. Secondly, it gave Lewin the opportunity to do some on-site research in his field, pharmacology, with special emphasis on intoxicants and hallucinogens. That explains his visit to an opium den in San Francisco's Chinatown and his interest in the Smithsonian Institution collection of flora. His concern for industrial hygiene and worker health is evidenced by his interest in the skin disorder manifested by employees of oil refineries. On his return to Germany, he would write up this last, feeling that he had, so to speak, "scooped" his professional competition in describing this disorder and its likely causes.

The third purpose was to attend the International Medical Congress held in Washington, D.C. that year, and, in that connection, to promote himself among his professional colleagues. He had not been scheduled to give a paper at the Congress,[24] although he was already then, in 1887, at age 37, one of the rising international figures in his field, but he might have attended the conference, just as we would today, to gain exposure and make valuable contacts in his areas of specialization.

At the time of their journey to America, Lewin's travel companion, John R. Warburg, was 77, 40 years older than Lewin. We are told in the letters that Warburg, referred to throughout in the letters as "Uncle," had already visited America some forty years earlier. He was an ideal travel-partner for Lewin, for three reasons: first, he spoke English well, while Lewin spoke it not at all, so that Warburg throughout their travels served as an on-the-scene interpreter for Lewin. Second, Lewin, while no longer poor, had not the financial resources to undertake a journey of this dimension. Warburg was, in contrast, financially very well-off, and undoubtedly picked up most of the costs of the trip. It was his wealth that enabled the pair to stay in the best hotels in every city that they visited. Thirdly, Warburg faced with equanimity the aggravations that one encounters as a traveler, in contrast to Lewin's irascibility and his impatience with such difficulties.

The journey served Warburg's interests as well: in addition to his obvious interest in again seeing first-hand how North America had changed in the four decades since his first trip, we learn from the letters that he had business connections in many of the cities that they visited, and sometimes allowed Lewin to pursue his professional interests while he, Warburg, met with his associates in the firm's offices across the United States and Canada. Having in mind his advanced age, one can truly appreciate his gusto on this lengthy trip, the culinary deprivations that he and Lewin suffered, and the stamina required to put up with oceanic steamship travel and transcontinental rail travel in those days. Since Warburg died three years later, in 1890, one can only hope that it was not this strenuous trip that caused or contributed to his death.

We learn from these letters that during their entire journey, lasting seven weeks and covering some 6,000 miles, a journey during which Lewin and Warburg spent much of their time together in the same stateroom or train compartment, they by and large enjoyed each other's company. There are hardly any references to a falling out between the two of them. The exceptions might be the episode in the San Francisco brothel (*see p. 183*), and Uncle's refusal, until the early morning hours, to spend the night on the train in Vancouver (*see p. 69*). With those possible exceptions, the two travel companions stayed on good terms throughout, notwithstanding Uncle's advanced age, which required an extra measure of care and solicitude from Lewin.

Lewin's wife, Clara, remained behind in Germany to look after their two small daughters. It is well for us that she did, because Lewin, intensely devoted to her, spent a good portion of his free time in writing these lengthy letters to her, describing what he saw and setting down his musings about his sights and experiences. Perhaps these letters were the condition under which the journey was undertaken in the first place. That is to say, the bargain between them was that if she could not travel with him, he would at least keep her as fully informed as possible about the journey, so that she would get the full flavor of everything that he saw and did.

It is also fortunate for us that Lewin was, as one used to say in speaking well of someone, "a man of parts," with wide-ranging interests. In the course of these letters, we learn of his interest in structural engineering, as evidenced by his curiosity about the fabrication of the New York elevated lines and the Brooklyn Bridge, and about the trestles which carried his Canadian Pacific train over the deepest mountain gorges; in botany, particularly the flora at the higher elevations in the Canadian Rockies; in the Native Americans of Canada and the United States; and in his fellow-passengers, whether on the trans-Atlantic voyage, on the New York elevated, on trains, and ferryboats and steamers. We are privy, too, to his speculations as to the exhaustibility of natural resources, the nature of matter, and the economic growth potential of the cities which he visited and passed through.

Lewin's letters would have been tedious reading if, like lesser travel-diarists, he had limited his observations strictly to what he and Uncle did, what they saw, and whom they spoke to. But it is evidence both of Lewin's trained eye and of his loving relationship with his wife that he hid nothing from her and shared with her his deepest thoughts and emotions, giving us, more than a century later, a glimpse of his innermost self.

Tourists from the earliest days of travel to the present time have measured what was new to them in their travels against what they were familiar with from their homeland. It is human, and utterly normal, that what one sees abroad will be judged harshly by that standard. The hotel beds are not as comfortable, the food inedible, the manners of the locals intolerable, the storekeepers rude and out to cheat the visitor. The list of complaints is seemingly endless. One of the charms of Lewin's letters is that he is not at all hesitant to make these judgments and to report them to his wife, even when he knows, and we learn from the letters that his tendency to express derogatory opinions of his fellow human beings doesn't sit well with her.

Travelers take an especially keen interest in the quality of the restaurant food that they eat on their journey, and that was certainly true of Lewin and Warburg. As Lewin sat down to recall the events of the past days and transmit them in his letters to his wife, the meals that he ate, and those that he was offered and rejected, seemed to be uppermost in his mind. This culinary emphasis is evident almost as soon as he boards the S. S. *Hammonia* on his outward journey.

Sometimes, as in his visit to the beach at Long Branch, New Jersey, he takes one bite, realizes that the food is spoiled and pushes his plate away. At other times, he turns his nose up at the food offering even before tasting it. He makes a point of rejecting the steak that is offered to him again and again on his train journey across the United States, and particularly when the accompanying beverage is milk. Oh, the horror of it! This combination must have stirred in him some primordial revulsion, because observant Jews are forbidden to eat dairy and meat at the same time; the combination is taboo, un-kosher. At the same time, his orthodox Jewish upbringing did not prevent him from eating lobster, as at Long Branch, had it not been spoiled, perhaps by a lack of refrigeration, or to buy and eat dried cuttlefish in San Francisco's

Chinatown, or a savory oyster lunch in Philadelphia. Again and again, he reports in his letters that he and Warburg have passed up a meal altogether, preferring a bottle of ale or beer and some crackers to what was otherwise available. Less frequently, he and Warburg eat with gusto, complimenting the chef and even, in one case, expressing to him their "*höchsten Zufriedenheit*" (highest degree of satisfaction), the compliment that the Kaiser himself gave to vendors of goods and services when he was highly pleased with them. All in all, it is easy to come to the conclusion that, for the most part, Lewin did not relish the food that he ate in his travels across North America, and that he returned with great relief to his customary German food.

The observant traveler, wherever he goes, takes in the people who travel with him, and those who inhabit the cities, towns, and rural areas that he passes through and sees from his train, car or bus. That was especially true of Lewin, who had formed from his years in the university and laboratories the habits of detached observation. Of special interest to him were men and women whom he did not encounter in Berlin: blacks and Native Americans. Fifty years earlier, Alexis de Tocqueville, in his *Democracy in America*, had identified these two groups as sharing a common misery:

> These two unfortunate races have neither birth, nor face, nor languages, nor mores in common; only their misfortunes are alike. Both occupy an equally inferior position in the country that they inhabit; both experience the acts of tyranny; and if their miseries are different, they can blame the same author for them.

Even though the Civil War had been waged and won in the intervening years, Lewin reports that little had changed with respect to the position of these two minorities. He writes to his wife of his admiration for well-built black men (he calls them "Othellos") and of the apparent fondness of black women for brightly-colored clothes. He is "alarmed" by the wide grins of the darker-colored African-Americans, more specifically in the contrast between their white teeth and pink gums and their dark skin. He expresses pity for the degenerate condition of the Native Americans, is saddened by their depressed economic condition and at the same time conveys a deep respect for their essential nobility as the original owners of these lands. He commiserates with them—"So now they must labor and serve here who once were the owners and masters of this land!"—but infers that, despite their degraded condition, these natives "perhaps live in greater contentment than the white man, who has seen better things than he possesses and cannot attain them."

Lewin also encounters representatives of two groups with whom he is only too familiar: Germans, or, to be more precise, German-Americans, and Jews, and neither group comes off favorably in Lewin's judgments. Within his first days on board the *S.S. Hammonia*, he compares the multi-colored, ethnically diverse passengers in the *zwischendeck*, or steerage, to his fellow-passengers in the cabin classes, to the disadvantage of the latter. He enjoys the democracy of the have-nots, and their lack of inhibition, again comparing it favorably to the lethargy and faux dignity of the cabin-class passengers, many of whom, he notes, are Jewish bourgeoisie as he is. He also encounters Jewish merchants in his travels, and makes plain his contempt for them: "They are easily recognized, even if they don't look like Messrs. Isaacson and Goldstein, by the exorbitant prices they charge for curios." Clearly, in his opinion, they are out to play him and Uncle for suckers, having that trait in common with the German-American storekeepers and restaurant-owners, who serve him and Uncle inferior food at exorbitant prices. Just as we Americans, traveling abroad, are embarrassed by loud-mouthed fellow-Americans when they draw attention to themselves in a store or on the street, so it undoubtedly pained Lewin when his compatriots didn't measure up to his exacting standards.

Lewin's observations go far beyond the mundane reporting of meals eaten, people encountered and sights seen. He uses these visual impressions to reflect deeply on their significance and draws conclusions as to what the visual data might hold for the future. So, for example, he comprehends, although he is not trained as an economist or geographer, that the city of Vancouver, British Columbia, then in its infancy as a port, is likely to grow enormously because it represents the shortest route to the port of Yokohama, Japan, and that Detroit, because of its position on the border with Canada, would grow to become a much larger city. Of course, he is not always correct in his predictions, but is still confident enough to express them to his wife. Seeing the endless forests of Canada as he passes through them on the Canadian Pacific Railway, he predicts that "at some future time, when the last bit of coal will have been consumed, there will be enough trees left in Canada to supply Europe and the other continents with fuel." In the same vein, he marvels: "What an immense industry will rise and bloom here in the future, based only on this wealth of trees! How many millions of dollars are lying here!"

He could not have foreseen the emerging need for gasoline, derived from refined petroleum, in powering automobiles and engines of all kinds. Some of his predictions may yet prove correct:

> [T]his region [*Ontario*] is a match for the neighboring one in the United States. The future is here. When America becomes overpopulated and exhausted, then it will be

Canada's turn to produce what until now still lies unused in its virgin soil!

His lengthy trip across the North American continent serves at last to reinforce his patriotism, his love for Germany and things German: He condemns the United States as the "[l]and of rascals and scalawags," calling it a "sanctimonious nation" with respect to its hypocritical liquor laws. When told in San Francisco of the corruption that attended the construction of the new City Hall, he concludes that

> Only big time graft, trickery and dishonesty can account for it. They are indeed prevalent here in America, so grossly, so directly, so openly prevalent as nowhere else in the world, not even in Russia.

As he nears the end of his travels, he sings the praises of his native land, even in so small a detail as the marching abilities of American soldiers. After watching them parading on the drill grounds of a fort on the outskirts of Detroit, he writes: "What a mess they made of it! A Prussian sergeant would have torn his hair out in despair at the sight." He writes to Clara:

> I have come to see that we live in a truly blessed country. Think of the pleasures that we can enjoy for so little!

and, later on,

> No, I wouldn't even want to be buried in this country, to say nothing of living here! How fine a country Germany is! I have learned a lot on this journey, and that is perhaps the best lesson of all.

He could not know that, 30 years later, the sons of those ragtag marchers, perhaps, would help their British and French allies to defeat the Kaiser's armies on the Western Front in World War I. Nor could he, this proud German, know that, in the 1920's, the last decade of his life, as hooligans assaulted Jews in the streets of Berlin and other German cities, he would be forced to retreat from his German patriotism, to conclude that Germany was no place for Jews.

We see displayed in these pages as well an all-too-human tendency towards immodesty, together with an unbecoming sensitivity to slights, especially from those who do not fully appreciate his accomplishments. Lewin obviously had a large ego that needed constant massaging, mentally recording even the smallest snubs and indignities. In the opening paragraphs of his very first letter, written evidently before his ship has even cleared the North Sea coast of Germany, he writes of his pride in his achievements and expresses his hope that he will not be considered immodest for doing so. Objectively speaking, he had reason to be proud, considering how far he had come from his humble beginnings in the *Grenadierstrasse* of which he writes, but yet, it is startling to see a man's ego thus openly displayed, if only to his wife.

In later letters he writes with pride of those occasions when his fame has evidently preceded him and opened doors for him and for Warburg. Visiting the McGill University College of Medicine, he is bemused to see that the annual report of the pharmacologist "places great emphasis on knowledge of the 'untoward effects of drugs,'" a reference to the book that he had written on that subject, which had only recently been translated into English. Even the janitor at the Harvard Medical School is aware of his writings, and his *carte de visite* seems to open doors as if by magic! He dwells on those occasions when he sees things that can become the kernel of a new article that he can write for publication in a scholarly journal, such as the aforementioned skin eruption that he observes on the arm of a refinery worker, and hopes that no other scientist will beat him to the punch, as it were.

We see his pride displayed most transparently in his reports to his wife of the international medical congress that he attends in Washington, D.C. Speaking of his impromptu presentation at the meeting of his section, he writes that "Two more people came up to me, expressing—in broken German—their pleasure with my lecture. One of them made me laugh when he said, 'It was so dull in our section until you came.'" Of a German colleague, also attending the Congress, he writes that "He showed me some of his experiments, including a new reaction to lead—which I had published five years ago." Listening to another German scientist, several years his junior, reading his scientific paper, he stands up at the end of the presentation, derides it as old hat, and is forthwith invited to take over as chair of the next session.

At one of the conference sessions he encounters Dr. Paul Gerson Unna, a contemporary of his, also Jewish, whom he knew from Hamburg. Dr. Unna was later to be recognized as the father of modern dermatology. The two of them, Lewin and Unna, try to arrange a time to get together again later during the conference, but Dr. Unna's schedule is so full that he can only suggest that they meet again over breakfast. This social put-down so offends Lewin's sense of dignity, his *amour propre*, that, as he writes to Clara, he knows instantly that this planned get-together will never take place. But there is also a sense of wonderment at what he has accomplished:

Here in this distant continent I have found respect and appreciation, perhaps more than at home; if I were to go to India, I would find people there, too, who knew my name and would show their regard for what I have accomplished by obliging helpfulness.

But we must not over-emphasize these negative aspects of Lewin's nature. He had come far in his life, would go still farther, and had reason to be pleased at his success.

More significant than this petty self-flattery and one-upmanship are Lewin's judgments of Canada and the United States, and his extrapolations from what he saw to what he thought was in the offing in the years ahead. Remarkably, for he was not an economist or one knowledgeable in the uses and misuses of natural resources, he had much of value to say on this subject.

He marveled at America's natural resources, but saw difficulties ahead in the profligate use that was made of them:

> Mankind here is living as the beneficiary of Nature's riches. . . but woe betide them if Earth's prodigal hand closes—then they, like everyone at home, will have to work for a day's pay. Even so, this nation is inventive! They will always make more out of barren soil and rock than the Germans and, likewise, they use their natural riches in a grander manner than we would have done.
>
> However, in the final analysis it comes to the same thing: where so much is squandered, exhaustion sets in before long. If at present the simple worker must work as hard as his counterpart in Europe, the time will come for America too when work-performance and profit are so abnormally disproportionate that, on account of the higher prices for commodities, social misery here will be greater than at home.

He described marble as

> an overwhelming plenty which, however, will come to an end one day as everything in this world does. Marble is already being quarried from under the surface. More work, more sweat, is required to haul the material out from the interior of the earth and it will get more expensive accordingly. What

was valued but little at first because it was obtained in plenty and without toil is now highly appreciated.

Traveling across Canada, he marvels again and again at the wealth of natural resources, the timber that he could see in the endless forests through which the train passes:

> Think of what human hands have created here! How admirable the perseverance of these workers! Granted, it is the struggle for existence that brings such works into being, and there is no delight in success, no striving without self-seeking. Be that as it may, we admire the outcome as a sign of spiritual and technical human development.

On his return from this journey, he expressed to his family and colleagues his opinion that, within twenty years, the United States would overtake Germany as the premier industrial engine of the world, and in that he was proven correct.

Certainly, it was not Lewin's purpose in visiting America or in writing these letters to undertake a thorough analysis of the rich tapestry of contemporary American society and to draw comparisons with the society and culture of Wilhelmine Germany. He had not been commissioned by any publisher to write a book on his observations, with particular reference to any one subject, nor was his journey financed by a foundation which would expect a report on his return, as might be the case for an academic traveling today. He was simply writing letters home to his wife, Clara. Within that limited framework, his letters were perceptive enough. That said, there are important omissions which we, as 21st-century Americans having the perspective of the 120+ years since Lewin's journey, and with an awareness of the full span of history since then, can readily identify:

- He shows an utter lack of interest in American and Canadian history, politics and current events.

- For a man with a strong social conscience, forged in the poverty in which he was reared, it is noteworthy that he expresses no interest in the class struggle then being played out in America, other than to register his disgust at the poor public sanitation in Chinatown and at the hovels that he sees from his train window. The previous year, 1886, had witnessed one of the watershed events in American labor history, the confrontation of striking workers and management forces in Haymarket Square in Chicago, which resulted in the deaths of police officers, strikers and civilians. Five of the men indicted were German immigrants, and the appeals process was being played out in the very weeks that Lewin and Warburg were traveling in America. Lewin indeed during the appeals period spent a brief time in Chicago, a city which he found unimpressive. If he was at all aware that this was a city that had witnessed enormous turmoil the year before, turmoil that was even then still being played out, it is curious that there is no mention of these events in his letters.

- One would have expected that, as a humanitarian and as a physician with a strong altruistic streak, Lewin would have shown a greater concern for the health and safety of the workers who toiled under brutal conditions in the factories, refineries and quarries that he visited or viewed from the passing train. Yet we see none of that in these letters, with the exception of his interest in the oil refinery worker's skin rash, and that seems to been motivated by a self-serving interest in describing the condition in a forthcoming article. What we glean from these letters, instead, is a frequently-expressed admiration for the technological prowess that makes these massive industrial facilities possible.

- Montreal's bilingual culture seems to have been of no interest to him.

- While he notes the widespread presence of Chinese men in British Columbia and in San Francisco, he appears not to have given much thought to the reasons for their presence, and to the absence, by and large, of Chinese women.

- The trans-continental Canadian Pacific Railroad line, a daunting engineering feat, had opened only one year earlier, in 1886, but, again, this is not considered worthy of reporting.

- Although he spent several days in Washington, D.C., his mind seems to have focused almost entirely on the proceedings of the Medical Congress held there. Yes, he and Uncle sought to gain admission to the White House, only to find that visiting hours were over, but we do not find him inquiring about American politics, or comparing American politics to those of his homeland, either to praise them or to deprecate them. He has some acid comments about graft and corruption at the local level, but he imparts no information to his wife about the American political system, nor, evidently, did he discuss the subject with his American acquaintances, perhaps because of the language barrier.

- He is uninterested (at least as far as we can determine from his letters) in the Jewish communities in the cities which he visited or passed through. He comments acerbically on the Jews he encountered, as fellow-passengers on the S.S. *Hammonia,* and as the shopkeepers, minor hustlers and grifters with whom he dealt in Canada and the U.S. Lewin and Uncle were in Boston on September 19, 1887, the day of Rosh HaShanah, the Jewish New Year. It appears that they attended the synagogue services held at sunset on the previous day (the start of the Holy Day by Jewish reckoning) and on that day, but we are told nothing of the identity of the synagogue nor of Lewin's impressions of the services and the congregants, nor does he comment on differences in the religious worship as he observed it in America and what he was accustomed to in Berlin. This is of a piece with his lack of interest in the burgeoning Jewish communities in any of the cities which he visited on his North American travels.

- Only on a few occasions did Lewin and Warburg meet individual Americans in social settings, and these were without exception business associates of Warburg's. We can presume that, as they were German-Americans, the conversation was in German. Never during their seven-week journey did the two travelers meet socially with an American family, German-American or otherwise. Lewin was therefore not in a position to report to his wife—even if had dared to generalize from one such experience—on the American family, the American woman in a domestic setting, and the differences between the bourgeois home life in New York, San Francisco or Philadelphia on the one hand and Berlin and Hamburg on the other.

- Finally, there is no evidence that he prepared for the trip by reading the accounts of earlier German visitors to North America.[25] To be sure, he may have done this preparatory reading, and had some knowledge of these matters, but he simply doesn't refer to them in the letters.

The matters that he does refer to are so wide-ranging that these omissions will strike the reader as all the more surprising. It goes without saying that the omission of these issues from the letters may mean only that he found no reason to mention them in these letters to his wife. Perhaps he felt that these were background issues which would be of no interest to her. The emphasis, understandably, was on what he had personally experienced in the course of the day. Yet, those are, in many cases, only the jumping-off points for wide-ranging thoughts, giving us an insight into the real man, so it is curious that the matters highlighted above are not touched on at all or only by the least of references.

As we weigh the strengths and weaknesses of these letters, we need to keep in mind that, in his travels across Canada and the United States, Lewin was not a journalist on assignment. He probably did not anticipate that his letters would one day be collected and published. He was, however, a scientist, trained in the scientific discipline and blessed with a naturally curious disposition. He saw and absorbed what he encountered, but he did not go out of his way to obtain and assemble a full picture of all he saw.

We also learn from these letters that, while Lewin was writing to his wife, Warburg was keeping a diary and writing letters home to his wife. That these have not survived is unfortunate, because Warburg was writing from a perspective that Lewin could not have: his advanced age, and the fact that he had visited the U.S. and Canada forty years earlier. That would mean that Warburg came to America not many years after de Tocqueville wrote of his travels through America in 1835. The intervening years had seen America change from a collection of states, each pursuing its own interests, to a "United States," as a result of a horrific four-year civil war, and, largely as a result of the victory of the Union in that war, from an agrarian landholding society to an urban industrial society. That must have been a breathtaking transformation, especially to a businessman like Warburg.

Letter-Writing as an Art

Travel diaries, written by men who have visited exotic far-off places and wish to report to the ruler who financed their voyage, or to their fellow-merchants, or perhaps only to their own families, are certainly an ancient genre of letter-writing. One thinks, for example, of ibn Battuta's 14th-century narrative of his travels from North Africa to China and back, of the travels of Marco Polo, of Henry Timberlake's account of his travels in the Near East, of the diaries of Captain Cook's voyages to the Pacific, and of James Boswell's *Journey to the Hebrides* (1774).[26]

Journals, written after returning home, based on notes taken during the journey, have the great advantage over letters written and mailed during the journey that the author is writing them at his leisure. He has the time to expand and expound, to winnow out, to edit, even to embroider, should he choose to do so. Conversely, the weakness of letters is at the same time their greatest asset: their immediacy. In most cases, they are written the same day as the events described, or within a few days thereafter. The recipient of the letter reads it, too, with a sense of immediacy; he or she reads what the letter-writer has written, unmediated by any editor's blue pencil, or even by the second thoughts of the writer himself. The letter writer's judgments spill directly from his brain to the pen, and thence to the paper, and are read by the recipient in the same way.

The intimacy and immediacy of letters is, however, their main drawback as well. They are written in hotel rooms, and aboard trains or ships, in many cases when the writer is already exhausted after a long day of traveling and after having received countless perceptions, all of them new to him. Letters end, oftentimes, not when the writer has exhausted his storehouse of recollections of the day's impressions but when he is simply too tired to continue. Moreover, because of the compressed travel schedule, there is often too little time left in one place to report more fully on what was to be seen. On their journey westward across Canada, for example, Lewin's train stopped in many places for only an hour or less, scarcely time for Lewin and Uncle to alight from the train and try to get the sense of the place before getting back on the train again. We wish that Lewin had spent more time in Montreal and soaked in the bicultural uniqueness of the place; that he had sought to understand more fully the role of the Chinese laborers in the construction of the Canadian Pacific Railway; that he had described in even richer detail what he had observed of life in New York, and so on. But it did not happen, and was not to happen. Letter-writers seldom augment their letters, once written, with additional observations and thoughts on the events already written of. Nor do they, with an eye, perhaps, on future readers, supplement their letters with additional details upon returning home. As a consequence, we often find ourselves begging for more information, for more elaboration of details and for more expressions of opinion, but our fervent wishes of course go unanswered. We want more, but there is no more to be had.

A traveler who keeps a journal, expecting to publish it on his return home, has the luxury of rewriting and editing it before he submits it for publication. One who, like Lewin, simply writes letters home during his travels has no occasion, and no motivation, to edit them afterwards. Consequently, we may find inconsistencies when we read the letters in their entirety. It reminds us of the tale of the blind men and the elephant: the blind man feeling the trunk one day and the tail the next, will naturally have to revise his views of the elephant after the second day. So, too, with Lewin. He seems to have been of different views with regard to the exercise of personal freedoms that he encountered in America. On August 29, he wrote:

Liberty! A poor misused word: everybody attaches his own meaning to it. I think that the way a person defines liberty may provide a clue to his character. That liberty also means a restriction on individual freedom is a point that Americans don't seem to have grasped, so far as I have been able to determine.

Ten days later, on September 9, he expressed a more favorable view of the subject:

I am glad that in this way everyone [*in America*] is vouchsafed freedom of action and opinion. This kind of personal liberty is well worth emulating in Europe—even so, this kind of Liberty will never prevail with us.

Here, too, we wish that Lewin had been more explicit in setting out to his wife, and to us, his grounds for these judgments, his reasons for modifying them over that ten-day period, and for his belief that "this kind of Liberty will never prevail" in Germany.

Professor Eli Nathans has aptly said that "Observations regarding a foreign culture can serve as a key to understanding the culture of the observer."[27] Scores of Germans visited America in the 19th century and wrote of their observations and experiences to the larger German audience avid for such reports.[28] For the Germans of that time, the United States "represented a challenge impossible to ignore," because

the United States seemed to embody forces that were transforming Germany (and much of the rest of the world), because of its great military and industrial potential, and because millions of German emigrants had chosen it over their own country.[29]

The two most common reactions of 19th-century German travelers to America were "fascination and horror."[30] Lewin, a left-leaning liberal (to use today's terms), shared that fascination and horror with other German travelers of every political persuasion. German travelers of that time had a "surprisingly accurate understanding of much of what they saw."[31] That was true of Lewin as well, but he seems to have differed from other German travelers in that "their judgments of America were 'astonishingly positive.'"[32] Lewin found much in America that was worthy of export to Germany, but we glean from these letters that, on the whole, his judgment of the United States, based on this journey, was not favorable.

Moreover, the letter-writer filters his travel experiences and impressions through his own unique psychological drama. Just as two artists, standing side by side at their easels, may paint the same landscape yet create two very different paintings, so too, will two persons recalling, for example, an encounter with a waiter in a restaurant, report the event in very different ways. These impressions will also change over the years, as the Zeitgeist changes. It is well to keep this in mind when reading of Lewin's visits to an opium den and a brothel in San Francisco. In his Victorian bourgeois morality, Lewin was very much a product of his time. One example is his prudish reference to a toilet as "that other place." More significant as an example is his description of his visit to the San Francisco bordello. It gives us an insight into Lewin's close relationship with his wife that he even mentions this visit to her, but, having undertaken to describe it, Lewin leaves us hungering for further particulars, but he discreetly draws the curtain over that episode, beyond reporting his revulsion at the scene. We find ourselves wishing he had lingered within, as Uncle did, instead of bolting out as he said he did. On the other hand, his Victorian sense of propriety seems not to have been injured as he describes walking through his Pullman car and observing women, not yet dressed, in various states of deshabille. Indeed, he seems to take pleasure in their lack of affectation in doing so. Finally, his dependence on Uncle as an interpreter also prevented him from experiencing more of those delightful encounters with the "locals" which add a special zest to international travel.

Lewin's letters are valuable precisely because he is frank to write of his impressions, whether for good or bad. He is writing for his beloved wife, and, evidently, they communicate well, because on several occasions he enlarges on some pet theory of his, but leaves it to his wife to fill in the blanks, as it were, because she knows him so well, and has undoubtedly heard him express these ideas many times at the dinner table. Furthermore, although he may have been pleased that she saved his letters, indeed, may have requested that she do so, there is no evidence that he had in mind when he wrote them an audience larger than his wife and immediate family. We know that because of the many passages in which he expresses his love for her, and passages, as well, in which he makes personal observations regarding various family members, which he probably would have omitted had he anticipated that the letters would be read by a wider audience.

We are fortunate, too, that Lewin and Warburg took their seven-week journey in the days before every tourist was armed with a point-and-shoot camera. Indeed, they had not brought with them even such cameras as then existed. Had that not been the case, we would not have had from Lewin the lyrical descriptions of what he saw—the brownstones of Manhattan, the woodlands of Ontario, the sun rising over the train-tracks in the Rockies, the seamy underside of Chinatown. We would have instead a photo album of historically-important photographs, yes, but we would have been denied the pleasure of his word-pictures, that is to say, the detailed letters that he wrote back to his wife, as reprinted in translation in this book.

The Historical Context

For American schoolchildren studying American history, and, perhaps, the American public in general, the three decades between the end of the Civil War and, perhaps, the Spanish-American War, that is to say, from 1865 to 1898, are a vast whiteness, a period when seemingly not much of historical note took place. The presidents, Hayes, Garfield, Arthur, McKinley and their ilk, were colorless and forgettable. We know them, if at all, because of their bushy mustaches and full beards, and because two of them, Garfield and McKinley, fell victim to assassins' bullets.[33] It seems as if the era began with America licking its wounds from the Civil War, then fell into a torpor, and woke up some 30 years later, now a power on the world stage. Of course, that was not at all the case, and these letters, written over a seven-week period in 1887, roughly two-thirds of the way through that period of great "whiteness," touch on some of the reasons why.

It was, in truth, a three-decade period of enormous social change, technological innovation and demographic upheaval,[34] marked by

- *Massive in-migration.* The number of immigrants entering the United States in the 1880's almost doubled from the number that had entered in the previous decade, from 2,812,191 to 5,246,613. In the fifteen years 1871-1885, 1,500,000 Germans came to the United States; Germany was the largest single country of origin during that period. These immigrants provided a ready source of labor, fueling the aggregation of enormous industrial organizations. When that cheap labor was unfairly exploited, it led to industrial conflict which at times bordered on open class warfare. New immigrants often experienced grinding poverty, leaving them prey to crime or to a life of crime.

- *Technological innovation.* Lewin in his letters alludes to some of the inventions that revolutionized Western civilization, such as electric street-lighting and the ceiling fan. Other transformative inventions which have served mankind for better or worse that were invented in the years 1880-1887 (by Americans and Europeans) include the two-phase induction motor (Nicola

Tesla, 1883), the punchcard sorting machine, forerunner of the computer (Herman Hollerith, 1884), the first patent for a gas-fueled motor car (Daimler & Benz, 1885), and the gramophone record (Emile Berliner, 1887). Truly, Lewin was traveling in a time when scientific knowledge, both basic and applied, was exploding, here and in Europe. One can scarcely contemplate our civilization today without the technological advances that took place, in the United States and in Europe, in the years that preceded Louis Lewin's visit to America.

- *Exaggerated cycles of economic boom and bust.* The great leaps forward in technology and science had their seamy underside: grinding poverty, economic chaos and social unrest. The winter of 1887, just seven months before Lewin's arrival, saw a panic, with runs on the banks, massive failures of mercantile traders and financial institutions, and bitter labor conflict. That winter, too, had been bitterly cold, resulting in crop failures and livestock losses all across America's farm belt. One woman testified that

> Of that long, wretched winter following the panic of 1887 the memory can never be erased, never grow less bitter. The poverty, the misery, the want, the wan-faced women and hunger- pinched children, men tramping the streets by day and begging for a place in the police stations or turning footpads by night, the sordid, grinding, pinching poverty of the workless workers and the frightful, stinging, piercing cold of that winter in Kansas City will always stay with me as a picture of inferno such as Dante never painted.[35]

There were not yet in place in those years the regulatory systems which were later created to mitigate, or to seek to mitigate, the impact of swings in the business cycle.

- *Natural disasters.* On August 31, 1886, a severe earthquake, measuring 7.7 on the Richter Scale, struck Charleston, South Carolina, killing 60. Tornadoes ravaged the South and the Midwest, killing an estimated 800 people; another tornado, in April 1886, demolished the town of Sauk Rapids, Minnesota and killed 72 people.

- *Urban violence.* The newly urbanized areas were equally turbulent. In addition to the riot in Chicago's Haymarket Square, already referred to, there had been in 1886 a strike against the Union Pacific and Missouri Pacific railroads, involving more than 200,000 workers. The failure of that strike had led directly to the collapse of the Knights of Labor and the formation of the American Federation of Labor.

- *Fires, industrial accidents, transportation calamities.* The widespread innovations of the 1880's and earlier had their downside, as safety considerations were often subordinated to financial pressures. Steamships caught on fire, or their boilers exploded, with great loss of life. Buildings inexplicably collapsed. Trains derailed or collided; shouts of "Fire!" in crowded theatres caused stampedes and death, as fire codes did not keep pace with the realities of crowded places of public assembly. Industrial accidents and deaths were everyday occurrences, particularly in the mines, the steel mills and the railroads. Long hours, miserable working conditions and the widespread use of child labor led to the cry for reforms that would culminate 20 years later in the first protective labor legislation. The headlines tell the story:

CUT BY THE CELTIC'S BOW,
THE BRITANNIC NEARLY SUNK BY COLLISION
New York Times, May 23, 1887

THE VICTIMS OF A PANIC; FOUR MEN KILLED
ON THE ELEVATED ROAD; . . . TEN ARE SWEPT
FROM THE STRUCTURE TO THE STREET BELOW.
New York Times, March 9, 1887

HORRORS BEYOND DESCRIPTION;
TERRIBLE WRECK OF THE NIAGARA
EXCURSION OF THE TP&W RY.
Chatsworth (Illinois) Plain Dealer, August 12, 1887

The last of these, taking place even as Lewin and Warburg were crossing Canada in such a train, occurred when a train crossed over a culvert on a trestle which had been weakened by a fire earlier in the day.

There were many other disasters, both natural and those caused by man. There were mine explosions with heavy loss of life in Wyoming on March 4, 1881 and January 12, 1886, and in Nanaimo, British Columbia on May 3, 1887. Near East Rio, Wisconsin, on October 28, 1886, a Chicago, Milwaukee & St. Paul train hit an open switch, telescoping the train and causing a death toll variously estimated at from 11 to 17. A devastating hurricane struck Indianola, Texas in August 1886, killing at least 25. As for bridge disasters, there were so many of them that, in the year of Lewin's visit, 1887, a book was written on the subject.[36] I

It is well for us that, if Lewin was aware of these disasters, they did not deter him from undertaking his journey, and that his wife Clara was evidently also unaware of them, else she might have convinced him that, as her husband and the father of their two children, he could not expose himself to such dangers.

• *Final subjugation of the American Indian:* Only a year earlier, in September 1886, the Apache chief Geronimo had signed a peace treaty with General Nelson Miles at Skeleton Canyon in Arizona, ending the last of the Indian Wars and sealing the "colonial" status of Native Americans.

Further Thoughts

In the course of a 50-day journey, of which some 20 days were spent in enclosed capsules, whether these were railroad trains, steamers or riverboats, and with only minimal contact with the inhabitants of the countries through which he traveled, Lewin accurately identified many of the strengths and weaknesses of these two nations, Canada and the United States. Among these we can list, first, the enormous wealth in natural resources, and their despoliation by man, resulting from the inability or unwillingness to recognize that these resources, however abundant, were finite and non-renewable; the suppression and victimization of the continent's indigenous Native American population and of the Chinese labor that was imported to build the railroads; the arrogance of investment capital; the over-reliance everywhere on locally-killed meat, especially steak; and the hypocrisy—the phony morality—of America's liquor laws. Of this last, he says, colorfully:

> Oh, you miserable water-drinkers! . . . [D]rinking [*of alcoholic beverages*] is no disgrace or sin. I myself am not a passionate drinker, but the conditions here make Germany appear in a kind of halo, compared to this milk-, ice cream- and water-absorbing people.

Some 35 years later, in *Phantastica*, he was to criticize the enactment in the U.S. of the 18th Amendment to the Constitution, the Prohibition Amendment, pointing out that, when done in moderation, drinking promoted good health rather than damaging it. He expressed concern that the prohibition on the use of alcohol would only encourage its users to shift to narcotics and other stimulants.

Born the son of immigrants, raised in poverty in an economic and religious ghetto, despised by the more comfortable Jews who considered themselves thoroughly German, Lewin was keenly alert to the nuances of social class and caste. Despising the pomposity of America's ruling classes, he nevertheless appreciated those who, despite their wealth, used it for good and were genuinely open to new ideas, especially to welcoming him as the personification, as he saw himself, of those new ideas. When men such as these, men of refinement and accomplishment, turned out often to live in impressive mansions, he seemed not to begrudge them their fine houses; indeed, he appears to have been mightily impressed and perhaps envious of their lofty station in life.

We must give Lewin and his elderly travel-companion credit for subjecting themselves to considerable discomfort and for taking risks that many of us would have shied away from as too dangerous and life-threatening. Lewin and Warburg descend in a jerry-built elevator and negotiate a perilous ledge to be able to stand behind the Niagara Falls on the American side; they risk traveling on the brand-new trans-Canada railroad, hurtling on wooden trestles across deep chasms, Lewin sleeps on the floor of his train compartment so that Uncle can have the only remaining berth, and, finally, he explores intrepidly San Francisco's tenderloin, all for the greater glory of science.

Lewin also shows himself willing in these letters to lay bare what to us seem his less flattering qualities, his negative images of those different from him, whether they were Negroes, Native Americans or whites who were, in his mind, of a lower class and lesser breeding than him. Not to put too fine a point on it, he shows a certain snobbishness to those whom he deemed inferior. At the same time, side by side with that snobbism, there is a sympathy, even an admiration, for what he calls the *zwischendecken*—the steerage passengers—on the ship coming over. He admires their earthiness, their natural exuberance and, above all, their willingness to leave behind their former life and stake everything on their new life in America. As a traveler, he is sensitive to those who make life easy for Uncle and for him, and, at the same time (and this is a much longer list), for those who make their lives more difficult. Especially, in the latter group, he constantly singles out German-American and Jewish retail merchants and restaurateurs for selling inferior merchandise or serving outrageously bad food at exorbitant prices, with an undertone of, "Well, what else can you expect from such as these."

One appreciates the keen eye and the coldly analytical mind with which Lewin assessed what he saw of the works of man, but one also appreciates how open—almost lyrical—he was in describing what God hath wrought: mountains, rivers, both wild and tranquil; stony cliffsides, forested hillsides and open prairies. He viewed these as an artist would, when, for instance, he tries to paint for his wife a verbal picture of the colors of the setting sun striking a cliff-face in the Canadian Rockies.

Despite his renown as a man of science, as a toxicologist and ethno-botanist, he was at the core, as his biographer, Brigitte Hoppe, has written, a product of his orthodox Jewish upbringing in the *Scheunenviertel*. Not for him that clear distinction between knowledge and faith, between science and religion, that 19th century rationalists argued for. He contended instead that

> there is only one basic religious thought, a belief in One God, an inconceivable incredible multifarious Power, a predominantly systematic order working in Nature, an omnipresence. I regard this Power as the basis of experimental biological research, and it has molded my scientific attitude towards drugs and toxins.

A man of science who accepts and contends for the Divine framework underlying all science—such a man deserves our greatest respect.

DS

Introduction Sources

For much of the text of this Introduction, and for its biographical material, I am indebted to Bo Holmstedt and Karl-Heinz Lohs, Introduction to *Louis Lewin. Durch die USA und Canada im Jahre 1887: Ein Tagebuch* (Berlin: Akademie Verlag, 1985 (2d ed.1990)) , and to

J. K. Aronson, "Historical Essay: Louis Lewin—Meyler's Predecessor," in *Side Effects of Drugs Annual No. 27*.

Wolfgang Heubner. *Louis Lewin, Nekrolog*. Münchner Medizinische Wochenschrift, 77. Jg (1930) 405.

Brigitte Hoppe. *Louis Lewin, 1850-1929. Sein Beitrag zur Entwicklung der*

Ethnopharmakologie. Toxicologie und Arbeitsmedizin. Dissertationschrift, Freie Universität Berlin, Fachbereich Medizin 1985.

Brigitte Hoppe, "Leben und Werk Lewins," in Hellerdorfer Heimathefte 3, *Louis Lewin (1850-1929) Leben—Werk—Wirkung,* a Symposium, 18 October 1992 in the Kulturforum, Berlin—Hellersdorf.

Internet

http://www.asmalldoseof.org/historyoftox/1800s.htox.php
http://en.wikipedia.org/wiki/Louis_Lewin (January 23, 2011).

Richard Koch, M.D. Obituary in *Frankfurter Allgemeine Zeitung,* January 24, 1930.

Bernhard Meyer. *Scharenweise strömte die Studenten zu ihm: Der Wegbereiter der Industrietoxicologie Louis Lewin* [*Students came to him in droves: the pioneer Industrial-Toxicologist Louis Lewin*], in http://www.toxcenter.de/artikel/Lewin-Prof-Louis-unser-Vorbild.php (January 23, 2011).

Eli Nathans, "Review of Alexander Schmidt, *Reisen in die Moderne: Der Amerika-Diskurs des deutschen Bürgertums vor der Ersten Weltkrieg im europäischen Vergleich,*" H-German, June, 1998,

www.h-net.org/reviews/showpdf.php?id=2085 (January 23, 2011), http://hsozkult.geschichte.hu-berlin.de/rezensionen/id=375

(January 23, 2011).

S.S. Hammonia, cover of salon passenger list

„Hammonia"

Capitain Hebich

von **Hamburg** nach **New-York**

am 31. Juli 1887.

Frau Schouda von Hein .. Newyork
Fräulein Shada von Hein . do.
Herr Fritz Hein. von Hein. do.
Herr Paul Tidden .... do.
Herr John Haase .... St. Louis
Herr Louis Wolff .... Chicago
Frau Auguste Wolff ...... do.
Fräulein Christine Wolff . do.
Frau Minnie Guntz ..... do.
Frau Sophie Lange, mit
    Tochter............ do.
Herr John Wolff, mit
    Familie .... do.
Fräulein Frieda Witte.... Rostock
Fräulein Johanna Fischer. do.
Herr Friedr. Lahl....... Chicago
Frau Doris Lahl......... do.
Herr Heinrich Lahl...... do.
Herr Ph. Kleeberg. mit
    Familie .... Newyork
Herr Louis Salomon .... Bridgeport
Herr Gustav Wuerth..... Newyork
Frau Kate Wuerth, mit Sohn do.
Herr John R. Warburg .. Hamburg
Herr Dr. Louis Lewin ... Berlin
Herr Albert Ives, mit Frau. Detroit
Frau Elise Schramm, mit
    Tochter u. Bedienung. Newyork
Herr August Sonnemann. Buffalo
Frau Amalie Sonnemann.. do.
Fräulein Sophie Sonnemann do.
Herr Chas. F. Johnson,
    mit Familie .... Cincinnati
Herr Clayton Rockhill ... Newyork
Frau Mary Rockhill .... do.
Herr Hans Jensen ...... Chicago
Frau Elise Jensen ...... do.
Herr Henry Iden .... Newyork
Frau Christine Iden..... do.
Herr Charles Drugelin ... do.
Frau Dina Drugelin..... do.
Fräulein Dina Törpisch .. do.
Fräul Johanna Heinemann Hamburg
Frau Minna Moser, mit
    Tochter............ Breslau
Fräulein A. J. Hartcastle. Maryland
Herr A. H. Bode .... Cincinnati
Frau Auguste Bode, m. Sohn do.
Herr Oscar Rose .... do.
Frau Auguste Rose ...... do.
Herr Ludwig Beise ...... do.

Herr E. Fernbach .... Chicago
Herr T. F. Carroll...... Boston
Herr F. Hoffmeister..... Cincinnati
Herr August Reinhardt... do.
Herr Henry C. Eibs ..... Newyork
Herr Albert Meyer ...... do.
Fräulein Johanna Sommer. Hamburg
Frau Johanna Maass..... Newyork
Herr John Hynemann.... do.
Frau Catharina Schäfer .. Husum
Herr C. Klinkhammer ... Buffalo
Fräulein Auguste Brauch. Altona
Herr William Wuerz, mit
    Familie .... Newyork
Herr Charles Boug. ..... Boston
Herr Hermann Leckebusch do.
Herr Carl Wagner . .Newyork
Herr Alfred Goldschmidt. do.
Fräulein Minnie Hemter Chippeway Falls
Fräulein Madeleine Portener Newyork
Herr Abr. Ober .... do.
Herr Edwin Germen ..... Prag
Herr Wm. Baumann ..... Maracaibo
Knabe Hugo von Peine . do.
Fräulein Doris Reimers... Helgoland
Herr Hans Manau........ Wayneboro
Herr Geo Freudenberg .. Chicago
Frau Wilhelmine Freudenberg do.
Frau Eva Schlehlein ..... Milwaukee
Herr C. H. Johannsen.... Augusta
Herr Otto Julius Wilde... Omaha
Herr Heinr. Voss .... do.
Frau Emma Anger....... Hamburg
Herr Bernhard Wischer .. Cincinnati
Frau Henriette Wischer .. do.
Frau A. A. Kendall, mit
    Tochter............ Ver. Staaten
Herr Alfred Repennig .... Newyork
Herr Ad. Wieber .... Giessen
Herr August Dolge ..... Leipzig
Herr Louis A. Freyer ... St. Antonio
Herr Henry Zuckermann. Hamburg
Herr Peter Lauer........ Rochester
Herr Georg Stratmann ... Hamburg
Herr Ernst Stratmann.... do.
Herr Conrad Schulz...... do.
Frau Sophie Schulz ..... do.
Herr Albert Schulz ...... do.
Herr Julius Regenburg, mit
    Familie .... do.
Herr John Peak Rich .... Toronto

Salon passenger list, S. S. Hammonia,
Hamburg to New York, July 31, 1887

Herr Oscar Nöldechen ...Hamburg
Herr Moritz Herschdörfer .Newyork
Herr Ernst Klimke ...... do.
Herr Dominique Lindenthal Brünn
Herr Vivian F. Gorrissen.. Newyork
Frau Victoria Wühelm ...Amsterdam
Herr Sally Abel .... Berlin
Frau Flora Abel .... do.
Herr Hans Hein ....Husum
Frau Wiebke Hein .... do.
Herr Adolph Hirsch...... Prag
Herr Ferd. Kreuler ......Newyork
Herr Hermann Held ......Schweiz
Herr E. P. Mowton .....Newyork
Frau Dr. Charlotte Löwenthal Hoboken
Herr C. J. Riedel ....Hamburg
Frau Kate Perazzo ....Newyork
Herr Stephan Dieckmann. do.
Herr John Dieckmann ... do.
Fräulein Anna Rose . ....Magdeburg
Herr Gustav Sassenberg ..Chicago
Herr August Carstens ....Omaha
Fräulein Lidwine Jarisch .Reichenberg
Herr Jacob Röhrer ......San Franzisco
Herr John B. Hoss jr. ... do.
Fräulein Pauline Wahl ...Stuttgart
Herr Carl Eschenbach ....Cincinnati
Herr Rev. Peter Abromavtys Suuwalk
Fräulein Barbara Strübin .Schweiz
Fräulein Alice Strübin .. do.
Frau Sarah Silberberg ....Newyork
Herr Joseph Silberberg... do.
Herr B. Metzger, mit Frau Frankreich
Herr Albert Saft......... Galveston
Frau Emilie Winn ....Woburn
Herr Moritz Schrier......Newyork
Herr August Starke ......Cincinnati
Frau Johanna Starke...... do.
Frau Louise Ehlerding ... do.
Herr Chas Balmer ....St. Louis
Herr Edward Mortimer.... do.
Herr Wm. Litzkendorf ...Newyork
Herr Wilhelm Plath .....Brooklyn
Frau Anna Plath .... do.

Frau Louise Rilling ......Newyork
Fräulein Caroline Rilling . do.
Fräulein Anna Rilling ... do.
Herr Chas. Rilling....... do.
Frau Philippine Soeffner..Boston
Herr Louis Süssmilch .... do.
Herr Adolf Schmille .....Herford
Fräulein Anna Schmille .. do.
Frau Marie Schneider, mit
   Familie ....Carlsbad
Frau Rosalie Brasch, mit
   Familie ....Zempelburg
Frau Regina Bry ....Michelstadt
Fräulein Clara Meyer.....Berlin
Herr John Eckel.........Mobile
Herr Felix Funger ....Alhnburg
Frau Jette Davis.........Newyork
Herr David Davis........ do.
Frau Auguste Müller..... do.
Fräulein Octavia Müller.. do.
Frau Hedwig Quensell....Berlin
Fräul. Philippine S. Wiesener Newyork
Frau Emma Dolge.......Leipzig
Fräulein Hedwig Tilltz ...Glogau
Herr Michael Hinger.....Wilmington
Frau Louise Hinger .... do.
Herr Chas. Kuper, mit Sohn Newyork
Herr Willie Katzenberg ..Chicago
Herr Pastor C. F. Schatz .Detroit
Herr Herm. Schneider, mit
   Familie ....Newyork
Herr Otto Merters, mit
   Familie ....Amsterdam
Herr Walther Uellner ....Newyork
Herr Walther Uellner .... do.
Herr Rich. Weyersberg ..Hamburg
Herr Chas. W. Rickerts ..Rochester
Herr Nicolaus Winkelmann St. Louis
Herr Wm. Brüning ....Newyork
Herr Ferdinand Martiensson do.
Frau Anna Sonne ....Milwaukee
Frau Rachel Fraenklin ...Newyork
Herr Arwin von Wigandt .Liegnitz
Fräulein Henriette Rosch .Berlin

Offiziere der „Hammonia":

1.	Offizier	P. Fröhlich	1.	Maschinist	A. Umann
2.	„	v. Bassewitz	2.	„	C. Pahl
3.	„	von Hoff	3.	„	F. Küster
4.	„	C. Schaarschmidt	4.	„	A. Peters

Schiffs-Arzt Dr. Mitzlaff
Proviantmeister D. Toosbuy
Ober-Steward C. G. Stark

*Second page of salon passenger list,
and list of officers*

Hamburg to New York

Sunday, July 31	Depart Hamburg, Germany
	New York
	Albany
	Buffalo
Thursday, August 17	Depart Niagara Falls

Prologue
Sunday, July 31, 1887

Surely it is forgivable if a person, with all due humility before God and spoiled by success, thinks of himself as something special? On Saturday, that kind of feeling came over me as I came down the *Heidereutergasse* on my way to the synagogue.[37] I passed by that same old dilapidated house where I had lived thirty years ago and where I had played as a boy. Today, just as then, a gang of barefoot, rough and unwashed urchins amused themselves on the street. I have freed myself from this environment, to be sure not only by my own merit; I have obtained knowledge and put my mental powers to use; I call a sweet wife and lovely children my own;[38] I am alive to the joy of being able to assist my parents and sisters by word and deed and to see them happy about me; and, finally, I know that others, too—a younger medical generation as well as the older one—think well of my work. Yet I am not self-satisfied and strive to be modest.[39]

The Journey Commences

Aboard at last! What a colorful crowd! Old and young, simple and smart. A bouquet as big as a carriage wheel caught my eye. It didn't take me long to recognize the person who was carrying it: it was the beautiful English girl (with her father and mother), whom we saw at Sylt[40] and with whom I danced. She recognized me and nudged her mother.

The ship, a paddle-wheeler, started out from Hamburg at 8:45 in the morning [*to reach the S. S. Hammonia, evidently anchored in the deepwater ship channel*].

At 11:00AM we reached the *Hammonia*.[41] The officers, stewards and crew were lined up in rows to greet us as we came aboard. Behind them I could see a mob of men and women in rags and tatters, the steerage passengers. They were prevented from mingling with the first and second class passengers by a line of braided rope. To get to our cabin we had to once again display our tickets. Shoving and being shoved, we were shown our way through the interior of the ship towards our cabin by the bearded Chief Steward. Another mandatory display of tickets and finally we gained entry to our cabin. As soon as we closed the door behind us, my first thought was that our luggage was not in the cabin! Then I felt under our beds, and there it was!

We settled in. At 11:20 the ship got underway. We felt the ship gliding forward almost motionlessly—no pitching, no rolling. Neptune, the evil-witch, was holding his trident horizontally. The sun sends its rays down, refreshing breezes allowed us to forget the all-consuming scorching heat of recent days.

We feel completely at ease. At 2:30 we passed Cuxhaven,[42] and the shoreline slowly vanished from the horizon. We had brought on board with us an elaborate breakfast. As we came back out on deck, the last evidence of man's work disappeared from our eyes; we are now surrounded by a vast expanse of water. We lie on our deckchairs and speak of this and that. I indulge myself in criticizing people, something which I know you, my dear heart, dislike. We praise Hermann's[43] attentiveness, for sending a friendly telegram to us that would reach us when we boarded the ship, which stands in sharp contrast to John's[44] senseless laziness and inattentiveness. Now we hear the ship's bell ringing. It's 4 o'clock, and soon we'll be eating dinner.

Naturally, we sought out the smallest table and had the good fortune of sharing the table with a couple of fine examples of mankind. I placed Uncle on a sofa to my right. On my left sat a young man who looks like a mail clerk or perhaps a schoolteacher; his family had apparently given him the money for this voyage. He was using his table knife as a fork, to eat with. He puts the food on his knife, lifts it upward toward his mouth, pauses for a split second as the food rests on his thick proboscis-like lower lip, takes a short, deep breath, and then the morsel of food disappears in his mouth. This process is repeated like clockwork, so that the calves liver and potatoes disappear in about 2 minutes and the roast chicken in about 1-1/2 minutes.

Now the sun has disappeared below the horizon, and gray rainclouds send a torrential rain down on us. It's much colder now. I drew my raincoat about me, Uncle put on his winter jacket. We walked around the ship out on the deck. Neptune had righted his trident, the ship commenced to shake and tremble—and the cook's arts reappear for the second time at daybreak, more or less altered, quite recognizably. I laughed, because I noticed that a Slovak, who was in the grip of the same *mal de mer* as I, was offering as a libation to Neptune the potatoes that he had just eaten for dinner. I started to feel dizzy and soon began to feel the pain of a raging headache. Ah, I thought: cocaine![45] Out with you, prophylactic phial! Your contents shall warm my chilly insides, just as the Peruvian sun once warmed you! 0.05 grams of cocaine disappeared inside me, dizziness and headache vanished magically; cheerfulness returned as I inhaled the refreshing seabreeze with delight. But wherever I stepped on the deck I encountered evidence of offerings to Neptune's caprices. But Uncle, like an old sea-dog, is immune from these dangers. Evening arrived. Like a red ball the sun dipped over the horizon against the sea. A second dose of cocaine could not dispel the prevailing dizziness and indisposition. At 8 o'clock Uncle went up for tea laced with grog. I wanted to hook up with him up on deck, but I didn't last long up there, and returned to our cabin, crept into my berth, and very soon sleep overcame me. I woke up again at 10:45, when Uncle came to bed, then went back to sleep right away and awoke feeling refreshed on a sunny morning.

Monday, August 1

So I'm sitting here, thinking of you with indescribable affection, and write you, while around me, in a constant hum, I hear voices speaking in every language. If I'm not mistaken, I was in the middle of describing the characteristics of my eating-table partner to my left. This man, of short and stocky build, is more mannerly and more refined in his table manners [*than the man on my right*]. This morning at breakfast he took a piece of toast, pressed it together, dunked it into a large coffee cup, put it to his mouth, which he opened, but not too wide and without showing too many teeth, and zippety-zap the toast disappeared. Uncle and I took generous helpings of food and beverage; whatever was offered to us. Meat, cheese, potatoes, eggs, etc. I'm feeling very well now. However, I think that by the time we get to the [*English*] Channel, which we are now approaching—we should be in Le Havre this evening—the illness which I feel coming on, and which I have so far suppressed, will become manifest. When that happens, I'll take some morphine to deal with it.

Uncle is such good company. It is really refreshing to observe him; he's singular in his good nature and his friendliness with everyone whom he comes in contact with. He slept soundly last night. This morning, I helped him get dressed. He didn't have the right buttons to go with his collar, so I gave him some of mine.[46] We haven't gone out of our way to make friends on the ship. An unsophisticated Holsteiner, who has lived for 15 years in Omaha, tried to start a conversation with us. He spoke constantly about how special it was that he was making this trip. I asked him how old he thought Uncle was; he guessed 65-67 years old![47]

Tuesday, August 2

I'm sitting on the deck next to Uncle, soaking in the sun's rays, a refreshing breeze in our faces, hearing around us many languages and countless dialects. We, God's chosen people, on whom, because of our alleged sins, the curse was placed to be dispersed among the peoples of the earth, are among those represented here in goodly numbers and in fine specimens. I track one of them as if I were his shadow. As we came on board and started making ourselves comfortable in our cabin, the door was flung open and a gaunt pathetic little man, wearing a little American jacket, with a finch-like beak sitting in the middle of his face, a toothless mouth, a drawn-back upper lip and a jutting chin, rolled his eyes and, from the enclosure where his teeth used to be, poured out in a very unfriendly tone, in a Posen-sounding voice: "Well, this is my cabin, Number 126, etc. etc. etc." We wanted immediately to set the man straight. I laughed out loud and told him, "Mister, if you were looking for 126 minus 100, then you could come back here, because this is Number 26." This man talks to everyone on board, but if ever the word "mauscheln"[48] was appropriate, it would be for this fellow, and for the buzzwords such as "marks" and "money-making" that spill readily out of his mouth.[49]

I also see a man wearing yellow shoes, and women with large diamond rings and earrings the size of cherries. More interesting than this company is my observation of life and of the goings-on in steerage.[50] Dirt and neglect side-by-side with false elegance, talmi-necklace, pince-nez and walking stick; but one can also see in various positions and movements people dressed cleanly and neatly, all of them thrown together as if in a kaleidoscope. Over there I see a ragged Polish Jew crouching, next to him two Turks squatting on fine kilim rugs; over there, a group of Slovaks, among them a youngster who sings, in mournful drawn-out tones, *"Polen ist nicht verloren."*[52] Another lad snatches the fiddle from him, and his unskilled hand plays "Yankee Doodle," which animates a few men into performing a sailor's jig. Then an accordion comes out; someone plays it and couples turn to the doleful tones of this instrument. Are there Jews among them too, I wonder? There are many Polish women on board who, with different clothes and in different surroundings, would excite admiration! No, these women are not among the dancers.

In their movements, their way of doing things, even in their features—though unconsciously—we see expressed the sense of their situation. In their old homeland, they were beggars, ridiculed and scorned by the crude and unfeeling mob which knows nothing but the lowest animal instincts; here, on this ship, they stand at the gate of a new destiny. What will it give them? Will they regret having left behind the Old World to catch perhaps a ray of sunshine which will make all their privations and toil seem light? Will that young woman, pretty as a picture, who again and again gives her limp breast to her emaciated baby, feeding it with her very life-blood—will she at least have the reward of watching it grow to adulthood? That gray-bearded old man with the long caftan, the big blue spectacles, low shoes and white stockings, who, true to the traditions of his youth, takes only potatoes and herring for food, no meat and other prohibited things, who is always greeted with mockery by the stokers and other rabble—will he bless the day or curse it when he had the courage to free himself of the conditions that he has known for a lifetime?

And how much higher does that man rank than the young lout with his pince-nez and walking stick, who, evidently in that moment where he outgrew his father's [*disciplinary*] rod, cast aside the bonds of his faith. Now he has become a cosmopolitan, laughing at these old Jews and feeling himself uplifted by his supposed intimacy with the crude, ill-bred Christian mob.[55] My hope for this young man is that his life takes a turn toward still a third metamorphosis, cleansing him of this artificiality and refining him.

When evening comes, the steerage passengers start to make music, with improvised drums and horns, tom-tom and triangle. Their melancholy song seems rather to accompany lovers' dallying than to express deep emotion, sadness, thoughts of home or nostalgia. Judging by their bearing and behavior, not many of them seem to have these feelings, but the sight of the sea's grandeur awakens their amazement as it does ours.

Since yesterday afternoon we have been lying in close to Dover. The sea, only slightly wavy, shows a lapis lazuli color. We came so near the English coast that we could see the white cliffs in detail, as well as roads, forts, houses, etc. On the other side, the French coast shimmers, veiled in a light mist.

This body of water, seemingly endless and yet so confined, is animated and enlivened by sailboats, steamboats and, over there, by a torpedo boat as well. If one wanted to prophesy from a seabird's flight what one's fate will be, one would be frustrated, for hardly a seagull came into view, nor have we seen any sea-creatures, or sea-lions, but we do have on board a deck-lion, a "swell" clad in a short blue jacket, light checked trousers, a tall gray hat, patent leather shoes with broad heels, yellow dog's leather gloves and a little cane. He amuses Uncle and me and the other passengers by imitating the way ladies with bustles sway their hips, swinging his rear end first one way and then the other. For myself, I'd rather see a real sea creature than one such as him!

[*They revel in their comfort, feel the fresh sea air in their faces, and think of the loved ones left behind.*]

The ship moves slowly forward, under a starlit sky, with Venus directly over the bowsprit. At length we see lights on the port side, first Dieppe, then Le Havre and Trouville and, ahead of us, Honfleur. Only when it is past midnight do we separate ourselves from these beautiful sights. The entire bay seems to be brightly lit. Unfortunately, the ship keeps on going, evidently because the shipowners are too stingy to enter the harbor [*and pay the harborage fees*]. The anchor comes down, and so we lie at anchor outside the harbor, and see the bright electric lights beaming out from the lighthouse, illuminating the blackness of the waters.

[*Tired, they make their way to their cabin, still irritated that they couldn't enter Le Havre. As the ship rocks gently, Lewin sprays Reseda perfume*[54] *on the beds and walls to counteract the odors in the cabin.*]

[*Waking to a brilliant morning, Lewin admires the sparkling sea, the crowded bustling harbor, the town climbing up the hillside, and the fishing boats, "each one with a gray and brown sail, spread like birds' wings, on their way to their destiny, in places where a silent war is ceaselessly waged."*]

The wonderful disposition of Nature! Nothing exists in its own right—everything has its purpose and exists to fulfill it. This goes as well for the animate world as for the inanimate, the world of iron-ore and marble. For a long time, men of little vision have smiled at this theory, but bit by bit they will be torn from their disbelief [*and accept the truth of that theory*]. Thus it follows that we exist for the shipping company and the shipping company for us. But we cannot let the shipping company get away with the misconception that we will permit ourselves to be fleeced defenselessly. Meager comfort, bad coffee, weak broth, so-so cleanliness, unpalatable beer and dreadful wine are abuses we have to contend with. There is no writing room; the so-called smoking room is so well ventilated by open doors and windows that one doesn't want to undergo such a hardening process. Moreover, these Americans and German-Americans spit so unpleasantly on any spot not occupied by a person, they scatter their cigar-ash and their matches and throw their legs about in such a way that this room is entirely out of bounds for us. There is no library. A bulletin posted by the management announces that there is a library on board under the direction of the chief steward. The books can be taken out in the morning from 7:00 to 8:00, but you have to put down the retail price of the book as a deposit. Such insolence! It's just too much!

Moreover, as much as one would like to follow the ship's course on a navigation chart, there is no such thing. If I hadn't brought my own pen and ink, I would have had to rely on the helpfulness of my fellow-passengers. The people in Hamburg (HAPAG-Lloyd) will hear from Uncle when he gets back, that's for sure! The ship's doctor is a pathetic figure. What intellectual depravity drives such a man to spend his life, year-in and year-out, doing nothing [*of benefit to mankind*]? Naturally, I made no effort to chat with him.

In the afternoon around two o'clock we cleared the Channel, as you may have read in the paper: "*Hammonia* passed Cape Lizard."[55] Now the ship is moving ahead for real! There is a strong wind from the northeast and we are grateful for the warmth of winter coats and thick gloves. The stars shine brightly in the sky. Until ten o'clock we enjoy this spectacle, inhaling the refreshing air into our lungs, which have been weakened by the urban air that they are accustomed to.

Wednesday, August 3

At about six o'clock, I awoke from a deep sleep. The ship was rocking so that I couldn't get dressed without bending this way and that.

> [*Lewin* describes *the cabin, the cleaning of the steerage deck in the early morning, his and Uncle's daily routine, singling out for mention the handsome Chief Steward, who, with an elegant movement of his wrist, rings the bell that summons the passengers to their meals.*]

> [*While they are lying in their deckchairs, the chatting and talking is suddenly interrupted—there are shouts, unusual activity, energetic leaping from the deckchairs—because there has been a sighting of flying fish leaping out of the water and back in. The fish, 18 inches long, leap from the water as if released by a spring, to a height of about one foot, and then dive back immediately. These sea creatures seem to live in families. They stay behind the moving ship, continuing their tricks in its wake.*]

The quiet on board is so refreshing and comforting. We're far away from the daily routine and work-a-day activity. No newspapers here to irritate me with their foolish chatter. One's thoughts, normally rutted in the track of the customary, glide further and further away and find their new track in ideas about Nature and all its wonders. But no matter where my thoughts wander in these transcendental spheres, they always return to you, my dearest, and to the children. Hopefully, your trip will be over tomorrow and you will have arrived at your destination. Remember always your promise to me: to take care of yourself and refresh yourself, not to socialize, and to tell everyone who invites you that you must have peace and quiet. Kiss the children for me.

Thursday, August 4

We arose early. The ship bounced around uncomfortably, so that I got dizzy in dressing myself. As I came out onto the deck, the dizziness disappeared. The skies were cloudy and gray, the horizon hidden in fog. A hard rain pelted me in the face. Nevertheless, I made my mandatory promenade around the deck. I pulled my hat down firmly over my ears, and the sharp southwesterly wind made my raincoat billow around my body. As soon as the rain stopped, I returned to my deckchair, and looked out at the foamy sea, with its remarkable play of colors, from inky black to dark green, to a deep blue. Where the ship's keel touched the water, I saw in the white foam of its wake a light blue hue so delicate that it would have been difficult for a painter to create it on his palette. On the wide sea, a person feels alone and abandoned. Not a sail in sight, nor another living being, except for a single diminutive tern. Always changing, yet always the same, the current foams, as it has done since the beginning of time. Those creatures who live in those waters, or who travel on them, are as transitory as the rays of sunshine that even now are breaking through the black rainclouds. These rays have always existed and will continue to do so as long as the Earth exists.

It's too bad that, even here, in the quiet of this ship, thoughts such as these are disturbed by unsought intrusions. A barrel organ plays an ancient melody, and a couple of women, of dubious origin, start to dance to the music. Despite all their efforts to get others to join them in this amusement, and despite the fact that the ship was moving well in calm seas, and despite the steady sunshine, they do not find any takers among the better people nearby. The latter—unfortunately I'm talking here about Jewish women—don't show any inclination to bestir themselves from their comfortable deckchairs. If only they could have gotten others to get up and dance! In steerage, they have put on a variety show, with drums and cymbals.[56]

A strong wind and steam move the ship along at speed. Gigantic sails are fully unfurled to catch the wind. The darkness is broken by the ship's lights, which illuminate the ship and the surrounding sea. The almost-full moon throws its chalk-white light over the sea as well, and Venus, the evening star, is once again visible again over the bobbing bow of the ship. We enter the ship's dining salon, Uncle for his grog and I perhaps for a glass of the inferior beer that they serve on this ship. But we couldn't go to bed until we had some kind of cultural pleasure. A nice English lady provided that for us, with a virtuoso performance of Chopin and other classical pieces. I went up to her afterwards and thanked her warmly for her fine recital.

Friday, August 5

Even while we were still in bed in the early morning hours, we realized that the sea was uncommonly turbulent. Never before on our sea journey had the ship pitched and rolled as it was doing now. The wind had shifted during the night to the northeast. The ship pitched not only along the length of the ship but across its width as well. We started getting seasick. Walking along the corridor, you could hear from behind the cabin doors the groans and moans of the passengers. In the dining salon you could see that, for the first time, the table settings had been secured, and bottles, etc. had been placed in fitted niches. It was obvious that many passengers were not there to take their breakfast that morning. The deck was a mess, and, even when you were still yourself in good condition, the sight of so much vomit could make you sick. I held myself in, managed not to throw up. I sought a place that was shielded from the wind, found our deckchairs, and there we sat, fairly steadily.

When we went inside for breakfast, I couldn't put up with it, because the room wasn't ventilated and one could feel the rocking of the ship much more than out on the deck. So I took my breakfast roll out onto the deck and bit into it with a hearty appetite. After breakfast we didn't move from our deckchairs, and I was pleased that, the rest of the morning, no urge to get sick came over me. As a precaution, I had taken a generous dose of cocaine. In powerful surges, the wave swept over the ship from the windward side to our sheltered lee side. I can truly say that I've never seen waves this high. With each climbing of the crests and plowing into the troughs, the ship's hull must have risen and sunk 20-30 feet or more. The sea itself looked a deep black, like an enormous seething, turbulent cauldron. And everywhere that white foam, the howling wind. First the ship shivers and trembles at the crest of the wave. Then, for about a half-minute, it shudders, then it plunges into the depths, rights itself, then, after 1-4 seconds of seeming quiet, the cycle begins all over again with a sideways motion.

There were only 40 people at lunch today, compared to the usual 90 or so. I allowed myself to eat well and enjoy the meal. Afterwards, we went out onto the deck again. Until late in the evening you could see people looking like lumpy packages lying around in every conceivable position. We allowed ourselves to get chilled through and through by the penetrating wind, and so to bed.

Saturday, August 6

Last night was splendid, and we awoke to sunshine this morning. The resurrection of the dead! From every porthole they crawled out, those who yesterday couldn't get far enough into their holes; the color has returned to faces that yesterday were ashen pale, and, where yesterday there had been only moans and groans, today there was the ring of laughter. The ship didn't rock much. Along with that, a hefty wind came out of the west. The late afternoon chill, when the sun had disappeared behind the clouds, made it necessary for us to get into our warmer outergarments. We got up from our deckchairs only at mealtimes. The monotony of the sea was broken in the afternoon by the appearance of three ships on the horizon. Otherwise, the day passed as all the others. After dinner, the same crude women danced around. That night, Uncle and I discussed our possible visits [*to friends and business acquaintances*]. Since I had made it clear that I didn't want to undertake any such visits, we agreed that we would not do so. You were much in my thoughts, my dearest, and my only fear is that family obligations will cut short your vacation time. Stand strong and don't let yourself be moved by any such considerations!

I forgot to write that I talked to the beautiful English girl. She has been staying with relatives in Hamburg for two years and now she is returning with her parents to Maryland. Of course, she remembered me. How could such a characteristic head as mine fail to make an impression! Are you laughing?[57]

Sunday, August 7

Today is even warmer and finer than yesterday. I have to say that my fellow-passengers are a source of discomfort to me. A goodly number of them are not familiar with the use of handkerchiefs, so that you have to give them a wide berth as you pass by them. Almost all of the Americans and the German-Americans spit everywhere in such a disgusting way that you would think you were among the betelnut-chewing peoples of the Orient. And their table-manners are dreadful! The other two passengers at our table have such bad manners that others nearby have already taken notice. Uncle quipped that the man on my left should go on a trip to the cannibal-people, to wean them from their man-eating passion. The way these men eat, and the quantity of the food they stuff in their mouths, is brutish and beastly, as if they were pigs at the trough. For example, at lunch today, one of them ate two rump steaks, together with liverwurst, potato salad, three pieces of eel, two pieces of herring, hot potatoes, endless helpings of bread and butter, cheese, etc.

It will amuse you that I have discovered on board ship here the very image of Mr. Toots.[58] Picture a young man of perhaps 20, with an unusually featureless face, covered with pimples; the lips are thick and grossly everted, and a silly giggle plays on them. He wears, ordinarily, a jockey cap, or, when he dresses up, a white hat with a broad black band. A pair of pince-nez glasses with black frames hangs by a ribbon from the hatband. He wears a light-colored suit speckled with tiny black dots. Green canvas shoes with leather trim and a colorful handkerchief peeking from his breast pocket complete the outlandish appearance.

After breakfast I went back to my berth to nap while Uncle sat in his deck chair and slept there. The ridiculous shipboard rules do not allow passengers to keep their own drinks on board, so our cognac and the Danziger[59] bitters have found their secret corner in the cabin and from time to time we enjoy them. In the evening, a young English lady, very distinguished-looking, who is on board with her mother, played the piano. I told her that I admired her piano playing and we got acquainted. I also introduced Uncle to her. She plays very well, was in Berlin for 18 months and studied there at the Scharwenka Conservatory. She is hoping to establish a similar institute in America. It was a pleasure to talk to her about all sorts of things—her German is not good—and to hear her play. I asked her to come and see us if she should return to Berlin.

Monday, August 8

I slept poorly, and was up six times. I tossed about and thought in my half-asleep state that I would be thrown overboard in my tossings and turnings. It was hard, what with the ship's pitching and rolling, to get dressed in the morning. I hurried up onto the deck as fast as I could. I, "hurried"? The ship's motions were so violent that I couldn't make any headway. On every step of the stairway [*to the deck*] lay violently-ill women, with ashen faces and a look of utter apathy to what was going on around them. It didn't take long before I started feeling not-so-well either. Only by pulling myself together in a concentrated way was I able to ward off an acute mood.

Up above, a ghastly picture presented itself. Even though I had only recently seen for myself the power of the sea, that was nothing compared to what I saw now. Waves reaching as high as the bulkhead pounded against the ship, which groaned and creaked from bow to stern. Combine that with the roaring and howling wind, a noise so loud that you couldn't get a word out nor hear one. The sky was a deep gray, and from time to time a skin-soaking rain-shower pounded the deck, then another wave flooded over the deck, so that the one side of the ship that offered shelter from the storm offered no such relief from this one. Many people stayed below-decks, in their cabins. Everywhere I saw women lying like warehouse-bundles, huddled in blankets and pillows, on benches and chairs.

Uncle and I stayed on the decks, but I was not in good shape at all. I had a terrible headache and every movement of the ship gave me an indescribable pain in my solar plexus and from my throat to my head I could feel my arteries throbbing. There was no let-up to the ship's bobbing up and plunging down. Then, all of a sudden, we heard a foghorn, giving out a deep mourning tone, drawn out, swelling, rising higher and higher and ending on a piercing note. After a short pause we heard it again, in shorter and shorter intervals. We're sitting in a fog that enshrouds everything that's more than a ship's length away from us. You can imagine how uneasy we felt. We were now in the area of the infamous Newfoundland Banks. I could hardly get down a cup of coffee. Uncle, in contrast, was chipper and had a good appetite. Slowly the minutes passed by—each minute seemed an eternity.

> [*Lewin tried to go for lunch, but he had to give it up. He slept for a while in the cabin, went out on deck again and managed in spite of his misery to admire the majestic aspect of the sea in its turbulence. Finally, the fog dispersed and the foghorn was silent.*]

Tuesday, August 9

This was a night that I won't forget as long as I live. From 1:00am until the graying dawn I was awake, and then, catching a couple of hours of sleep, I had nightmares the likes of which I've never had before. The ship's movements, as it pitched and rolled from one side to the other, were so frightening that my head felt like it would snap into pieces. I felt as if I were mortally ill. The ship's clock bell struck every half-hour. Still no daylight! I turned to my right side, then to my left. I held my breath, then breathed deeply. Nothing helped. I sat bolt upright, then tried again to sleep—still nothing helped. More and more the ship-colossus pitched and twisted, ever louder the roar of the tempest, the howling of the wind. I could hear the water in the holding tank sloshing from one side to the other, the wooden cabin-walls creaking and groaning in their frames—it was enough to drive you crazy! And sleep just wouldn't come. Around 3:00am the seamen started working on the deck, and that of course did nothing to lull me to sleep. At long last came daybreak, and with it sunshine.

So now, here I am on deck, looking out onto a beautiful sea, feeling physically refreshed, warmed through and through by an almost tropical sun, and writing of my ghastly recollections from last night, recollections which, as I'm hearing from my fellow passengers, I share with them. I was speaking a while ago to an elderly gentleman, a man from Hamburg, an acquaintance of Uncle's, who has made these trans-Atlantic voyages so often he couldn't keep count of them. He said that he had never experienced a storm such as this one in mid-summer and that he would scarcely have thought it possible that it could happen. It is still uncertain when we are going to arrive. I am ready to feel the ground under my feet.

Silently the ship glides over the water. We look at the glowing furrow the ship's keel is plowing. Those millions of animate beings who, torn from their placid stillness by that same keel, perhaps responding to their excitement by glowing, will soon come to rest again when the black monster of a ship with its laughing, chatting and, for the moment, cheerful people has passed by. Here, in the microscopic workings of the world, is repeated what, 24 hours ago, could be observed macroscopically in the so-called "lords of creation": how small and humble before the elemental power of nature, and how brutal in their joy, when no enemy threatens! Happy the man who fears only external enemies, or, rather, woe to him who thinks he has only those. To live means not only to fight against exterior harm, but to a much greater degree to fight against oneself. A worthy striving! I can say of myself that I stand guard watchfully and fight myself bravely. Let me hope that it has already done some good. You, my dearest, would be the best judge of that.

Wednesday, August 10

I awoke feeling refreshed and renewed in strength. The sea is calm, with hardly any wind. We often use the term "smooth as glass" in speaking of the surface of water even where there is a slight movement in the waves, but here there is absolutely none. The last bit of wind that remains is enough only to cause the gentlest of ripples. The blue of the sky, the blue of the sea, as far as the eye can see! The only reminder of the past days of extreme weather can be seen up on the ship's funnels, which are encrusted with salt almost to their tops by the impact of the giant waves which pounded them during those storms.

At about eight o'clock a distant dot is sighted. Great excitement! Some powerful telescopes have made out a sailboat—perhaps a pilot boat. Soon you could make out with your own eyes the ever-growing dot on the horizon. We found a good spot on the rail to watch all this happen. Pilot boat! Pilot boat! People were betting on the serial number of the boat and I bet Uncle on the time that it would take the boat to reach us (I lost). "I bet you . . I bet you"—over and over I heard those words. People were even betting on whether the pilot would have a beard and, if so, on the type of beard. The ship's steps were lowered, and he came on board. He gave us the latest news and then disappeared onto the bridge. The prospect of a secure harbor beckons. The temperature is 23 degrees Reaumur.[61] Some of the passengers have warned us about the August heat in New York. Meanwhile we found out that draft beer was being given out to the passengers. Bottled beer was not to be had. It appears that the stewards get higher tips when they dispense draft beer; that's why they don't sell it in bottles. The day passed in harmony, as it had begun. We drank a glass of sparkling wine to your health, grateful to have sensible wives who did not oppose our plans. If we continue to be of the same opinion tomorrow, we may again confirm it with wine; perhaps your ears will tingle.

Thursday, August 11

Again a fine day! Everything on board is splendidly decorated. People are wearing their best clothes. Everywhere the polishing cloth has extracted a brilliant shine from iron and brass. We are scheduled to arrive at about 4 o'clock. The first errand will be to inquire after letters from you. Again the sea is marvelous, sparkling under the sun's rays and glittering in a deep blue. We are feeling very well. We hope you will quickly get the news of our safe arrival.

Observation: 10-11 August
                 Three o'clock in the afternoon
At sea: 9 days, three hours

We first saw land at one o'clock. Shadowy outlines materialize more and more, and at last we discern the wide Hudson [*Lower New York*] Bay. After a lot of waiting and checking—it is now 6:30—we have finished dressing on the fifth floor of our Fifth Avenue Hotel [*in New York City*].[62] There was nobody to meet us, and we allow the impressions to act upon us in all their massiveness.

New York, August 11

My beloved Clara! Not an hour has passed since I sent you two heavy letters, each of them, I think, some thirty pages long. But now I am sitting again, pen in hand, in order to enjoy my greatest pleasure: talking to you.

The excitement among the passengers grew, as the sun hastened to her ocean-home. We had had lunch—a very skimpy one, the Company being stingy—and then we patiently waited on deck for further developments. As early as yesterday the proximity of land had been heralded by floating seaweed and single sea-anemones in beautiful violet shades. All at once a comedian started to shout, while pointing to the right with his finger. The whole steerage and many first-class passengers joined in the cry, "Land! Land!" It turned out to be a hoax, but, in the end, we did see land. Gradually, very gradually, outlines appeared to the right: first, the lighthouse of Fire Island, to which the name of our ship was signaled for transmission to the telegraph. Then the contours of Long Beach and Rockaway Beach became visible. To the left, land appeared as well, which could be discerned through the light mist as wooded heights. The water now showed intensely green, whereas in past days it had been a splendid blue.

More and more the shores come together. Villas built in a mélange of strange styles lie amidst the most beautiful greenery. We are in the bay of New York, or rather Lower New York Bay. Every house on Staten Island can be seen distinctly, and the same goes for Coney Island to the right of us. The water is wonderfully alive. All sorts of vessels glide past. Slowly we steam onwards, passing the quarantine island with its barracks-like buildings housing those with contagious diseases. Now the shores from left to right seem almost to touch. To each side of the Narrows, a fort guards the entrance to the harbor proper. The steamer stops. A boat with a yellow flag appears. The port-doctor wants to make sure there are no passengers with contagious diseases on board. He steams away satisfied, we dissatisfied because of the loss of time. Again the sound of another whistle, again the ship stops. A small customs-launch lays to alongside, and customs officers emerge. The passengers rush to the dining hall, which has been converted into five offices for the customs formalities. We stay on deck in order to enjoy the sights. Ahead, in a choice position close to all the ships' routes and visible from afar, is little Bedloes Island[63] with its "Statute of Liberty Enlightening the World."[64] We thought the pedestal too high [*in proportion to the height of the statue itself*].

On past the statue and past very many big and small ships! Some of them, the ferries, are in fact 1-1/2 or 2-storied houses; they give a curious impression when they pass. On the left side are giant elevators for loading and unloading grain, 7-9 stories tall.

At last we see the pier [*in Hoboken*] of the *Hamburg-Amerika Packetfahrt Gesellschaft* (HAPAG) looming ahead of us. Much waving of handkerchiefs, pushing and jostling, an incredible excitement. It makes Uncle angry, and for good reason. We decide to wait and see what happens.

After the customs officers had finished with everyone else, we went down into the converted dining room, and signed a statement that we had nothing to declare. Then we looked on from the deck, as hundreds of trunks were pushed helter-skelter along the wooden gangplank into the customs clearance hall.

At last we left the ship. In the huge floating hall [*the pier*] we had to pick out our luggage; it took us more than an hour to collect the pieces. And now for the customs examination. But then we saw that people were already standing there, in such a long line that our heart sank. We felt faint, hungry and thirsty—the stinginess of the Company hadn't allowed us a final meal before leaving the ship. So we went into Hoboken and had an ale, which we enjoyed. Back to the Customs. The punctiliousness of the examination defies description. They pulled out Uncle's business papers, shaving gear and ties, hoping for booty. In my luggage they groped under the strap and so on. At last we sat in a carriage [*on the way to the ferry*], then by ferry we crossed the Hudson and eventually ended at our destination, the Fifth Avenue Hotel on Madison Square. Here we were lodged on the fifth floor. A refreshing rain cooled the air. Iced water refreshed us.

Fifth Avenue Hotel, New York City

It was by now too late to go to Sallenbach's for your letters. We longed so very much to have them. We retired early to our rooms, from where I wrote these lines to you.

Friday, August 12

In the morning we rose early and went down to breakfast at 7 o'clock. It would take up too much space if I were to try to describe even in the broadest terms the interior of this hotel. The stairways and corridors are covered by carpets of excellent taste which, in their turn, rest on some kind of padding, so that one sinks in at every step. The dining rooms—there are three of them—have a wide foyer, fitted with marvelous carpets and, before you get to the dining rooms, you pass through two reception rooms furnished with regal luxury. In the center is the dining room, a vast ellipse with a fine ceiling, and, round its entire periphery, columns of dark brown granite with handsome capitals. At the door two ushers are posted to lead the guest to his table, whether he wishes to be so guided or not. Each two guests are provided with a waiter who, tiresomely, stands near the table all the time, waiting for orders.

"Now, what will your order be?" Uncle acts as the interpreter, but it's difficult to choose from among the 12-14 dishes to which we are entitled. Unlike other guests, we chose not to order the melons, which are eaten sprinkled with pepper, nor did we order fish or meat, and so on and on, but only coffee and eggs.

It is still too early to go out for your letters. We look about. The streets with their 7-9 story buildings give you a strange feeling, but when you see the really high ones, they seem downright gigantic. The façades—in places quite handsome—reveal the purpose of the building. Some look like warehouses, but the lower stories of the buildings next to them are pleasing to look at. Then, higher up, the distribution of story-heights gets so irregular that one is amazed as much by the magnitude as by the lack of taste: rows of bulls-eye windows alternate with attic windows, arched with rectangular ones, and so on.

If you walk further into the town, but still not at its center, the uniformity in the construction of dozens of fairly recently-developed streets strikes you. It would indeed be impossible for me to find the difference in these one-family houses. In spite of this uniformity, they are at once more graceful and more solid than those in Pöseldorf.[65] They are all built of finely-shaded brownstone, and, on street after street, staircases lead to the front door of each of them, all of the same considerable height and made of sandstone. It looks strange, because the eye does not register these 100-300 arched staircases as such. Windows, doors, metalwork, all are well-made and of the best material. Nearly without exception the windows are made of crystal glass, with beveled edges. No small gardens anywhere.

In the commercial streets you find many red-brick houses, often uniformly built, as you also find along the Hudson. What surprises us is the great amount of sandstone, granite and marble fitted in everywhere, in every imaginable form. Even more remarkable are the cast-iron balconies frequently fixed to each floor, connected by iron ladders, so that in case of fire you can get from the first floor up to the seventh or eighth.[66]

Now let me tell you about the advertisements. They surpass anything that people in Europe can imagine. When I look out my hotel window, my eye catches an ad that occupies the entire wall of a house: "Robertson's, M.D., Electric Corsets." Uncle said we could go into the store and ask about their prices. I think I would burst out laughing when he does that. He told me that he had a secret intention to present each of you with one of those "electric corsets." In return, I shall give him "Richardson's Electric Cigarettes." A man, dressed in black and white, slowly paces the streets, clad in a long coat that touches the ground and has these large advertisements printed on them. Maybe that is not so extraordinary; but what is more surprising is that Levi & Goldstein have stretched ropes across the street, about 50 feet above the pavement, and have hung from these ropes 10-20 colored umbrellas and parasols. But what really gets to you is that no post, no chimney, no wall and no tree is free from "Pritchard's Castorian," a children's medication, or "Pearl-line," a detergent, which we saw advertised in the same spot seven times, side by side, or "Hood's Sarsaparilla," with a charming girl's head, or "Tutt's Liver Pills," or, lastly, "S.O.S. for the Blood." Wherever the eye roams, it encounters these advertisements.

Many black people in all shades—the word [*black*] is very appropriate here—are to be seen in the street, some of them with the build of an Othello! * * * On the other hand, few of the women are good-looking. They are usually overdressed and seem to love gaudy colors.

At 9 o'clock we went to Sallenbach's. We had to wait 45 minutes until Mr. Schlesinger came back. Letters? None! The *Eider*,[67] a mail-boat, has arrived, but we should come back after the mail had been collected from the post-office. I had so much counted on letters from you that their non-appearance was more than a major disappointment. Only Uncle's equanimity calmed me a little, at least outwardly.

We used our time to experience the Elevated Rail-Road.[68] There's a station near Sallenbach's, at Grand Street. You hardly know how to respond to such bold simplicity. Even in the narrowest streets you find iron pillars perhaps 1-1/2 feet thick, spaced at intervals of about 15 feet, reinforced here and there with diagonal members. Small iron steps, roofed over, lead to a platform the width of a city street. You buy your ticket, and then a few steps further you come to a man sitting next to a glass box. You throw your ticket into the glass box, the man presses a lever and the ticket disappears, and the train comes a few minutes later.

A New York elevated train

You sit down on a cane-woven seat and travel wherever you want, unimpeded and uncontrolled. One station comes after another, just minutes apart. As the train arrives at each station, the name of the station is called out, and, after the train gets underway again, the name of the next station is called out. On these trains, every passenger, short and tall, male and female, white and black, is reading a newspaper. It seems to be a national malady here. On the train and on the street, on every park bench and on every steamship, everyone is occupied with such reading matter. What a waste of time, and how much silly, incorrect and superficial stuff is absorbed in this way.

We wanted to have a look at Central Park.[69] The sun was burning hot and we were perspiring, but only because we were walking in the sun. It was actually no hotter than Berlin at this time of year. Central Park is similar to our *Tiergarten* and similar in layout to the Brussels park, with trees, shrubbery and great meadows and footpaths, but also a few roadways. Nor is it lacking in more formal gardens. The American penchant for moderation is evident in small details here as well: "Keep off the grass" is written in big letters on wooden signs three feet high.

After more aimless meandering through the park we came to the obelisk, only recently arrived from Europe, which had been created roughly in Moses's time.[71] Now it stands in the New World and stares at times and people which it could never have imagined in its time. It knows so much, which can never be wrested away from it, because it has seen Alexander [*the Great*] and

Napoleon—it has seen the downfall of empires and the vanishing of splendid cultures, the intrusion into the desert sands and the breaking-through of its lands, in order to give the sea-current a new pathway through those lands.[72] But now that its script [*the hieroglyphics*] has been deciphered, we can read its history just as millions upon millions of people read it in ancient times. Poor granite! No Egyptian priest wanders past you now; only an American policeman with his leather truncheon is there to stand guard over you. And your view no longer scans that which the rising sun illuminates, onto those sacred precincts where persons honoring you stand, but onto the tasteless Metropolitan Museum[73] and on the little people like us, who criticize you. Criticize you! If we could only hear your sarcastic laughter! But we [*Lewin and Warburg*] are laughing, too, laughing over the American who, in order to create a link between the obelisk and the pedestal, has created as a substitute for the missing cornerstone something out of bronze, on which is inscribed in Greek the story of the obelisk's origins.

Catty-cornered from the obelisk stands the aforementioned museum. Although brand-new and luxuriously outfitted, it seems from the outside as if it had been built in the fifteenth century. There are many fine objects inside, particularly among the modern paintings and sculpture. For example, a painting by Rosa Bonheur,[74] a Brozik,[75] a marble Medea from Latona and so on. Close by are swords and Assyrian masks, textiles and porcelains—this is, after all, an American collection!

Very tired now, we go back to Sallenbach's. Still nothing! That was a blow, but what could be done? We couldn't understand it, but comforted ourselves with the thought that tomorrow morning we would certainly have letters in hand.

It was past lunchtime at the hotel. We headed to a friendly neighborhood bar and, for a small glass of beer (about two wine-glasses full) paid one Mark! Impossible to convey how expensive everything is here. One may well say that a 10-pfennig coin at home is worth exactly 10 cents (40 pfennige). The only thing that's cheap here is baked beans.

Once we got back to the hotel we undressed and napped, then we went back downstairs and I persuaded Uncle to accompany me to a barbershop. It was very funny. As is the custom in America, I stretched out on what looks like a surgical chair that you would see in a hospital, while Uncle sat next to me and read. In the chair next to mine a man was having his shoes shined while his hair was being trimmed.

Dinner at 7:00! It is incredible how much there is to choose from on the menu, and as a hotel guest you are entitled to all of it. However, we had decided ahead of time to be prudent in what we chose to eat and to be moderate in our eating. An interesting item: we noted with amusement that, after having ordered only a half-bottle of wine, we had to move to another table, so that no one would be scandalized by our consumption of alcoholic beverages. We were tempted not to give in to the demands of this sanctimonious nation, but in the end we decided it was better to take it as a joke than to get steamed up over it. At table, people drink only ice water, while, in secret, they consume every kind of alcoholic beverage you can think of.

You ladies could not have traveled with us, even if it were otherwise possible. The jewelry alone—without which even the simplest lady would not dare to be seen in public—would cost about $10,000, and that doesn't even include the cost of the dress! I pointed this out to Uncle, and from then on we amused ourselves by checking out every passing woman and putting a value on her from the value of her diamonds. There are women who shine only through their jewelry, but some by their beauty as well. Women seem here altogether to be more highly valued than men. In the hotel they have their own "Ladies Entrance," a special entrance reserved for them.

At 8:30 we went to the Madison Square Theater.[76] I've already sent you a view of the theatre. It's a little jewel box, the likes of which I've never seen before, with many loges on the two sides. The carpeting is so thick that you can't hear any footfalls. There are three entrances to the theatre from the street. The stage curtain is embroidered in the Japanese style. There's a stork at the edge of a blue pond, tall ships in the background, a blue sky above. The walls of the theatre, on the left and on the right, are mirrored, so that, if you're sitting in the orchestra, you can look to the left or the right, and see clearly the people sitting in the first row. The play was stupid—I couldn't understand what they were saying, but I could follow the action very well—but the acting was outstanding. In the end all the loose strings in the plot were neatly tied up. Satisfied, we returned to the hotel.

Saturday, August 13

Although our beds are very comfortable, we were up this morning by 5 o'clock, and it was still early when we boarded our favorite means of transport, the elevated, which brought us to the Battery, the southernmost point of Manhattan Island, on which New York stands. To one side flows the East River, on the other side the Hudson. We looked for Castle Garden,[77] the place where all steerage passengers must land, either to find work here in New York or to be sent onward into the interior.

The weather was wonderful. The fresh sea-breeze reminded me of our passage. We felt no discomfort from the heat and laughed at those who had warned us of the tropical heat of New York. To pass the time until one o'clock, when we were scheduled to ask again for our mail, we took one of the huge ferry boats to Staten Island, past the Statue of Liberty. There we saw towns made up almost entirely of stately wooden houses, surrounded by trees and beautifully situated high above the road with a view of the Upper Bay and New York itself. Then back again. On these boats there is almost always a trio of musicians playing, two violins and a harp, or a violin, a lute and a harp. When they stop playing, one of the musicians goes around to collect money from those willing to give some. On the ferry, as in the streets of the city, we see many ladies dressed all in white, with finely embroidered ruffles; it makes a very good impression.

At last we returned to Sallenbach's, full of expectation, but, again, no mail. Mr. Schlesinger (who, it seems to me, has the first signs of a brain infection), went to the post office with us. The firm's box was empty. Inconceivable! I was and am very much put out about it. Uncle kept me from sending a wire. Of course we are not going to start [*out, on the trip,*] until we have had mail from you.

With Mr. Schlesinger, we went to Cook's Travel Agency and let him show us the itinerary that they had arranged for us. I shall send you the maps you will need in order to follow our progress. Here it is:

New York > Buffalo > Niagara Falls
Suspension Bridge > Port Dalhousie
Port Dalhousie > Toronto
Toronto > North Bay
North Bay > Port Arthur
Port Arthur > Vancouver
Vancouver > San Francisco (by steamer)

From Niagara Falls we are going to make a side trip to Montreal, and then perhaps in the other direction, to Detroit. The way back will probably be by Atlantic Pacific, as noted.

Mr. S. gave me the key to his post office box, so that I could look for letters myself, this afternoon and tomorrow morning. Back at my hotel room, I studied the maps, because I was not in a mood for letter-writing. In the afternoon, on our way to the post office, we went to a saloon (Hoffman's). We had noticed its splendor yesterday and wanted to have a look at it. We each had a glass of beer, so as to be able to sit down and see the inside. I can't describe the place to you in detail. It's enough to say that, next to a genuine Correggio,[78] under glass and illuminated from above like all other originals by an electric light, even in daytime, are a life-size Bacchante,[79] in bronze, and paintings by modern masters, marble statues, small bronzes, etc., etc. There is no way to put a price on the value of these furnishings, but there is nothing in the world to equal it. When we went back to the post-box, we found many letters for Mr. S. but none for us. I will spare you a description of my reaction.

We took the elevated onto the Suspension Bridge.[80] It makes a powerful impression. One simply can't fathom how such enormous masses of stone and iron can be held in suspension! The cables that help to carry the weight are non-rigid. The bridge sways when the railroad passes over it—but it holds. We went over by rail in about four minutes, and walked, at a moderate pace, in about three-quarters of an hour from one end to the other. It is a wonder-work and a triumph of the human mind and mathematical calculation.

In my bad mood I wrote a postcard to you. Please be more conscientious about writing, for you know that I cannot live without news from you. We were in bed by nine o'clock.

Sunday, August 14

Early in the morning we were at the post office. Eureka! At last! At last! You are well! How happy I was to have received your mail! Heaven be praised that everything is alright. You women of course did more talking than thinking. Via England, although you knew that the *Eider* sailed on the second or third. But I am happy to have my letters and I am not going to argue. May God keep you well—that is the important thing.

[Here Lewin discusses a personal matter.]

Even so, my dear heart, I beg you to refrain from making social calls and undertaking visits [*while she is on vacation*]. The old aunts are not waiting for your calls! It really distresses me that you have already lost a half-week. Be egotistical! Think of yourself and your duties! *Mens sana in corpore sano*! Be strong, and be willing to say no. Let others gossip—they have nothing else to do!

As a celebration we made a trip to Long Branch, the most elegant seaside resort. There were about 1,200 people on the ship that took us there. We couldn't help but think of the possibility that the boat and its passengers might encounter some misfortune.[81] Such thoughts were provoked by seeing the words, "Life Preservers," stenciled everywhere to indicate where those rings were stored.

On the Elevated, there are advertisements for insurance companies, stating how much you get for losing a hand or a leg, etc. These notices are particularly pertinent on the Elevated because habit can make people so indifferent that they use this ostensibly most dangerous of all means of transport with complete unconcern. It is difficult to convey the boldness of the structure, the recklessness of the driving. There is a greater sense of safety on these large steamers. There is room for everybody, and everyone enjoys the sea-breeze. Outside the bay two sailing boats circled around our ship, with the sails imprinted on both sides in enormous letters: "Use Dr. Scott's Electric Corsets" and "Liver Pills." One has to laugh!

We are enthralled at the beauty of the seashore that we pass. Once we pass Sandy Hook, the beaches are flat and white; one resort follows another. Everywhere one sees airy wooden structures, boardwalk jitneys, people. After a two-hour trip we arrive at a handsome pier, made of iron and jutting far out into the sea. It took about a half-hour for all the passengers to disembark. Neither Ostend[82] nor Sylt[83] can compare with this seaside resort.

Men and women bathe together in abominably ugly bathing suits. Intending to swim in the salty ocean water, I got a token for 25 cents and a shabby blue bathing suit and the dirtiest, most unappetizing and flimsiest dressing area that I've ever seen. On the ticket-taker's advice, Uncle took my watch and wallet for safe-keeping. I undressed quickly and dove into the sea. I had a fine swim—the sea reminded me of Sylt, but with that dreadful suit on, swimming gave me only half the pleasure.

There is life and animation everywhere. On the beach and in the resort proper; that is to say, there is a string of resorts that extends for about a mile along the beach. Hard by the sea there is a big restaurant, but not for us. It proclaimed itself to be a "Temperance Restaurant," with milk-drinking men, lemonade-drinking women! We were thirsty for beer. A German *bierstube* beckons. We enter. Beer and lobster salad! The dish arrives, Uncle takes a bite—ughh! Spoiled and rotten! If even Uncle is disgusted, then you know it had to be really bad! We returned the dish but even so we had to pay this German scoundrel about 3 marks, over our strong objections.

We wandered through nearly the whole town, which stretches quite a long distance along the beach. All the houses are surrounded by greenery. On the return trip to New York, we couldn't leave the pier until five o'clock, and when we got there, we were among the first to disembark, but, even so, we didn't get back to the hotel until 8:15PM. At that hour, we were too late for dinner, although we had paid for it; all we got was cold cuts and tea. Afterwards, we went upstairs and busied ourselves writing letters until bedtime.

We decided, since the boat to Albany wasn't scheduled to leave until nine o'clock in the morning and we had to see Mr. Schlesinger first, that we wouldn't leave until Tuesday.

Monday, August 15

Today we booked our return passage on the [*S.S.*] *Wieland* [84] for the 28th of September. Then we went to see Mr. Schlesinger, who will forward our trunks to Washington [*D.C.*], leaving us to travel with our hand luggage only. Later we packed and prepared everything for an early start. So, tomorrow morning at nine o'clock! On into the wilderness! Perhaps we shall go to the theater again tonight.

Tuesday, August 16

We didn't undertake anything yesterday, as we had thought we might. Uncle felt weak. On Sunday we hadn't eaten much and today he had no appetite at all, even though on our voyage across the Atlantic he had been as normal as could be in this respect. He wrote in his diary for about two hours, then we went out for a short walk, then came back to the hotel and put the finishing touches on our packing. I included in my bag a little German-English dictionary, which I had bought so that I wouldn't have to ask Uncle

Hudson River Line, S. S. Albany

all the time for the meaning of a word. We went out for dinner, but Uncle had only a little soup and we went to bed early. He even passed up his usual after-dinner cigar.

We woke up at 5:00AM. Uncle was coughing a great deal, whereas on the ship coming over he had hardly coughed at all, and he was worse off today than yesterday. At 8:00 in the morning we left for the boat, which departed on schedule an hour later. You just can't get over the sense of astonishment you feel in seeing this vessel. If I had thought I had seen the largest ship before this, I learned now that it was not as big as this one.

It isn't just the size of the ship that is so remarkable, but its layout and furnishings—you'd think you had been set down in a palace. Wherever you look, you see wonderful boldly-grained lemonwood, such as you and I once saw in a bedroom furniture suite. You see the same wood in the stairways and corridors. On all three decks and on the stairs there is thick carpeting, which deadens the sound of footfalls. Your feet fall deeply into these floor coverings and they're also pleasing to the eye. Throughout, there are practical ornamented Smyrna carpets. On the first floor you find wide and deep elegant leather-upholstered chairs and comfortable easy chairs, covered with the finest silks, that you don't just sit down on, you sink down into them. At the foot of the wide stairways that lead to the ground floor, there are two wide fountains, surrounded in that same boldly-grained wood and with porcelain bowls, and with cups hanging from silvered chains.

S. S. Albany, interior

Rounding out the picture is a large luxuriously-appointed dining room, and, off the main dining room, smaller rooms which can be had for private dining, at extra cost. A band in uniform plays dances and marches. The cleanliness of everything from the engine room to other unidentifiable rooms is absolutely astounding. Most of the people on board are well dressed, when they aren't running around in their shirtsleeves and without their vests. We've seen many elegantly-dressed women, most of them dressed in raw silk, with little hats on their heads and carrying small sticks in their hands, shaped like this [*Lewin drawing omitted*].

These people are headed for Saratoga,[85] the finest spa in America. And now, should I try to describe for you the scenery that met my astonished eyes? I've seen Switzerland, the Rhein, the Elbe and so on. Nothing compares to the banks of the Hudson. That majestic wide river, dotted with countless vessels of all kinds, discharges perhaps double the amount of water into the ocean as the Elbe does. As far as the eye can see is the most magnificent greenery. For mile upon mile, these green forests beckon to the eye as a soothing resting-place. Where the ship can't get close enough to the shore, you fix your telescope on these forested vistas, to see these continuous stretches of steep mountain cliffs, accessible on foot only with difficulty, or not at all. These are the nourishing ground on which the majestic deciduous trees and shrubs grow. High up on the rocky cliffs—this is particularly true on the left side—and a short distance back, are villas. I say "a short distance," but it's hard to judge, because the ship moves with a speed, a breakneck pace, that's unique to steamships. On the right [*eastern*] side of the river, the view is not so wild. Here the houses are larger, the cliffs not as high and not as steep. Even on this side there are exceptions, and one can see here, too, at times falling away to the water's edge, partly covered with foliage, masses of granite and sandstone rock formations.

Where the shoreline permits it—that is, where the cliffs don't come right down to the water's edge—we see villas, houses, cities. Many, like Yonkers, are built up on the heights like Blankense,[86] but on a much larger scale and perhaps, because of the scale of development, more pleasing to the eye. Where the eye can see beyond the cliffs, you can glimpse beyond them, in the distance, shrouded in a blue haze, far-ranging high mountains, the likes of which you can see elsewhere only in Switzerland.

On both shores, on tracks running close to the water's edge, you see trains, here dashing across bridges, there cutting behind the cliff-masses. On the left side you see them only sometimes, on the right side, with short interruptions, almost the whole time.

The Hudson and its shores produce their own unique effects. No legends, no traditions, are connected to these rocks. No Lorelei[87] sings her siren song here, to give rise to a myth, but many a red-skinned siren may have intoned the eternal song, the song of love, from these rocky ledges. No crumbling robber barons'[88] castles look down from the heights, but many a modern robber-baron sits up there and, refreshed for new action by his rest from Saturday at

1:00PM, descends on Monday morning to his store and gets ready to skin the public all over again. The Rhine is very beautiful, but everywhere you must listen to its tales. The aura of olden times, embodied in legend and history, belongs to that river, as the young cities, the chimneys, the factories and the villas belong to the Hudson.

The sharpest bend in the river is at West Point, the famous American military academy. There are also forts here, to defend the Hudson. We also pass many islands, like in the Pfalz,[89] but, again, without the legends. The farther the ship travels up the Hudson, the lower the cliffs and shoreline. The cliffs and rock-formations attempt here and there to reach the shoreline, but for the most part they retreat farther into the countryside or are transformed into smaller hills. I had wondered in New York [*City*] about the great use of stone in the buildings. Now I have the answer: a thousand cities the size of New York could not use enough stone from these mountains to make a dent in the cliffs along this river!

As wonderful as it was to see the ever-changing scenery at every point along the river, and as strong an impression as it made on me, I couldn't really enjoy myself because of my anxiety over Uncle's condition. As soon as we had taken our place on the boat, he fell asleep, then awoke, then nodded off again. I stayed next to him and noticed that his face was very pale and his hands cold to the touch. I found the last available private sitting room and paid a steep price to take it—a marvelous space with a chaise longue, armchairs, three windows, all positioned so that one could enjoy the scenery. Once we were in the room, I suggested that he take off his coat and lie down. He fell asleep right away and slept from 11:30AM to 2:00PM. He felt ill, admitted that the previous night he had had cold sweats. He was totally apathetic, which is not his usual disposition. I kept after him, until he finally ate a bowl of soup and drank two glasses of ale. Then he went back to sleep until 5:30. I decided not to continue on past Albany and he agreed. I gave him some pills to take [*evidently a laxative*]. As we approached Albany he told me he felt weak in his legs, but his overall weariness seemed to have gone and he appeared to have regained his spirits.

At six o'clock we arrived in Albany. A crowd of Negroes, shouting over each other to be heard, surrounded us. One of them pushed us into a hotel-bus; we rattled over the bumpy cobblestoned pavement to the hotel. There another crowd of perhaps twenty Negroes surrounded us. Neither of us had an appetite for dinner. Uncle decided that we should continue on [*without spending the night in Albany.*] It seemed from his renewed energy that he was feeling better. We noticed here, as we had in New York, the unbelievable dirt that can be seen in the streets of American cities, even though this is the state capital. In contrast is the cleanliness of the State Capitol, all in stone and beautifully proportioned. Nothing in Berlin can match it. A horse-tram takes you up the steep hill to the Capitol. By the illumination of electric street lamps we made our way on foot back to the train station. This city, like other cities that we have been in and passed through, is lit by electricity, although the amount of light leaves much to be desired. At the train station we reserved places in the sleeping-car. We had tea at the hotel, and were outrageously cheated in the process. At 10:00PM the train departed for Niagara Falls.

I should mention that I encountered my first mosquitoes in Albany. They didn't bother me. Much more unpleasant and repugnant was the plague of flies, which are to be found everywhere, and nobody does anything about it. Neither in New York nor anywhere else have we seen flypaper or anything of that sort. The flies "stick" to people, covering the food on the sideboards and at the dining tables. In Albany we noticed that an inventive landlord had put a fan-contrivance in motion, driven by a motor;[90] it serves as ventilation and also drives away the flies. In the middle of the ceiling there is an axle with 5-6 wheels. From these wheels rope transmitters run to side-wheels, which are connected to movable propellers. [*Lewin drawing omitted.*]

When we entered the sleeping car we couldn't believe our eyes: we were going to share our car with twenty other people, with no partitions! Each section contained an upper berth and a lower berth, the two beds guarded from profane gazes by a curtain which could be drawn across the opening.

This was not at all to our liking, and even less so our discovery that this sleeping car had berths for both sexes, i.e. women sleeping among the men. And, to top it all off, it turned out that Uncle and I both had upper berths, in different parts of the sleeping car! This was most awkward, because Uncle cannot climb up to the upper berth, and moreover it was to be expected that the pills I had given him would have their effect during the night. As I was on my way to seek out our reciprocal bed-companions, an Englishman came up to me and said something, but I was preoccupied and didn't pay attention. But I soon learned that this man had been separated from his wife in the same way that Uncle and I had been. As neither Uncle nor I cared to have the lady as a companion in our section and were not interested in the secrets of her toilette, the exchange was soon agreed upon.

At bedtime, I played the valet for Uncle, who wanted to sleep fully dressed. I undressed him a little, by force, and then scrambled up to my pallet. Even though I was clad like Adam, the heat was oppressive. But the berth was wide and comfortable. These carriages have no outer corridors [*as in Europe*], and all the berths being laid out longitudinally, the space saved improves the width of the berth. Both of us slept well. By 6:30AM, we had arrived in Buffalo. On the way to the washroom, one catches glimpses of the men and women still in bed, because the curtains do not draw tightly. But the women do not seem to be prudish in this country, in spite of their seeming seclusion in "Ladies Parlors."

Wednesday, August 17

The stop in Buffalo lasted a long time. I studied physiognomies, especially those of the Negroes. If one of them speaks to a "brother in color,"[91] he gestures with his hands and arms and shows a lot of gleaming white teeth. With the very dark ones, this gives them quite an alarming appearance.

Newsboys were hawking their newspapers, the be-all and end-all of American existence, their cries mingling with those of the bootblacks: "Shine! Shine!" Two of these shoeshine boys jumped onto the train, and one of them jumped down with marvelous dexterity while the train was already underway and picking up speed.

At about 8:00AM the train pulled into Niagara [*Falls*], a large city. When Uncle had been here before, the town had no more than thirty houses; today one hotel adjoins another and one villa stands near another. There are big stores, electric lighting and other prerequisites of a booming town, complete with all manner of cabs and carriages as well. "Cataract Ice" is advertised in big letters, and a fine building bears the name, "Cataract Bank." I for one—*nomen est omen*[92]—wouldn't care to entrust them with my money. "Pearline" and "Tutt's Liver Pills" shine from every fence, every wall; and Barnum, the Great Barnum,[93] announces his activities in gigantic larger-than-life pictures. In the middle of the enormous posters that announce his arrival is his portrait, with the legend: "I Am Coming! Wait!"

We put up at Niagara House, for Uncle thought this was where he might have stayed on his first visit here forty years ago. This wood-frame house indeed looked ancient and decrepit enough to have served as his hostelry so long ago. We got a room which had just been vacated, were served bad coffee and took off for the Falls![94]

> [*Here is inserted what is evidently a tourist brochure, in English, entitled "Niagara Falls, The Great Cataract."*]

We hired a carriage, because I didn't want to expose Uncle to the strain of having to see all the worthwhile sights of Niagara on foot. The waiter at the hotel, who spoke broken German, had given us to understand that only people with money should come to Niagara, and that such people shouldn't mind hiring a carriage for 4-5 hours if they were traveling for pleasure.

First we drove to the whirlpool.[95] The roar of its waters can be heard from afar. An enterprising American has built a wooden shaft extending down from the edge of the cliff for a distance of 100 feet. This shaft is enclosed with wooden boards on all sides, except the side facing the cliff-wall, which is open. Inside the shaft two elevators move up and down, powered by a gas engine.

We stepped into one of the elevators. The descent caused me some anxiety. Here in America, more than elsewhere, life hangs by a thread. That realization comes, unless one lacks common sense, especially in an apparatus such as that one. After a while, we reached the bottom of the shaft. One can hardly find the words to describe the impact that this seething cauldron of water makes. How many people have experienced the Falls! Niagara Falls is something quite extraordinary. With incredible velocity the waters come crashing down from the heights and into the rocky bed below, where they encounter all kinds of hindrances to their onward progress. There the waters foam and tumble and, no sooner has the first wave overcome those hindrances, than the second, and then the third and the fourth. The water spray shoots up to unbelievable heights. The first quiet sounds of the eddying water are then amplified a thousandfold, as the water roars, thunders, screams and howls, so loud that you can't hear your own words. And then, again and again, the water crashes down into the rock, one wave upon the next, and so it will be for thousands of years, and for thousands of years men will wonder at and try to recapture this same water-spectacular. And yet men will profane their impressions, the grandeur of which should still be imprinted on their minds, through all kinds of silly irrelevancies. To pose for photographs at the Falls is a profanation, and I am of the opinion that those who pose in that way don't have a true comprehension of this unique nature-scenery.

The ascent back to the top, in that elevator, was also uncomfortable. Happily, we did come to the top in one piece and made our way towards Goat Island, saw the rapids from that vantage point and then, again, the cascading waters as they plunged over the falls and into the depths. The impression that made on us as we stood there was as powerful as what I've already described. Where the water plunges over the edge of the cataract, it takes on a beautiful light-green color, before turning into white foam, and the thundering roar in the depths announces that the water has reached its destination.

It was a glorious day; the sun shone over the scenery, causing two rainbows to appear, near the bottom, where two of the mighty torrents were dissolving into the finest mist. Many people enjoyed the sight together with us, making it seem almost like a small Barbarian invasion.[96] Within the fenced-off area, from which you could enjoy the view, Uncle scrambled confidently over both the rough and the smooth terrain. From there we went to Luna Island, where the Niagara, all small eddies, whirlpools and rapids, can be viewed in its entire mighty expanse. There I picked a few red leaves, thinking of you.

After visiting a few more of these observation points, we drove over the new Suspension Bridge,[97] paying the dollar toll, to the Canadian side. Here, from the roof of a hotel, we saw the much more imposing Canadian Falls, and also the American Falls, leaving us with an indelible impression and an unforgettable memory.

In preparation for a trip to the bottom of the falls, and underneath them, we put on an outfit made of sailcloth [*canvas*]—trousers, coat or cloak, muffler, cap and galoshes. You can imagine how funny we looked. Wearing that outfit, we had to cross a busy street to the flight of stairs which leads about 150 feet down. As soon as we stepped off the stairway at the bottom, we became aware of a fine penetrating mist. Unlike the American Falls, under which a wooden walkway has been built, here there is only a boulder-strewn pathway, three arms-lengths wide at the start, but gradually getting so narrow that there is hardly room to put one foot next to the other. The guide went ahead, Uncle followed, then I brought up the rear, forming a kind of chain. We got past the first and second cataracts and were already soaking wet but the guide wanted to go on. Then we were told to turn and put our backs against the face of the cliff, so that we could see the masses of water streaming down. At that point I was seized with such a sense of dizziness and anxiety that I yelled to the guide to turn back. Uppermost in my mind was the concern I felt for Uncle's safety. The slightest slip on the wet loose stones with our rubber-booted feet was bound to bring instantaneous death. Uncle laughed at my fear, but nevertheless I had the guide clamber past us and step by step we went back. I was happy to feel solid ground under my feet once again.

Hot and perspiring, we arrived at the top. Our return drive took us across the suspension bridge, a structure which boldly and lightly spans the river, through pretty groves with numerous sumac shrubs, and so back to our hotel, where we revived ourselves with refreshments and wrote to you. In the evening, at 8 o'clock, on to Montreal (Uncle had gone out by himself that afternoon and purchased the tickets).

*"The Guide went ahead, Uncle followed, then I
brought up the rear, forming a kind of chain."
(Louis Lewin drawing)*

After endless ticket-checking and ticket-punching, we arrived at our sleeping car and found our own compartment, the Stateroom. We were glad to be by ourselves, and both of us in splendid spirits. Uncle demonstrated his good humor by hearty renditions of *"Le Senateur"* and *"Le Roi d'Yvetot."*[98] By this time it was 11 o'clock, and other people on the train were already sleeping. I asked a black porter to make our beds. It wasn't his job to do that, he told me, adding that the porter who was responsible for our compartment was drunk, and that he was not willing to do his job for him. In the end he condescended to do as we had requested, and made up one bed. The other one? There wasn't one; the bed he made up was to serve us both. I made a good German fuss, but in the end, despite all the talking on both sides, and although I made a row that drew the attention of all the train employees, no second bed was to be had. The rascals had sold the other bed "under the counter"—you could see that in the look of embarrassment on their faces.

I made Uncle stretch out on the one bed. I asked him to tell me what the word *"beklagen"* was in English; he said it was "to complain." "I complain about this," both of us reiterated high and low, but if there is no bed to be had, even a negro cannot supply one, so in the end I lay down on the floor and slept—as Uncle found out when he got up in the middle of the night to go to the bathroom—slept so soundly that I didn't wake up when he forcibly pushed my legs over to one side so that he could get out through the door. Early the next morning I heard a loud knocking and demand for tickets. Responding to this request, I learned that we were in Clayton [*N.Y.*], and that it was time to get off the train; the steamer was waiting.

At this point Uncle was still sitting, undressed, on the bed, with our hand luggage and its contents scattered all about. We made it to the steamer in time, but only with the loss of the bag that Aunt [*Bernhardine Warburg, John Warburg's wife*] had given me, with our opera-glasses and my cigars inside. We left the bag hanging somewhere and there is little chance that we shall see it again.

It was about six o'clock when we boarded the steamer. A light rain was falling, but it did not obscure the view, another one of those exceptional views that you find only in America.

Crossing Canada

August 18	St. Lawrence River
	Thousand Islands
	Montreal
	Toronto
	Winnipeg
August 29	Vancouver

Thursday, August 18

One never encounters a wearisome uniformity here in America. As soon as you have assimilated an extraordinary impression, a new and quite different one replaces it. The steamer was to bring us to Alexandria Bay. We couldn't believe our eyes when we saw an ocean-like expanse of water with hundreds of islands with beautiful groves and equally beautiful villas, usually only one to each island. We were near Lake Ontario, and bound for the basin-shaped extension of the lake which leads directly into the St. Lawrence River, the waterway that Uncle had so longed to see.

The Lake of the Thousand Islands with its Alexandria Bay is once again, like so many things here in America, overwhelming in the sheer scale of its scenic beauty. There are in all 1,692 islands scattered far and wide, sometimes separated by narrow straits, others widely separated like the Hallige Islands.[99] A refreshing quiet pervades everything. If one didn't already know that, wherever there are human beings, there is terrible suffering, in many forms, one would think of these islands as an Eden-like refuge.

Some of the islands have huge wood-frame hotels and summer boardinghouses with balconies and porches. Graceful little boats go back and forth between the islands and the mainland. From Clayton on up to Alexandria we saw very few of these specks of land that were not inhabited. Even if there is barely room on an island for a little wood-frame house, you will find one there, mostly built in the Swiss style with steeply-pitched gables and porches. Only the tiniest of the islands are uninhabited. The enclosed picture gives you a faint idea of these islands and how they are distributed in the waterway.

[Lewin inserts here his sketched map of the St. Lawrence River with its Thousand Islands.]

At about 8:30 we reached Alexandria Bay. There we had about a one-hour layover before the steamer was to come which would take us down the St. Lawrence [*to Montreal*].

Uncle amused me greatly. He admitted that he was tempted to buy a pair of oars which stood outside a shop, on account of their exceptional beauty, but he was afraid of being laughed at. I bought an egg-beater for your kitchen and a screwdriver for myself. Here in Alexandria we became acquainted with a new vocation—that of hotel salesman. An elegant-looking gentleman sidled up to us and handed us a brochure for the Windsor Hotel[100] in Montreal. This same hotel had been recommended to us as the largest in that city. We gave our assent, so were immediately entered into his order-book, and just a few minutes later the staff at the hotel would receive word that a pair of distinguished travelers would make their appearance there. Shortly thereafter, a second gentleman came up to us with the same request [*for a different hotel*], and I may as well add that this individual gave us not a moment's rest during the entire trip. He sensed in us tasty morsels, though we were neither appetizing nor fat.

At last the steamer came, built along the same lines as the Hudson River boat that we had traveled on, but—as we could readily see from the moment we stepped on board—bearing about as much resemblance to those vessels as a not overly-clean village room bears to a royal palace. A numerous company was already on board, so all the best seats were taken. But we did find seats and now we watched as the ship steamed past the thousand and more islands into the St. Lawrence.

The weather was splendid, and we enjoyed the scenery to the fullest. The first hotel salesman annoyed us—indirectly, because he planted himself in the middle of the company and gave a monotonously unbroken, evidently humorous talk about the visible island-world. His audience laughed and applauded after every longish discourse, and he was not long in presenting his order book to those applauders, and its pages filled up noticeably. This is how people do business in America. This man makes the same journey day after day, delivers, unbidden, the same talk day after day and gets his commission on each hotel-victim that he has hooked.

> [*Lewin writes that among the passengers on the boat are a group of lodge members, the "Foresters"* [101] *men with outsize badges, fancy-dress hats, etc., a whole hierarchy.*]

In order to finish with this description of American peculiarities, I will only mention that I have frequently observed that American women seem to have a strange predilection for lemons.[102] Sitting next to us on the deck was a good-looking young woman who, not being content to suck on the lemon, finally ate the whole thing, leaving only the seeds. Coming over on the *Hammonia,* we had already seen young girls sucking on lemons.

The journey was wonderful. The farther down the St. Lawrence we traveled, the larger some of the islands became. On the smaller ones we saw only one or two tents. Americans go out to these islands in the summer months, leading the life of Indians and applying themselves principally to fishing.

[Lewin describes the St. Lawrence River, its banks and its islands.]

The price of our ticket included a meal on board ship. It was pitiable, but we comforted ourselves, as we always do, with ale, sat down at the stern of the boat and chatting amiably, enjoying the changing scene.

There are still some interesting things to come, especially the famous St. Lawrence Rapids.

[Lewin inserts a detailed map of the river and its rapids.]

The plan shows you where they are located. You will also find on the plan, better than I could have recorded them, the facts concerning these rapids, which can be a danger to smaller vessels. Larger ships, too, especially if they are scratched, rotten boxes such as ours, can easily go to pieces if they run aground on the rock masses which cause the whirlpools. As soon as the prow touches one such eddy, the boat heels over, the engine shuts down, the water foams and boils. But, after all, these are not ocean waves! Still, the steamer rolls and groans considerably during the entire passage. Once we get past the rapids, the river current is so strong that the steamer moves along quickly without using its engines.

Before reaching Montreal, we passed under two bridges spanning the St. Lawrence River, remarkable not so much for the boldness of their arches as for their enormous height and length. One of these is the Canadian Pacific [*railroad*] bridge, the other the Victoria Bridge, the latter closer to Montreal.

Shortly before our arrival in Montreal, Uncle was accosted by a gentleman who told us he was a doctor; he talked a lot, pressed closer and closer, so that, in spite of his badge announcing himself as a "Forester," which he wore inside his suit, we suspected him of having sinister intentions and kept our hands tightly over our pockets. He shook hands with me as with a person well known in America through my writings on the "untoward effects of drugs," and said he looked forward to seeing me again in Washington.

At last, at 8:30, we docked [*in Montreal*]. We were glad to be rid of that dangerous trap of a steamer. The *commis d'hotel* placed us in a hotel car, the other pirated victims together with us and in numerous other cars besides ours, and—*nous voilà à l'hotel de Windsor.* I arrived at the hotel with an intense migraine headache.

Hotel Windsor, Montreal, Canada, circa 1887

The hotel is an imposing-looking building with a pillared lobby, very wide corridors, foyers, a suite of ladies' rooms, a profuse use of sandstone and stucco. One senses an effort to imitate the Fifth Avenue Hotel, also with regard to service, etc., but the place falls rather short of this ideal. We had a room on the ground floor, each bed large enough for a family. For all that, I didn't sleep well because I felt indisposed, and dreamed much of you.

Friday, August 19

I woke up feeling fresh and well, and first of all asked for letters—again nothing! I can only suppose that you haven't been writing often and that you mailed the letters the wrong way. We set out for some sightseeing.

From the picture of our little hotel, you can get an idea of its dimensions.

You will get a few factual particulars about this town from the enclosed small clipping and the longer description.

[Lewin inserts here an excerpt from a tourist brochure, with a brief description, in English, of the City and its highlights.]

Having heard of a college in this city—McGill College[104]—we decided to make it our first destination. After much direction-seeking from passersby, we found ourselves standing next to a large park with splendid trees. We entered at random, and found a custodian standing in front of one of the buildings. He took us on a tour of the premises, showed us a poorly equipped chemistry laboratory, simple and serviceable lecture halls, a pretty library, very well-stocked. He talked a lot, of which I of course understood nothing, and then took his leave, directing us first to a neighboring building, the medical college. Here we met another caretaker, a shabby-looking and loquacious but friendly person who held a large number of keys, who was willing to take us around. First the anatomical cabinets: two rooms furnished with only a few cases. In these cases some bones, some preparations in alcohol: *Spiritus preparata*, an anatomical model, a skeleton, a few models of the human brain which didn't seem to be bad, and in glass boxes the brains of different animals, conserved, so it seemed to me, in glycerin.

From there we went, at my request, to the Pharmacological Laboratory, a high-ceilinged room, lit by one large window, with several benches and three-legged stools, perhaps 12 of them, a lecture desk and two cases for the "collection." This is the skimpiest exhibition you can imagine. The few *preparata* standing there looked dirty. The best thing in the whole place was a collection of medicines in green bottles from Parke, Davis & Co.[105] In the background I found, in small vials, a few pathetic remnants of alkaloids. In the same cabinet there were about ten bottles of medicine filled with all sorts of mixtures. Our guide explained that they were left over from the previous semester—the students had prepared them for practice. Of instruments, a separate study for the professor, etc.—nothing.

Still worse was the furnishing of the Physiological Laboratory. This discipline can only be taught and made understandable if at least the most fundamental things are shown. But in the instrument cases here I saw only a kymograph[106] and some smaller knick-knacks. There was also a big room for individual research.

More impressive than these is the relatively large and well-furnished Chemical Laboratory, with many work-stations for the students. Some of the necessary equipment, for example the kiln, looked as if it had been out of use for a very long time. Also in this same building was a room for Histology, with many good microscopes, and one for Anatomy. This latter, though somewhat primitive, serves its purpose adequately, especially since material for dissection is said to be available in abundance. We also had a look at the cellar, the library, etc.

Finally, we were provided with last year's report of the College. As to the entrance examinations, the elementary course requirements, and the questions asked of the students in the year-end examinations, the report is apt to cast a most peculiar light on the training of American doctors. It amused me that the report of the pharmacologist places great emphasis on knowledge of the "untoward effects of drugs."[107] This is said to be an excellent college. If that is so, what about the less well-known ones?

From there we went to see Mr. B., who was away on a trip. His brother-in-law talked a lot without saying much. His purpose, as near as I could tell, was to depict his brother-in-law as a business genius.

We left him very soon and took a carriage for a sightseeing trip around the city, but only after our host had provided us with a few French novels—German ones are not to be found in all of Canada. Our first destination was Notre Dame de Lourdes,[108] a large church with three naves, the interior decorated with gold everywhere, but also with very fine wood carvings. From there we went to the Jesus church, with several large paintings of saints hanging on the walls. Someone was playing the church organ while we were inside. Then we stopped at a tavern for some ale as a restorative and passed the architectural showplaces of the town on our way to Mount Royal Park.

Three-quarters of the way to the park we passed a large building which, we were told, was the French Hospital. I decided to take a look at it. In my broken French I communicated my request to the Sister of Mercy who received us. She took my calling card and, after a while, a young doctor came who spoke fast and with whom, of course, my French was doubly broken.

The wards are separated according to nationalities—English, French, Irish—men and women apart. They are still old-fashioned, but clean throughout. Each bed can be enclosed on all sides by a curtain of flower-printed calico and over the bed is a sort of canopy of the same material. The patient lies on a good spring mattress. The floor is snow-white. Most of the patients lying there seemed to be suffering from chronic afflictions. There is no one in this hospital suffering from infectious diseases. These patients have ample opportunity for spiritual edification: in many of the wards I saw large crosses and rosaries.

The Sisters attend to the pharmacy. It looks impeccable, the containers spotless, and the same goes for the equipment. In one ward I saw the sisters handing out the medicine, using a method I think very appropriate. The patients who are ambulatory approach the table where the sister sits with the requisite medicine bottles. She pours out the dose, the patient drinks it and moves away, then the next patient steps up to the table.

The operating theater is well-lit, clean and well-equipped, the seats arranged as if in an amphitheater. I learned that this hospital is also a medical school, and that this one, as well as the other one that we visited and two others still, are autonomous corporations licensed to train doctors. It seems there are many institutes of this kind in Canada!

As is typical with Frenchmen, the man who took me through the hospital was remarkably amiable. Later, a second doctor joined us. He had many questions to ask, which I could answer only in fragments, so to say, on account of my insufficient knowledge of their language. What a pity that one neglects language instruction in school! It is only when you travel in a foreign country that you realize how helpless you are, even if you were able to convey your wishes by all sorts of language-scraps. I intend to fill in this gap [*in my knowledge*].

After leaving the hospital we drove through a magnificent park, in one part of which are all the cemeteries of Montreal, including the Jewish one, and then higher and higher up Mount Royal to a very beautiful observation point, which allows you to see the whole town, lying in radiant sunshine at your feet, and as far as the eye can see the beautiful plain through which the St. Lawrence flows. It is not often that one enjoys such a bird's-eye view, and with it a restful quiet, where, down there, as in the whole world, the fight rages on between God's children. Old World or New, human desire and striving are the same everywhere.

At the hotel we again met Mr. B.'s brother-in-law, whom we invited for lunch. In the afternoon we wrote and had dinner. Meanwhile, it was getting late, so we had to abandon part of our meal and make haste for the train station and our rendezvous with our Canadian Pacific train. The agents of R.D.W[109] welcomed us. We settled down in our compartment. Noiselessly, without signaling its departure, the train which was to house us for the next six days and seven nights moved out of the station.[110]

My sweet Clara! In spite of the excitement that gripped us in anticipation of our forthcoming experiences, I thought of you all the time and realized that it would be almost mid-September until I would hear a word of love from you. Echoing Uncle's frequent prefacing of a sentence, let me say: "Next time I make this voyage," I would give you other instructions before I leave! For the moment, there's no use reasoning.

Compartment No. 8, exactly in the middle of the car, received us. In the accompanying picture, it is on the left side, the seats clearly drawn. One of the double-seated couches is mine, the other is Uncle's. The window is between us, and a table can easily be set up underneath it. Now we have our books lying on that table, but, because of the way that the train jerks this way and that as it speeds along, I can only write by holding the writing pad down with my left forearm. Uncle's bed consists of the two lower couches which can be connected by an upholstered centerpiece. My bed is released and comes down from the wall of the compartment by pressing a spring-release button. This is a real Pullman car which, according to Canadian Pacific officials, costs $20,000-$25,000, or about 100,000 marks.

The lavatories are exemplary and their fittings as practical as can be imagined. The smoking room, ladies-parlor and the many mirrors complete the equipment. To keep out the dust, the windows are double-paned, and tooled leather blinds protect you from the glare of the sun. The passenger's every conceivable and attainable wish has been anticipated and executed with solid workmanship.

Soon we grew thirsty. At dinner we had had only ice water, which lay uncomfortably in our stomachs. But a dining car is only attached at eight o'clock in the morning, runs with the train for twelve hours, and is replaced by another car which stands ready at the next station. Our porter, who looks very Jewish but is a Negro with a light complexion— probably the result of repeated racial intermixing—and who even speaks some broken German, beckoned to me on the sly to come to the stateroom

Canadian Pacific RR *Pullman sleeping car*

and offered me gin. I quickly fetched Uncle and we were both revived by this beverage. We asked for a small supply and went to bed.

Saturday, August 20

I slept poorly last night, with many interruptions, mostly because I felt cold even with a heavy woolen blanket, and even after having put on my underwear before dawn. Uncle slept so soundly that I had to rouse him at 7:30. A priest, one of several on the train, had arisen even earlier than I had. He had a real stage-priest's face, on the portly side, with eyes whose glance must have had a piercing effect on those who came under his scrutiny. He wore a long clinging soutâne with reddish-violet edgings and buttons of the same color, reddish-violet stockings and Oxford shoes. An enormous golden cross, hanging on a golden chain, gleamed on his chest. His head was covered by a hat of silken felt with a twined sea-green and orange cord and a tassel to match. He soon got off the train.

What a feast for our eyes lay outside the train! For several hours we had been moving through woodland. Wherever you looked, nothing but splendid leafy trees, no somber shadowy pines, but rather light birches, shimmering in the sun, and among them primeval groves.

But in spite of that, much of what you see is depressing. Everywhere, near the train tracks and at a distance, as far as the eye can see, are burnt, half- and entirely-charred tree trunks by the thousands and millions, sticking out of the ground or lying there in a tangle like weeds. They show manifold ways of destruction: here hundreds, rid of their bark, lift their bare boughs and branches toward the sky, over there everything up to a man's height is charred to the core; further on you have only jagged lumps of coal, pathetic remains of what were once magnificent trees.

"They . . . lift their bare boughs and branches to the sky."
(Louis Lewin drawing)

Where you see, here and there, cultivated soil, hundreds or thousands of such stumps crop up. At first you think you are traveling through a cemetery. With all that, you must keep in mind that these burnt-down trees were still comparatively young. The old giants that once stood in these regions, extending for miles on end, have long since found their way into the world by various routes on the Canadian Pacific.

The Canadian Pacific—or, as people say here, the Ci-pi-ar [*C.P.R.*]—has used millions of tree trunks for trackage, for telegraph poles and for the numerous station buildings. All things considered, this railway, which is unique in its grandeur, has had everything coming its way. It received five million acres of land from the Government as a gift, and that's without taking into account other subsidies. This is so vast an area that all of Prussia could probably fit into it twice over. The most splendid forests were—and probably still are—in this region.

From right and left trees have been felled for railroad ties. These ties have only two parallel planes, and the rest is left rough-hewn. On the level ground they are laid fairly close to each other; the track lies on them in a shallow indentation, held in place by hook-shaped nails which grip the track smoothly and are driven deep into the wooden cross-ties. Miles of forest have been used up in order to create this link between the oceans.

Where a farmer put his hand to the clearing of the wilderness, he of course could not fell each tree. Much was burnt off and it may have happened often enough that the fire caught onto adjoining trees and then raged unchecked, destroying all in its path until it died down or was finally put out. How often might a railway crew have set fire to one tree or more, just to cook a meal!

This fertile soil gives back without human assistance what has been lost, and new forests rise from the old, fertilized by the ashes from the old stands, but these, too, if they are nearby, are not spared. In the course of the day we saw many a bare mountainside, now scorched by the sun, which formerly, and not so long ago, provided shade, and many an arid plain, which must blame its lack of water on the destruction of its trees. For all that, we still saw on this one day's journey alone the mightiest and most beautiful forests of deciduous trees to be found anywhere in the world. What a sight it must have been formerly, when man had not yet wreaked havoc with his uncontrolled fires.

We passed many a farm and sometimes stopped at one of them. One, two, sometimes three houses, a pond from which burnt stumps peek out, with ducks swimming busily about, a barn—these are the buildings, but, under the economic conditions now prevailing, they presuppose assured means, especially when, as at the first farm we saw, the fields are dotted with sheaves upon sheaves of grain.

Why don't these people clear their fields of the tree-stumps? Granted, for the time being they still have enough other sources of firewood. It is a fact that the locomotives of the CPR—up to three-quarters of the entire six-day route—are fueled by good timber!

Bringing lovely variety, one lake after another appears in these mountainous woodland regions, most of them framed by leafy forests which perhaps have known only an Indian's tread. These lakes are enormous in size; there are dozens as large as the *Starnbergersee*[111] or larger. Then again we pass smaller, quiet waters, and speeding past us once again are rustling forests where silver birches predominate. On both sides of the right-of-way, and further out as well, the land here, as in the Old World, is subdivided—here too, we see fences and other means of enclosure denoting ownership and possession.

Small settlements have their churches too, and of course their parson, for whom they provide. In Mattawa, where I again picked some leaves for you, three clergymen got off, but this is, by local standards, a rather big place. Even in Rockcliffe, which has only about eight houses, a wooden church rises above man's dwelling-places.

At 11 o'clock we reached North Bay. In spite of the sunshine the temperature was autumnal. In the splendid forest through which we passed after stopping at this junction, we saw the first leaves in their autumn hues— yellow and beautifully reddish-brown among the light green ones. Soon after that, we came to Lake Nipissing,[112] with its large tree-bearing islands, but without visible signs that human beings seek pleasure or gain there. Along the entire length of the lakeshore, we saw not one canoe, not a soul. And so on and on with maddening speed, always the same picture: forests upon forests; mud-huts; log cabins, deserted, perhaps erected only for a few days' use. They are all uniformly built. The soil is leveled off, and log laid upon log. At the corners a rounded indentation gives the log above it a firm point of support. Such a construction is half a man's height; the doorway is even smaller. In those cabins that are destined for more permanent habitation, the gaps between the logs are plugged with clay, and they have some sort of protection against the rain entering from above. The logs used for roofing are halved lengthwise, hollowed out in the form of grooves, and then laid close one to the other. So as not to let the rainwater get through between the logs, every two logs are covered by a similarly hollowed-out one, laid perpendicularly to the first two.

[Lewin inserts his sketch of a log cabin with its split-log roof.]

It's a hard and miserable existence that these hut-dwellers lead, most of them workers employed on the adjacent section of the railroad. What for? For food and clothing. They indeed eat their bread in the sweat of their brow—removed from all that refreshes and diverts even the poorest of men elsewhere. The solitude of the forests, year after year, the passing of the trains, over and over again—this is all these people see. Perhaps they are content!

We have reached mountainous terrain. Night is falling, we go to bed, tired from looking out continuously at the passing scene.

Sunday, August 21

I got up at 7 o'clock and found Uncle already dressed. His innate vigor is astonishing. I told him today that he was to be admired as much as the phenomena which Nature offers us here. What mental and physical keenness![113] His way of enjoying is quieter than mine, more phlegmatic, while mine is sanguine. But impressions have the same powerful effect on both of us and indeed they are of a nature to capture all the senses.

Nothing here bears the imprint of human beings. We speed through a wild rocky region which has been forced by dynamite to make way for us.

After Peninsula, where we arrived at 7:15, and beyond, the identical scene presents itself over and over again: precipitous cliffs and trestles bridging rivers and ravines. To our left, hidden only occasionally by rocks, lies the largest of the American lakes, Lake Superior, for the dimensions of which I find no adequate comparison. I am convinced that Lake Geneva and Lake Constance, and a few Swiss lakes thrown in, could comfortably dance a quadrille in its expanse. Mighty islands dot its surface, all of them wooded—quiet refuges for the animals which not so long ago lived fairly securely in the Canadian woods, but which are today relentlessly pursued by day and night, probably to their extinction, by the eager English huntsmen who can frequently be seen at the train stations in their outlandish sports apparel.

One hardly knows which of my many impressions it is most important to convey: that raspberry-covered hill from which, while the train was stopped at Gravel River, I quickly gathered a handful of berries; or, after Mazukama, those jagged granite masses, more than usually impressive, in whose clefts tall trees have taken root; or the work of man, the railroad construction itself; or that large blue lake—kaleidoscopically the scene changes. In awe I stand on the observation platform of our car, full of reverence for God's creation!

At the Nepigon station, I saw my first Indians, looking decrepit in their seedy clothing. I was nearly left behind there; I had to run for about fifty paces to reach the high step of the passenger car.

We continued to speed through the rocky defiles created for this railroad. Many boulders hung dangerously over the tracks, threatening to fall to our left or our right or on top of us. Woe unto us if one of them should lose its balance! Because of the unbelievable magnitude of this work, the workmen who built these tracks had no time to secure these overhanging boulders. They lie on the steep mountainside, held in place only by the weight of the one on the other. But there is scarcely time for fear; one encounters almost immediately a smooth cliff face, climbing to the height of an immense tower, seemingly as smooth as the palm of your hand. The clattering steam engine and the cars behind them stir up an unbelievable echo as they roll past these remarkable multi-colored masses of stone. About 15 minutes after leaving Nepigon, I saw cliff-masses uniquely colored by the reflection from the evening sun.

Through Ontario by rail, via "rocky defiles" and over viaducts

In the course of the day, splendid forests alternate with burnt-out, charred areas and rocky terrain. Creaking and groaning, groaning and growling, the lightweight wooden bridges spanning the deep gorges bear their heavy burden [*the train*]. An uneasy feeling overcomes me when I stare down from the window of the train into the depths below. Seldom is there a stone foundation to provide a secure anchoring for the many-storied wood structure [*the trestle*] above. Instead, the wooden pylons are usually anchored directly into the ground, intricately arranged so as to distribute evenly the impact of the weight that they must bear.

Around 3:30 in the afternoon we arrived at Port Arthur,[114] a big place, but you can't call it a real town. We were both hungry. The dining car, which had been hitched onto the train that morning (as I said earlier, they change every day), offered us for one dollar such a miserably inedible meal that we decided we would rather go hungry than give the dining car manager any money for such a lunch. A few left-over biscuits helped to allay the worst of our hunger pangs.

The next station was Fort William, formerly a place fortified against the Indians, with an imposing high granite fort placed on a dome-shaped rocky height in the midst of a plateau. Here we had a long stop for the repair of a wheel. I seized the opportunity to send a little boy out to get us biscuits from a bakery—a funny flat and dry sort of pastry with jam worked into it, and two bottles of beer. That was our dinner.

On the way to Fort William, we always had Lake Superior in view on our left. But once we left Fort William, the lake disappeared from view and the scenery changed; it was no longer as wild, but flatter and more cultivated. We saw extensive grassy plains, though, before long, rocks and forests with their familiar aspects returned. At 7:45 I saw an Indian tribe with tents grouped in a cluster on the open plain. They had lit fires and we were close enough to be able to recognize two canoes with their singularly-shaped projections at the prow.

At nine o'clock I left the compartment for the platform. An unusual sight awaited me there. On the horizon were deep-red stripes against the sky, of a dusky dark-blue hue. The train stood out against it as a black shadow, while in the foreground a large lake melded its silvery-gray surface to the overall picture in a harmonious blending of hues. The boundless plain is clad in darkness. Silence reigns everywhere—even the tireless cicadas are at rest. A sharp wind blows over the prairie. I go to bed thinking of you, of my beloved children and of my far-away parents.

Monday, August 22

I arose early, dressed quickly and got myself ready for the day. I was freezing last night, despite the extra blankets which the obliging porter had fetched for me. We were approximately two hours east of Winnipeg, the largest city in Manitoba. Manitoba is a heavily settled area in comparison with what one sees elsewhere in Canada. The prairie stretches as far as the eye can see, with grasses in abundance, fragrant herbs and pretty flowers. The farms become more numerous, one sees great herds of cattle, and large barns next to the homesteads which, so far as I could tell, were still rather crudely built. I also saw haystacks in the fields and handsome horses grazing. At the Birds Hill train station I saw two Indians, dressed in outdated and ill-fitting European clothing. I felt some sympathy for them and gave them a few cents; Uncle did too. You can immediately recognize an Indian by his unique brown complexion, the straight black hair and the prominent cheekbones.

This beautiful area gave Uncle the idea of sending John here and to push him into farming. We spun this plan back and forth and finally came jointly to the conclusion that this would offer us the only opportunity to see Canada again, in the event that John were to come over here, and marry here, and we would then come back to attend his wedding. Then it came to me that I should send this young man with the prominent cheekbones over here. Here he would lose his slothfulness and become a self-supporting man, one who could stand on his own two feet, while in Europe he would always be a little momma's boy and would never become a regular businessman.

We arrived in Winnipeg at 9:30AM, and were told that we would lay over here for forty minutes. For my dear wife, I decided to buy a couple of items which we were told could be had in this city. So we rushed in a carriage to the store that had been recommended to us, but we didn't find what we were looking for. Nevertheless, we took this opportunity to see the city, the largest on our route between Toronto and the Pacific Coast, and, by our standards, the only place you could truly call a city. We were particularly impressed by the streets on which we walked—actually the main streets. Most of the houses are made of wood and are typically four stories high. More striking than the houses are the enormous shop signs and outdoor advertisements which are to be found everywhere—naturally one encounters here the ubiquitous ads for Tutt's Liver Pills. The streets are very wide and very busy. Almost every third house contains a "land office." Many many people, one could say the majority of the population here, are engaged in the buying and selling of lots, not just in Winnipeg and the immediate vicinity, but also elsewhere in Manitoba. At the train station I saw a man dressed in red shirt and trousers, the shirt imprinted in the middle of the chest with the letters "S.A.," that is, the Salvation Army. He served as a kind of walking advertisement.

In a hurry now, we ate our breakfast and bought some brandy as provisions for our journey. I took the risk of sending you from here a long detailed letter which, I hope, will reach you. I also had the opportunity during our stopover here to observe the unique hairstyle worn by women and girls, which consists of cutting the hair short at the back like a man's up to the top of the head and arranging it in front pony-like, parted in the middle.

And now, off to the prairie proper. For mile after mile the prairie is beautifully cultivated. It seems to me that even ordinary people enjoy a certain degree of financial comfort here. They earn, in proportion, much more than their counterparts in Europe, but, on the other hand, everything is much more expensive here than in, for instance, at home in Germany. I have come to see that we live in a truly blessed country. Think of the pleasures that we can enjoy for so little!

[Here follows a description of a short conversation with Warburg about a private family matter.]

Considering what I have seen here up to now, I feel no desire to live here. I had rather come to terms with red-tape bureaucrats and Prussian drill than to endure American conditions of life, American heartiness and American crudeness. An individual is free wherever he has the courage to be himself. It is true: one is often vexed by the irrationality, the vanity, the complacency of self-important fools and shallow-brains, but I must say that our entire education is opposed to the American one. The absence [*here*] of pedantic Privy Councillors[115] and antiquated professors does not make up for the greater material and spiritual benefits which we in Germany undoubtedly possess.

At bottom these Americans and Canadians, free as they are, have all the same hankerings for honors and decorations and the same thirst for power that can be observed elsewhere. Savages and civilized man alike have certain inborn qualities which await only the opportunity for their activation. If the opportunity presents itself, then the European decorates himself with an order that has been given to him indirectly by God, that is, by his deputy on earth, a man "by the Grace of God." The free Canadian fashions his order to his own taste and wears crosses[116] several inches long, hanging from colored ribbons; and the savage, finding a rare feather, puts this fortuitous decoration—*par droit de conquête*[117]—into his hair. It is like that everywhere and always will be! Here, as there, many an ox is worshiped, and perhaps here more than there—the [*new*] Golden Calf!

True humanity is the same all over the world, has the same aspect and the same rarity everywhere. Rational man, knowing the meaning of true humanity, endeavors to make himself better and better so as to come nearer to perfection in this respect: no boundaries of land or sea will separate such people, and they will see as a form of slavery the life they lived within the common compass before striving to attain, to a certain measure, this true humanity.

Such thoughts often come into my head in the course of this journey. I cannot fix them all here, and also need not do so because they live in me, and I want to leave something not yet said for the long winter evenings with my sweet and beloved Clara.

In the afternoon, solitary rocks brought some relief to the monotony of the prairie scene. A light rain obscured the view briefly, but soon the sun came out, showing the profusion of flowers to brilliant effect. Such burgeoning and blooming, such fragrance! And there is no work of man involved!

At every station I jump down from the train platform to pick something at random. That species of mentha[118] which I plucked for Aunt[119] in List,[120] and which she grew at home, fills the air here with its aroma. For our refreshment we put up bunches of this herb to the left and right on our platform.

At 4:30 we reach Brandon and note with surprise the elegance of the women and children in this hick town. The suits of the gentlemen as well would not be out of place on a Paris boulevard.

On one side of a wood-frame hotel is a sign with the inscription: "Farmers' Home—one dollar per day—Meals 25 cents." How much must such a farmer earn in order to be able to pay a dollar just for lodging! In every one of these so-called townships, such hotels are recognizable from afar by the big lettering of their grand-sounding names, most frequently, "Queen's Hotel."

In Regina, the Mounted Police entered our car, in the person of a handsome spur-clanking young man. In Berlin he might have passed for an odd sort of "Corps-student." A little black skullcap, kept in place by an elastic at the back of his head, a red hussar's jacket, riding breeches and riding boots, round the waist a belt with around 50 cartridges, and a pistol in a police leather holster on his left side. He checked every piece of hand luggage, lifting every bag and shaking it. The purpose, we learned later, was to look for alcoholic beverages. Fortunately, I had stowed my brandy bottle behind my seat cushion, so it escaped his attention.

The porter puts one of the night-pillows on each seat of the couch to make sitting on it more comfortable during the day. We are treated to fresh sheets and pillow cases every night.

Our company of travelers, most of whom came on board in Montreal, consist at this point of:

- an incredibly-talkative gentleman from Yokohama, who inserts "What?" after every third word even when no answer is expected, and has a classic "Posenish" accent in German[121] and a Yiddish one in English, and his nephew, whom we called "Guggenheim";

- a stout English ship's captain with a ruddy complexion who eats and drinks a lot, was the skipper on the *Alaska* and is traveling to take command of a steamer which is to sail from Vancouver to Yokohama;

- a lame young man from San Francisco, who, for health reasons, has been cruising about at sea for 17 months—he reminds us of Emil Warburg;[122]

- another young man, an American, who wants to try his hand as a farmer in the Northwest Territory;

- and, since yesterday, a portly Reverend travels with us, who releases every word slowly as if it were a precious pearl.

The Englishmen speak loudly, so that they can be heard from one end of the car to the other, and they spit very deliberately on the carpet even if the spittoon is there right in front of them. Others have developed the impressive ability to hit the dish-like opening of the metal spittoon from a great distance. If by chance—as has happened to me—the missile hits the neighbor's overcoat, well, that's just too bad.

Uncle smokes his cigar, usually without taking part in the conversation, in the smoking room. I enjoy the cool—rather too cool—evening air and then make for my lofty bed.

Tuesday, August 23

I passed a bad night, tormented and frightened by confused dreams, causing me to long for the morning. I got dressed and watched the sun rise as a blood-red ball, a really rosy-fingered sunrise it was, with those singular mighty red rays spread out like fingers far off in the east over the prairie.

As late as ten o'clock we got our morning coffee which, with few exceptions, is of every poor quality here. But one has to depend exclusively on the meals served in the dining-car, or rather, one has to depend entirely during the whole long trip upon what the management of the Canadian Pacific offers. The station-buildings are ramshackle structures consisting of nothing but an office, a waiting room and a bench. No refreshments, no food, no cigars can be had. You are forced to take your meals with the Canadian Pacific. It has a monopoly. Soil and forest, cars and equipment—all belong to the Company. Every coffee-pot, every butter-dish bears its monogram. Wherever you look, CPR rules.

In Swift Current we saw, not far from the station, some Indian tents and a considerable number of horses close by. One of them trotted over a rise, roped to the others. The train had a longer stop here, and soon we saw the Indians circling the cars. I saw them for the first time in their native dress. They were all wrapped in blue- and red-striped blankets, covering the body from top to toe. I saw a woman carrying her baby on her back in the deep fold of her shawl. The baby looked no way like a redskin; it had beautiful dark hair. It sucked its thumb very prettily and reminded me of my two thumb-suckers at home. Nearly all the Indians carried buffalo horns which they offered for sale. An old hag refused to sell me a pair for a dollar, demanding double that amount.

The Indian women wore all sorts of ornaments. A young woman sitting on our car step had a chain of beads twisted round her neck and in the middle she had stuck a bead through a piece of roundish white paper to make a kind of brooch. Some men wore 6-8 metal rings of different sizes through their ears. One was entirely naked under his blankets, another had a yellow color, maybe curcuma,[123] rubbed into his face, and the women had various colors rubbed into their cheeks. These were members of the Cree Indian[124] nation, who have their reservation nearby.

In the prairie [*these Indians*] collect the heads of buffaloes, pursued to extinction by their forebears, so that this animal has practically died out in these territories as well as in the United States. We saw heaps of such bleached bones lying near some of the stations. The Indians polish the raw bones with sand and oil until they look smooth and elegant. In the end I bought a pair, while our porter bought twelve. They fetch a price of 5-6 dollars in Montreal. Mine were only a dollar.

I walked around a bit on the prairie, with thousands of chirping cicadas hopping around. A fabulous quiet reigns on the sunny plain. As far as the eye can see, not a house or human being anywhere!

At lunchtime a young woman of about 23 appeared in the dining car, wearing a blue woolen dress, smooth and fitting tightly at the back. Collar and sleeves were decorated with parallel red braid. Where a lance corporal in the Prussian Army has his button, she wore a silver-plated S. She was a missionary for the Salvation Army. I asked Uncle to find out a little bit about her. In reply to his questions we learned that she traveled for the conversion of non-believers, approaching people not with sermons but with instruction [*in the faith*].

A priest with a tonsure, a pale young man in a long soutâne, sat at the table next to ours. I would have liked to have heard an exchange of views between those two [*the Salvation Army lass and the priest*]!

Reading, dozing, writing, looking out the window, I passed the time until the afternoon. Now and then, wave-like swellings crop up in the ground, looking like large burrows. The plain, dead level until now, shows slight elevations from time to time, the first faint signs of the mountainous regions that lie ahead. At 4:15 we arrive in Medicine Hat,[125] a fairly large settlement by local standards, or, as the German-Posenish-Japanese gentleman says, "a place," or "a good place." Here, too, the stop is of such long duration that I can get off the train and walk around the town, which consists of a row of houses near the station. A "General Store," drug store, bakery, etc. etc. are to be found in these wooden shacks. Several handsome houses with little gardens gleam from the other side of the train tracks.

Some black pigs are rooting around under some railway cars standing on rail sidings. To the west, the eye fixes on huge posters pasted onto the wall of a large wooden shed, reading "Wilber's Lyceum Co." Two wooden churches rise over the houses, one completed and the other under construction, and off to the side of the finished one is a large cow pasture.

At the station we saw some more Crees, wrapped in blankets of gaudy colors, some of the men showing frightening ugliness, savagery and cunning, qualities enhanced by the paint-dye on their faces. I saw one Indian, armed with a heavy stick, his figure bent and both his jaws painted brick-red up to the nose. He skulked about without speaking, had nothing to sell. Another one, whether male or female I couldn't decide, had as his or her only decoration red lines painted thickly around the eyes.

A young man, squinting disagreeably, spoke the native Indian language without pause and, as we could gather from the laughter of his companions sitting with him, mocked the palefaces in their finery or perhaps insulted them. He had yellow rubbed in all over his face. This seems to be some kind of grease paint, because the Indian men's faces all had a greasy shine to them.

Though some of the Indians have a few dollars and a few horses, it is a really pitiable end that has befallen this nation. They were surrounded and gawked at as if they were rare animals. Men and women laugh when they see such a figure stalking about, mostly without much dignity, wrapped in a blanket, with those singular pieces of cloth on their trousers and the strangest head-coverings, of felt or straw, but without the rims.

They who once were masters of this wonderful land are now here only on sufferance and must put up with strangers staring at them. Do they understand this thing called civilization? That they hate the intruders is certain, but they are powerless, and even if they should once or even ten times try to shake off the yoke of foreign domination, they will not prevail against cannons and alcohol.

Soon after leaving Medicine Hat, the train rolled over the Saskatchewan River on a long bridge, past the entrance to a coalmine, past splendid wheatfields and large potato patches, past cypress groves, gentle elevations and steep inclines overgrown with cypress. This seems to be a very fertile stretch of land. Slowly we are nearing those mountain ranges which cut across British Columbia.

In the evening it was as cold as it had been in the morning. I was too tired from last night's tormenting dreams to stay awake for very long. I would have loved to see the approaches to those mountains that rise 2,000-3,000 feet above sea level, but my body protested. I managed to see some of the mountains, was aware of the panting of the engine as it pulled us upwards, then fell asleep.

Wednesday, August 24

I got up at 6 o'clock this morning, eager to get a glimpse of the first rocky range into whose spurs we had penetrated during the night. Indeed, what was laid open before me in steady development until noon and from then on until evening surpassed anything that I had hoped to see or had altogether thought possible in my imagination. We were already in the midst of the Rocky Mountains, about 4,000 feet above sea level. Beside us a wild mountain stream roared seaward, winding now to the right, now to the left; here, having left its old bed which lay now unused, covered with millions of pebbles, over there separating into a new bed with 3-4 arms, further on streaming around an island, everywhere rushing, tumbling and foaming against the obstacles which tree-roots and boulders placed in its path.

This abundance of water produces as if by magic a luxuriant growth of grass. Among the numerous cypresses, silver firs, larches, the grass stands two feet high, a welcome gift to the railway officials who have settled here among the mountains. In its turbulent race forward, the Bow River has uprooted many a tree which now lies in the riverbed at the mercy of the onrushing waves.

And now, what about a description of the mountains? I can hardly do them justice. Soaring skyward to the right and left, these stone colossi, densely covered with conifers, look down on us. Now and then there are wide expanses of snow, not only in rifts and crevices, but also atop the smooth dome-shaped summits. It is a rugged sight and a rugged region, stirring, grand and formidable.

We humans always seek a congenial point of rest in scenically overwhelming areas. Here everything is abnormal, from the mournful remains of former forest-beauty all along the railroad right-of-way to the torn riverbed and the wildly-clefted gigantic mountains, and we tiny humans shiver in these heights, near the eternal snow, where we can see every black dot with the naked eye.

Following closely the windings of the river or bridging it, the railway keeps climbing. The rocks—more and more irregular in shape—rise before our eyes, letting their summits—wildly jagged, or pointed, or dome-like—sink into the clouds, which now begin to envelop this majestic creation of Nature in their dense veils. Deep ravines and depressions, stratifications and caverns, may be seen everywhere, before receding again into the distance.

"Following closely the windings of the river or bridging it . . ."
(Lewin drawing)

Up there, from the peak of one of those thousands-of-feet high rocky cones, a torrent forces its way in a headlong fall from crag to crag along a perpendicular rock-face; from afar it looks like a flat silver thread on the dark brown of the stony background. Then again the scene changes, as it does near Banff, famous for its springs. The place consists of several wretched shacks, one of them a general store and another a billiard parlor.

From one mountain valley the railroad rushes into the next. They are all intensively cultivated, in spite of the enormous elevation. Mightier and mightier the mountains rise into the skies, wider and wider the snow spreads over their heads and bodies. Fearsome if one comes close to their ragged surfaces or speeds past their base on iron rails, whose passage has been forced through them by dynamite. The bridging of deep abysses is getting bolder— standing on the rear platform, I shudder when I see underneath me the yawning chasm with a depth often more stupendous than that of the largest on the Rigi mountain railway.[126]

The wooden overpasses moan and creak, crackle and rattle. Of such trestle-bridges there are certainly nearly a hundred, each one spanning the depths more lightly and more frighteningly than the last. And close besides us, sometimes under us, the Kicking Horse River rushes over rough soil, tearing trees and shrubs from their roots as it does so.

Yet bolder than the windings that Nature has created are those which man has here prescribed for the railroad's path. Now in almost-circles, now in eighths, [*the river*] winds back and forth time and time again, moving to the right or the left to avoid obstacles, shrubs and fallen trees, forming one eddy after another, one set of falls after another. The name [*Kicking Horse*

River] aptly characterizes the activity of this wild stream, and it certainly lives up to its name. Such turbulent vigor one does not often find in a mountain stream. Making use of the terrain or building up its own way, always upwards, the train passes through tunnel after tunnel until, shaken by the impact of the awesome scenery and the frightening depths that we have passed over, we arrive at Stephen, a stationhouse named after the highest peak in the Canadian Rockies.

Mount Stephen and CPR station, British Columbia, Canada
(contemporary photograph)

Mount Stephen
(Louis Lewin drawing)

The station building of course belongs to the Company. It stands quite near the rock-face, almost leaning on it. A very wide staircase of only a few steps leads to a platform and thence into the building, which is made of timber and looks very welcoming. A large dining hall was at the disposal of our small company: the tables well-set, plates and dishes clean and appetizing. For a change we chose freshly caught salmon today to complement our typical egg-dish.

I looked for alpine flowers outside and, finding them, picked a few. Then we started again, this time with two locomotives, one in front and one at the rear, on our way down, and sometimes back up again.

Before reaching Leanchoil (we are now in British Columbia), at about 11:45, we passed in quick succession two valleys surrounded by snow-covered peaks so gigantic that they were awe-inspiring.

Everywhere we encounter railway workers who repair, inspect and—most important—remove overhanging rocks and boulders. Their living quarters are pathetic—often they live in tents, sometimes in wooden shacks sealed up with clay [*in the cracks*], while the Inspector has a more substantial house which is also used for the storing of provisions. These workers, and the numerous lumbermen whom the railway employs, get free board and lodging and in addition about 1-1/4 to 1-1/2 dollars a day, wages which would surely not be found anywhere in Europe on this scale for this sort of employment.

In some places the valleys through which we now pass, in spite of their towering surroundings, are more pleasant in appearance, so that one could be tempted to spend a few weeks here. For some time we had seen only mountaintops, while dense clouds obscured the slopes. The indescribable abundance of trees is amazing. Here one can substitute for "as numerous as the sands of the sea" as "numerous as the trees in Canada." I believe that at some future time, when the last bit of coal will have been consumed, there will be enough trees left in Canada to supply Europe and the other continents with fuel.

Although the height of the mountains on one side of our route had been decreasing somewhat, we saw them getting higher and higher on the other side. We were nearing the Selkirks,[128] a mountain range which, in its wildness and the ruggedness of its rocky masses and the beauty and fertility of its valleys, is by no means inferior to the Rockies.

Soon we reached the Columbia River valley. Our route leads along the river. We saw it come into existence from small beginnings. Now it whirls and tosses in such a way in its rock-built rock-bound bed that its noise makes conversation impossible. Where boulders lie in the riverbed, it forms beautiful cascades—so far, the river tumbles over such obstacles, but in the end it will smash those boulders to pieces!

The river makes so many frequent bends that I had to turn seven or eight times from one side to the other in order to keep sight of it—that's how often

58

the river is spanned by bridges. At last the train gains the open country and we reach Golden, a station consisting of a few houses, and encounter the inevitable "Queen's Hotel," a wooden shack, and a "Golden Saloon."

After Golden we reach a fertile plain, rich in greenery, with fine leafy trees and shrubs, but also again in some places burnt, felled and rotting timber. The train is still running along the Columbia, which is narrow here, but nonetheless has islands clad in green, with sandbars as well. To the left are the snow-covered Selkirks, to the right the Rocky Mountains.

Our next stop is Donald,[129] the terminal of one of the twelve divisions of the Canadian Pacific. It was raining lightly. A numerous company of men was standing on the train platform. Giant trunks of cedar trees were lying there, ready for export—they too are the produce of the Canadian forests. The Company's houses look very neat—painted olive green and attractively ornamented. But what about the other living quarters? Log cabins, rickety wooden sheds, and caves. Liquors, wines, bakery, and "Chinese Laundry" are advertised everywhere in giant letters on these hovels.

Once again we cross the Columbia River, which here appears remarkably wild and shows again, as it did in its upper course, a singular blue-green color. We rush past forest and field, through rock and close along the riverbank. One never tires of looking, of marveling, of absorbing impressions like a dry sponge, which still has the capacity to absorb and also strives to transmit part of what it carries to other media. You, my beloved Clara, are the medium to whom I hope to communicate, better than in writing, the many things I still have stored away in my mind.

Another turbulent stream, the Beaver River, now splashes the wheels of our car. It looks like it has mill-sluices in its course every 2-3 minutes. It roars and foams, flinging its waters upwards, lets them disappear in rocky chasms, races over giant boulders; with all that, in some places it is no wider than a room!

What a residence of beavers! Indeed, under rocky ledges, lying only a little higher than the water's surface, the traces of their work on tree trunks can be seen everywhere. In the place called Beaver, where the Company has a sawmill going, we saw near this establishment a lot of cackling hens hopping over the huge centuries-old trees that lie half-burnt on the ground.

From here the railway once again starts to ascend; before arriving at Bear Creek, we have already gained a considerable height, and we are traveling along precipices which produce a vivid sensation of imminent danger. Here we meet the Columbia again, only now it is a wide and mighty river. We cross it at breakneck speed on a bridge 750 feet in length and 295 feet high, which cost 1,000,000 mark to build. Thousands upon thousands of trees had been felled to build it. It is an enormous technical achievement, worthy of these surroundings where everything appears gigantic, larger than life-size. Soon the Hermit looms up before us, no less imposing than the other mountains we have seen. Here we reach Rogers Pass,[130] at 4,000 feet the highest point in the Selkirks, arriving at last at Glacier House, a Company refreshment house.[131]

On our way there we saw the most amazing construction! To prevent snow-slides and rocks from falling onto the railroad right-of-way and on top of the trains, tunnel-like sheds have been constructed in great numbers at the places most exposed to danger.[132] Logs as thick as arms are used as girders; on top of these are carrying beams which lie as cover and further support thick boards and trunks of brazil-wood, which, on account of its cost, is used in Europe only as veneer for decorating furniture.

While we were traversing Rogers Pass, Mount Carroll, with its craggy peak, stared down at us. On the mountains round about us lies snow, deep snow, but where we are is wonderfully verdant woodland. But these impressions, however powerful, are surpassed when we reach Glacier House.

"Tunnel-like sheds" at Rogers Pass, B.C. (Louis Lewin drawing)

Glacier House (at lower right) (contemporary photograph)

After the train twisted around seemingly impossible curves, rolled past precipices and over ravines, we found ourselves (at around 2 o'clock) on a sort of plateau, for below us, or rather, in the distance, we recognized valleys. All around, forest-clad mountains loomed over us, but this was the most impressive of all: close to the station building, about a half-hour's walk away, was a glacier—a large sheet of snow and ice, wide, and dazzling white against the sky. Yet the boundary between woodland and ice is not well-defined. It is a strange sight: here eternally ice and snow, there a beautiful forest.

In front of the station building is a fountain with three jets. It is bitterly cold outside, but the glowing stove in the dining room comforts us with its radiant warmth. After a few minutes, the breakfast we had ordered appeared. After we finished eating, we had time to examine at leisure this wonderful picture. The lushness of the vegetation is surprising. Wherever we tread, verdant ferns several feet high burst forth; numerous blossoms also appear along the forest growth up and down the mountainside.

CPR line through Albert Canyon, B.C.
(contemporary photograph)

Now we are underway again, over audacious bridges, through those wooden tunnels [*described earlier*], past mountain streams, woods, fields of snow—it's impossible to enumerate all the variations for you. It seems the same but it isn't. The individual features change every moment, thus altering the whole picture. The entirety of the impression cannot be imparted; it can only be seen and felt directly.

A moment ago we were wedged in a wild gorge; now a bend in the train track and a panoramic view over mountains, forests, and rivers presents itself. Think of what human hands have created here! How admirable the perseverance of these workers! Granted, it is the struggle for existence that brings such works into being, and there is no delight in success, no striving without self-seeking. Be that as it may, we admire the outcome as a sign of spiritual and technical human development.

Now it is four o'clock and almost dark. Heavy rainclouds press down upon us. Look! Lightning! A hundredfold the thunder echoes among these rocks. From overladen clouds a deluge of rain pours down. Even rain is on a gigantic scale here; it seems we are going to become acquainted with everything! An unforgettable experience for me, this thunderstorm. We reach Illicilliwaet,[132] a small settlement of the Company. There is no end yet to the terrible weather. Lightning flash upon lightning flash, and the rocks tremble under the rolling of the thunder. The foaming and lashing about of the Illicilliwaet River underscores the frightfulness of the scene.

An hour later, the sun is shining brightly. We have left the rainy region behind us. Here and there a mountain shows its peak, the raindrops break the light into beautiful colors and the mountain stream still hurries on besides us. It cannot keep pace with us, for, wherever the terrain permits, the train rolls along at breakneck speed in order to make up for the time lost in the slow travel through the rainstorm.

Everywhere around us are the traces of destructive human work: the pathetic tree-stumps, trunks felled and burnt. What an immense industry will rise and bloom here in the future, based only on this wealth of trees! How many millions of dollars are lying here!

In the evening Uncle and I speak of all these things; then, tired out from the multitude of impressions that have rushed upon us in the course of the day, we go to bed.

Thursday, August 25

What a horrible night! Better not to have experienced it! At around 11:30PM, near Notch Hill, I was roused from my sleep by a very forceful jolt. I jumped down from my berth and immediately slipped into my clothes. The porter came in from the outside and told me that the engine and the baggage car had derailed and had plunged down a not-very-steep slope; that the coupling to the three passenger cars had been detached, so that we had escaped disaster; that some people had been injured. Would I help them?, he asked. Several other passengers had also been roused and we left the car. Uncle was sleeping soundly and I didn't want to wake him.

Outside, an unforgettably gruesome scene presented itself. Trees were on fire, illuminating the devastation. The engine was lying in a ditch, wheels upward, hissing, smashed and twisted. Higher up on the slope, the baggage car was broken into many pieces, its platform splintered, but on the whole not looking too bad.

On one side of the embankment a crushed cow lay dying, on the other side an injured one, which was shot by the conductor. That was the cause of the derailment: these cows had bedded down on the railroad tracks to sleep that night.

In the first car lay the man with the worst injuries, pale and bloodstained.

He looked terrible. I stitched up the wound in his forehead, which had been torn open. In addition, both his legs were scalded up to the knees. There was no skin left on them; it was just hanging down in shreds. With great difficulty some oil was found, and a bedsheet from the sleeping car was torn up into bandages. I dressed his wounds, made him more comfortable. Wood was cut to make a frame for his blanket. It was 1:30 in the morning before I was finished with my medical duties there.

The second man had two bad injuries to his nose and forehead. Luckily, some sewing thread and wax were found, which I used to stitch up his wounds. He too was bandaged up as well as possible under the circumstances. In the meantime, the superintendent of the railway, who happened to be on the train, had gone by trolley to the next station and ordered another engine by telegraph from a Divisional Point higher up.

They delayed the departure until I was ready. At about 3:00AM we started on our way backward [*from the scene of the crash*] so that the rails could be cleared. I didn't get back to bed until 4:00AM, with a headache starting, had scarcely any sleep, got up again at 6:00AM —the train was standing on a siding—the headache not allowing me to do anything. The line wasn't cleared until noon. We passed the scene of the accident, where Uncle could have a look at it, and went out into the sunny morning. The railway doctor thanked me, but nobody from the railway management did. My migraine was so bad that I could scarcely talk to him; I had to lie motionless. The sun and the rest helped me, but the impressions of the night kept vibrating in me so strongly that I couldn't tear my thoughts away from them.

Now the landscape is no longer mountainous. On both sides of us only domed, rounded hills, one melting into the other, were to be seen. At Kamloops, the badly injured man was carried away to a hospital on a stretcher, and the doctor left the train.

Now we were in the Thompson River valley. Kamloops[133] is a big place with many wooden houses and a Chinese quarter. The Chinese can be seen everywhere, as the train passes through the settlement, and standing in front of their houses, mute figures who stubbornly pursue their objective. They have evidently taken root firmly in this country, for one sees them everywhere.

Leaving Kamloops behind, we travel along the Thompson River, which seems to be endless, always traveling to the left of the watercourse, close to the bank, over numerous bridges, through defiles and tunnels. What a colossal stretch of water! Perhaps it is only a lake which later flows into the Thompson River—I was not able to ascertain which.

Occasionally, we see, usually in a dip in the ground between two hills, a clump of trees emerging from the yellowish, clayey-looking rock-masses. How deserted this region is! Occasionally, a canoe is to be seen, lying small and frail at the riverbank, the only sign of human habitation. This is all we've seen for hours; sunbaked and rocky, these parts seem to be calling out for human habitation, but in vain!

Now the breakthroughs in the rocks are to be seen more frequently, or rather, I should say the "break-ups"; because the rocks at the water's edge have not been carefully pierced [*to make way for the train tracks*]; they have simply been blasted away. In this way rocky passages have been formed: one wall at the lakeside, the other on the land side, and between the two the train roars along.

By this time we have been slowly leaving the plain and again making our ascent. At last we encounter a village, just a few huts, really, a settlement of gold-diggers or gold-washers. The lake disappears and a river with a strong current takes its place, the Thompson River, its rocky banks to the right of us oddly-fissured, so that the eye is tricked into seeing crenellated fortresses, windowed castles, etc. As we approach, mighty strata of red granite come into view, with a fir-tree here and there. The river breaks noisily at the foot of these granite rocks.

We ascend to a height of 150 feet above the level of the river, so close to the precipitous cliff-face that looking down makes you dizzy. The trestle-bridge viaducts over the gorges are so numerous that I couldn't keep count. It is the frequent change in speeds, from slow to fast and back again, that causes anxiety. The steam-brakes are working overtime, but as soon as they are released we progress at such a mad speed that one thinks the train will surely plunge into the abyss at any moment.

We pass a miserable Indian hut, scarcely two feet high above the ground. A man and his wife, brown figures, are occupied in doing something on a small field near their hut; I couldn't make out what they were doing. I doubt that they can get much out of this soil. Probably it supplies them with enough for their sustenance, together with the wealth of fish in the river. Nevertheless, these people perhaps live in greater contentment than the white man, who has seen better things than he possesses and cannot attain them.

At 3:15PM we arrived at Ashcroft, a fairly big place by British Columbia standards, with stores, etc. By now my headache had improved and I could again take interest in my surroundings. On our side of the river I see a Falstaffian figure on horseback approaching the town, pulling a pack mule after him. Dusty and dirty, he looked like a gold-digger intent on turning his lucky finds into cash. His horse is saddled the Mexican way: the stirrups wider than a hand-breadth, embellished with broad ornate leather strips; the saddle, also ornamented, raised in front; the harnessing is also unusual.

The banks of the Thompson River are getting more and more imposing. On a rocky cliff my eyes came upon an isolated tepee, impossible to see how and from which side it is accessible. Everywhere the rock is bare and barren. No grass, no shrub, not a bit of green anywhere. While absorbed in the contemplation of the rocks on the opposite shore, which get higher and higher, raising their contours into the sky, I hear the sound of our passenger car rolling over a bridge—a three-story structure over a gorge—and not a moment later the train takes a curve of such impudent audacity that the pulse quickens.

The sun was so scorching hot that one could not blame the Indian woman who did her work naked—she could be sure that the train would pass her at such speed as to keep her brown beauty safe from lusting eyes.

Before long some growth can be seen on the heights—here and there a shrub, a flower, and trees along the river banks. The rocks rise very high here, form sharp-edged ridges, are piled one on top of another, or blend softly into each other—manifold formations can be seen, but everywhere the same roughness of scenery.

In the midst of the mule-track mentioned earlier, where the rocks recede somewhat, leaving a small space for a settlement, someone has evidently established a small ranch. It is surprising that from this apparently bare and sunbaked soil, a small oasis has been conjured up, which pleases the eye and—to be sure—its owner. Probably it is a stopping point for those who travel their weary way on foot or on horseback up and down this road.

A similar pleasant break awaited us at Spencer [*Spence's*] Bridge, where we arrived at 4:30. Here the Thompson, until now very wide, encounters rocks so massive that it cannot break through. It narrows down now to a mountain gorge in which it whirls and foams, with our railroad track running close alongside it. The passage is made awesome by the road itself and by what faces us: rock and yet more rock, granite in all imaginable hues from yellow and gray to a rich reddish-brown, cleft and fissured and dropping down to the river in compact blocks with smooth surfaces 100 feet in height. What a difference from what we saw only yesterday! I cannot adequately describe this ruggedness. It is as though a stony world had been hurled down from the sky and was still showing the scars of its precipitous fall. And the railroad! People should make a pilgrimage here to look in amazement at the wonders of Nature and of Man.

At 5:15 we pulled into Lytton, a village of gold-prospectors and Indians. The Indians are Christianized, their homes enclosed by a widely embracing fence. Some of them approached the train. The women, dressed European style, prefer gaudy colors. Their faces are a reddish-brown. The men look strong-boned. We saw a company of riders leaving the village. The leader of the company had his long rifle slung over his back and led his pack-horse by the bridle. He was followed by another man on horseback with a wide-brimmed hat, his rifle held across the saddle. All the horses were heavily laden; perhaps the riders were on their way to exchange gold for money. Their settlement looked clean. The wood-frame houses I saw had projecting eaves around all four walls of the structure. The site of that settlement is well chosen, being at the confluence of the Thompson and the Frazer River. I found the Fraser to be no wider than the Thompson.

The scenery stays the same. Sometimes we stay close to the river, then we ascend again, crossing ravines and gorges, following the river all the time and never losing sight of it. Foaming brooks tumble down over the rocks into the turbulent Fraser. They cannot undermine the narrow track bed on which we move forward, because they are caught and carried through wooden conduits. Thus rendered harmless, the current is allowed to find its way downstream as it pleases.

On the opposite bank, that is, to the right of us, we see snow-covered peaks again. In some places, which are especially dangerous, we proceed so slowly that even my little Gertrud[134] could keep pace with us. Suddenly, we come upon a sharp bend, and find ourselves on a bridge across the Fraser, with no time to get dizzy or to express amazement at our lofty height. Faster than I can write this down, we are across the bridge and have entered the darkness of a tunnel.

Now we are following the right bank of the Fraser, and discern both on that side and the other several Indian settlements, the huts half a man's height, mostly under foliage, which is again copious here. We see their fishing-gear at the river's edge or, where the river is inaccessible, on rocky ledges jutting out over the water. Fascinated by this part of the world, we enjoy the happiness—alas, not given to many—of widening our horizons.

It is better not to look out, or, rather, to look down, so narrow is the path on which we travel between the face of the cliff to our right and, to the left, the edge of the precipice.

We pass another Chinese settlement—ramshackle wooden huts looking terribly dirty—on our way to North Bend, which we reach at 6:30. This is a Divisional Point of the CPR, situated on a plateau-like enlargement of the rocks. What a site, embedded in green trees among the rocks! We see handsome wood-frame houses here, about six to eight of them, some of them near the rocks, fitted out for the use of summer guests. We had some refreshments in the Company House. The prices are fixed at 75 cents (that is, 3 mark) for dinner or breakfast, 65 cents for lunch. At that price the food is plentiful, clean and good.

Meanwhile, dusk had fallen. We rush along between rock and water, in mad pursuit of our goal, which still lies 132 miles distant. Evening mists are rising in the valley, so that we can distinguish only what lies directly opposite or close at hand. The waters of the Fraser roll by in a uniform gray.

At a dizzying height a man moves along on the parallel track. Dangerous wandering! On the track—I can see it distinctly—wooden boles have been laid, jutting out over the face of the cliff, their free ends supported by cross-ties so that man or beast can find a foothold for walking. But heaven help him if he slips! Smashed into atoms, he would find his grave in the rushing waves below. There are no rails, no hand-grip for him to hold onto. This part stretches for more than 200 English miles.

Quite near the water, in a rocky cleft, I now see a light: Indians are panning for gold here, in a brook that runs down off the mountain.

Like a curtain the evening mist has now come down over the awesome beauty of the riverbank. Now and then a tent still gleams in its whiteness through the nocturnal gray, and then we see only our nearest surroundings: to the left the precipitous cliff-face dropping down to the river, and to our right rocks whose upper reaches are no longer discernible. The moon sits reddish-gold in the sky, waiting for the last vestiges of the sun to disappear before shining in its solitary beauty. Night falls over the Columbia. The piercing sound of the locomotive's warning signal rings out sharply when the engineer encounters an unusual condition on the roadbed, the warning signal echoing a hundredfold across the mountain walls.

I am thinking of you, my own world for which I yearn, you dear and beloved creatures. And, as I do now, my sweet angels, I thought of you every minute of this eventful day.

Friday, August 26

During the night, while we were sleeping, the train arrived at Vancouver, the western terminus of our Canadian trip. We rose early to get a closer look at the town. From here, at around noon or one o'clock, we were to catch the steamer to Victoria.

Vancouver is a town in its very beginnings,[135] its deep harbor allowing entrance to ocean liners. We were disappointed that the post and telegraph office had not yet opened to the public; the gentleman [*the postmaster*], we were told, did not deign to arrive until 8:45! We wanted to send you a telegram, and managed to do so later—to set your minds at ease in case news of the train accident should have reached you, although this seemed unlikely.

We strolled through the town. The streets are laid out in a very broad pattern, the houses nearly all of wood, with many empty building lots, from which huge stumps or charred remains of trees stick up. In one place the Chinese were occupied with burning them down completely. Plenty of saloons, each one dirtier and more distasteful than the last, many loiterers, speculators, land-agents, gamblers and so on; dealers who sell second-hand pistols, clothes, harness tack and boots. We see Chinese women hanging up laundry on the flat roofs of their wooden shacks. The roads are paved with the finest redwood; the same is true of the sidewalks as well, which sit on each side of the road about two feet higher than the road surface. These pavements are not made from bits and pieces of wood, but from slabs of lumber nearly six inches thick, reaching from side to side.

Everywhere there are telegraph wires, telephone connections, streets lit not by gas lanterns but by incandescent lights,[136] big advertising posters full of humbug; young girls walking about with canes—pooh!—how disgusting this all looks! In front of many houses stand transverse sections of tree trunks up to 3 meters in diameter, reminders of and memorials to the vanished forest-glory of the place; staggering prices for the simplest and meanest articles, quite inferior, and unpalatable and rotten food in the best hotel—all this is what Vancouver offers, a place which is surely destined to gain great importance as the starting point for the shortest route to Yokohama.[137]

Here we took leave of our railway traveling companions. We ventured to hire a boat and rowed out into the bay. It was not dangerous, else we wouldn't have done it. Uncle took the rudder, I the oars, both of us did our jobs badly, but Uncle was definitely the less efficient of the two. In the end one of the oarlocks fell into the water while I tried to fish something out, and we had trouble retrieving it. But, all the same, it was a nice experience and we felt much refreshed afterwards.

We had seen everything that Vancouver had to offer. The hour of our departure neared, but no steamer appeared. We hadn't had any lunch because the price of our meals was included in the steamer ticket. We waited and waited, and still the boat did not come. Time passed—two o'clock—three o'clock—four o'clock—there we sat, Uncle with patience, I without. Nobody had any information to offer. At six o'clock the rumor spread that the steamer had broken a shaft and couldn't come. Pleasant prospect! Tomorrow at noon the boat for San Francisco leaves from Victoria. If we miss it, we shall have to wait a full week until the next. I take an interpreter—it is already seven o'clock and still nobody has given us a word of explanation—and go into the office. The gentlemen are sorry but don't know anything. We feel keenly our empty stomachs but can't afford to leave the wharf, because the steamer may yet arrive this evening!

At long last Uncle also gets indignant. I ask him to accompany me to the CPR office. Our tempers are at a boiling point. When we get to the office, Uncle threatens to publish a "paper" about the affair if there is no transport for us. We are assured that we will be taken tonight to Westminster by rail and from there to Victoria by boat, so that we can get there in time for our connection.

Neither of us had much of an appetite, though we hadn't eaten anything. We entered a "Dining Room" which, from the outside looked tolerable, in order to at least have some soup before we departed. It wasn't long before we were back out on the street again, having left the restaurant full of disgust. Uncle and I were quite sure: he had tasted that lobster back in Long Branch, and I today the apple pie!

Time passed slowly. The train was to leave at ten o'clock. As we were entitled to a bed and were tired out, I asked for a sleeping car, the boat for Victoria not being expected before morning. The answer: there were ladies on the train, and they had priority for the beds. By that time I was fed up with this hypocritical and ostentatious preferential treatment given to the ladies. I protested, insisting on two beds, and they went about finding them for us. But now Uncle declared—and it was the first time that I had seen him so obstinate—that he would rather sleep on the wooden benches [*of the train station*] until five o'clock in the morning. The lame young American entreated him, the Railway Superintendent who had given us the information in Vancouver came over and invited him to go to bed—but all in vain. I was annoyed because I had seen how bad the effects of an uncomfortable night could be for him. The train stopped, people got off, but he didn't budge.

Only when we were told that we might pass the entire night on board did Uncle get up. We squeezed through a narrow passageway, two feet wide. I asked the purser for our cabin. Ladies! *Himmeldonnerwetter!*[138] I was in the right mood and told the man in no uncertain terms that I couldn't care less about the ladies and that I wanted sleeping quarters right then and there, on the double. The purser just shrugged his shoulders. Uncle tried to deal with him, with no greater result. At long last something may have dawned on the fellow, or maybe by that time he had found accommodations elsewhere for the high-and-mighty ladies, because we were led to a small compartment with three berths arranged one above the other about two feet apart. Uncle took the middle berth, I the one on top and the lame American the lower berth. Sleep was out of the question—all night long they were taking on cargo, with a lot of shouting and bumping.

Saturday, August 29

The morning was rainy, so there was not much to be seen of the coastline. Only by degrees could I make out the numerous islands scattered here and there in the Gulf of Georgia and Puget Sound. But what I did see bespoke an extraordinary fertility. Covered in trees and grass, in manifold forms and sizes, completely flat and allowing the sea to cut into its shoreline, rising up over the sea in granite rocks, swarming with birds, and wherever the eye probed huts and tents and log-cabins: that is how this island world presented itself to the observer.

There are big salmon fisheries here which can and ship the salmon as soon as it comes off the boat. We stopped at one of these and saw Indians employed there. So now they must labor and serve here who once were the owners and masters of this land! But many of them still live on these islands and support themselves as they have in the past.

We were lucky again today with the weather. The sun appeared and we could see and enjoy the beautiful sea and its rocky outcroppings—after forest and wilderness, the beloved sea in all its bluish splendor. Some of the rocky islands—they are all wooded—seemed to be strewn with white sand on their slopes: fungi or, rather, lichens cause this singular coloring.

Unfortunately, our fellow passengers spoiled our pleasure somewhat. What annoyed me was not so much that the steamer-blackguards made us pay for two meals (which were dirty and bad in the bargain) under the pretext that this was not the boat that we had originally bought tickets for, or that the part of the ship that we had to pass in the morning was so filthy that I had to turn up my trouser cuffs; and that a certain place [*the bathrooms*] was in such an offensive state that only my strong protest caused the problem to be remedied; or that an unpleasant stench pervaded this rotten shell of a boat; no—it was the people in the boat who really annoyed me.

A lanky beanstalk of a young man with a monocle squeezed into his eyes—a sure sign of a good-for-nothing—fired at seabirds without taking any heed of his surroundings, just for the fun of killing. This is a dirty and brutal lot, from the monocled "gentleman" down to the porter! In the so-called "salon" where ladies are relaxing, the grubby waiter sits down without his jacket, exposing to view his dirty shirt and oily waistcoat, and nobody throws the bum out, presumably because everyone behaves likewise in his own way and because we are in the Land of Liberty!

Liberty! A poor misused word: everybody attaches his own meaning to it. I think that the way a person defines liberty may provide a clue to his character. That liberty also means a restriction of individual freedom is a point that the Americans don't seem to have grasped, as far as I have been able to determine. But enough of this!

What lies around us now is more attractive. At about 12:30 the island of Vancouver comes into view. It is named after its discoverer and is larger than England, to which it belongs. More and more of its features appear: rocks, trees, huts, houses; indeed, we are now so close that we can see the flowers among the rocks. The island sends rocky spurs out into the Pacific which, at this location—we are at the southern tip of the island—surges up without hindrance from the west. At 2:15 we land at Victoria in bright sunshine.

We had been told that our steamer to San Francisco would be waiting. We scanned the horizon but saw no sign of it. When is it due in? Nobody has any information! We move off about a hundred paces from the pier to a place where big boulders face the harbor proper. Here, the explorer Vancouver may have rested, knowing that his ship was safe in port, for, from this vantage point, man, harbor and land can be surveyed, a fine and restful observation point. The town with its towers, factories and houses invites us, but we dare not go there. I gather mosses, which I hope to bring back to Europe alive. Suddenly we see a ship leaving the harbor under steam. Momentarily we panic, thinking it may be ours, but we are mistaken.

I suggested to Uncle that we walk in the direction of the town unconcernedly, if only to get a little exercise. We set out at a good pace. Walking is easy, the road being well-paved and the sidewalks, as in Vancouver, consisting of fine split logs, set crosswise. And how charming the houses we pass! They are the villas of rich Englishmen who have their homes outside the town. After such a long time we encounter tidiness again! In the garden we see pansies, peonies, begonias, aconite.[139] Suddenly our young American comes by in a carriage. He invites us to accompany him into town, for, according to information that he had from the driver, the ship is not due in until 6 o'clock and maybe later.

We accepted his offer, and had no reason to regret it. A pleasant sea breeze mitigated the heat of the sun. We find ourselves in a big town of a distinct character. Big shops with mostly European goods at comparatively low prices, people dressed as we are, restaurants, schools and churches; all very much like home, but bearing a stamp of its own, which I am at a loss to define.

Everywhere people stand about with apparently nothing to do; men and women ride through the streets on horseback using saddles with wide stirrups or the usual ones. Over here, Chinatown begins, a quarter inhabited exclusively by Chinese. I notice a man carrying bundles of firewood at the end of long poles. Over there, a shop that has grotesque Indian idols large and small, carved from slate, for sale.

Very often you encounter light carriages with one or two seats, mostly driven by ladies. You might think that all these people are on a holiday at this attractive place and that everyday cares are as remote from them as they were from Adam and Eve in Paradise.

There are Jews here, too, as everywhere.[140] It may be difficult to fulfill the [*Biblical*] prophecy that on the day of the coming of the Messiah they will be ingathered from the farthest corners of the earth. On the other hand, they are easily recognized, even if they don't look like Messrs. Isaacson and

Goldstein, by the exorbitant prices they charge for curios. I wanted to buy there, but left my businessman-coreligionists laughing and, mindful of the Second Commandment, refrained from buying idols.

Our driver was a capable guide. After having had a look at all the streets and the residential suburbs, and having driven past the citadel-like residence of the Governor, and after seeing many poorly clad Victoria Indians, we were brought by our automaton to the Corso. Imagine being suddenly in the shade of centuries-old oaks, which line an avenue. On one side lies a large open space where—surrounded by many spectators—young and old men ply their rackets; while on the other side the trees get denser and form a grove where the uniformed Navy Band of the warships lying in the harbor perform operetta airs. Imagine, further, young and old pressing around the musicians, gentlemen and ladies on horseback in elegant or simple riding costumes, listening to the music, others dashing along at a daring gallop or letting their mounts make courvets;[141] add numerous cabriolets driven by ladies; and you may perhaps get an idea of the scene, but not of the mood that it induced in me: *bon gré mal gré,* [142] one must be cheerful and gay in such company. You could picture all these people leaving, after having so fully enjoyed themselves, and saying, as King Jerôme [*Bonaparte*][143] and your Aunt Flora did: "Merry again tomorrow."

During a further drive we came upon ferns as tall as a man, not singly but growing there unnoticed in their hundreds and thousands. There was still time left, for, from where we were standing on the heights, we could see our steamer, far out at sea.

We drove to the Post Office, mailed a postcard to you and looked in a few shops. In a shoe-shop I noticed men's boots, made of thick cowhide with three soles put together, one on top of the other. The shopkeeper told us that people here needed well-built boots such as these.

We stopped in at a restaurant for a refreshing meal. Not since we left New York have we had such excellent food at such a cheap price. I had a chat with the proprietor, a Frenchman, and assured him of my highest appreciation.[144]

At seven o'clock we drove to the dock where the steamer lay that was to take us to the Land of Gold. The S.S. *George W. Elder*[145] was to house us for the next three days. There were cabins on deck, but they were all taken, by ladies. We were assigned a cabin below-deck, and, of course, the very worst; that is to say, the cabin right above the propeller screw. At least, we were pleased that we had the cabin to ourselves; the third berth was unoccupied. The light of the moon appeared magically over a wide area of the Pacific, or, rather, the Straits of San Juan de Fuca, through which we now steamed. We stayed on deck until 9:15, enjoying the scenery from the cabin as well, until the vessel, having left the straits and rounded Cape Flattery, entered the ocean.

Eastward Across
the United States

Sunday, August 28

Yesterday, our young American had warned us that the S.S. *George W. Elder* was known in San Francisco and up and down the Pacific coast as a "roller" and that we would soon know why. Last night and today have proven this all too well. I hadn't a moment's sleep and was listless all day. The sea was splendid, smooth as a mirror, but nevertheless the ship rolled maddeningly and incessantly, from left to right, from right to left. The ladies were not to seen at mealtimes today, and of the men only about ten, although the ship was booked to capacity. Everyone was seasick.

How right these people were not to come down for the meals! The table linen, knives, forks, etc. were dirty, the food appalling. In all our lives, Uncle and I had never seen the like. We didn't bother to ascertain the nature of the distasteful items that were set out on the tablecloth, preferring to have a slice of bread with butter; to be precise, it was margarine butter. I had not been seasick until six o'clock. Then I went in to dinner, saw the repulsive food and had to hurry back onto the deck and pay my tribute to the good peaceful ocean. From then on I felt well, smoked a cigar, and fasted. The rolling of the boat didn't stop for even five minutes, and continued until bedtime.

Monday, August 29

Last night was just like the night before. The noise of the propeller, the rolling of the ship from side to side went on night and day. I had very little sleep and my head felt leaden when I woke up.

The sun shone brightly over the blue mirror-smooth sea. Gulls cavorted around the ship, snatching up the bread that passengers threw out to them. There was quarreling and bickering over which of them should have the morsels, exactly as we have seen them do at Sylt.

I am not a bit seasick. I took only coffee, bread and a bit of cake and was careful not to look at the tablecloth, the cups, plates, etc. The filth was indescribable.

My thoughts, dearest Clara, are concentrated on you and upon the children. I wrote to you the whole day, having found the writing posture which made me as much as possible independent of the rolling of the ship and which minimized my aches and pains. For, as a consequence of the ship's movements, I had such a fall from my armchair in the cabin that my backside is still sore.

At lunch I asked for two soft-boiled eggs, offering to pay extra for them. I couldn't get any, but they did serve scrambled eggs, very unappetizing in appearance. That's why I'm still fasting.

Tuesday, August 30

One gets accustomed to everything, within certain limits, even to the rolling and pitching of the boat. I slept fairly well, quickly downed a cup of coffee, or, should I say, dishwater. But I preferred it to cold water, which might have been even worse; and then came up on deck to be refreshed by the sight of the ocean. Instead of the gray seagulls which we had seen until now, white ones gracefully circling above the boat. At about 8 o'clock, land became visible to the left—it was California. A white lighthouse gleamed over the sea from a rocky height. Beneath it on a cliff could be seen the whitewashed house of the lighthouse-keeper, high up like the nest of an eagle, and seemingly so lightly attached that a gust of wind might have blown it into the sea.

The rocks are wild and without any vegetation. We sail, or rather roll, along on a course parallel to the shore. Our boat seems to have something wrong with its spine, or rather with its constitution, like a person with a nervous disease who trembles and has lost control of his movements.

The sea is so calm that the positive of its name could well be changed to the superlative.[146] It is so calm that one might venture out onto it in a rowboat. The stretch of land comes to an end. The sea now opens to a very wide-mouthed bay, so wide-mouthed that the shore surrounding it cannot be seen. But soon land reappears on the right, the outermost limit of the Bay of San Francisco, or rather the tip of the peninsula on which San Francisco lies. Forts stand on each side of the narrows to protect the city. Now land can be seen to the left as well, and soon we find ourselves steaming into the sunny harbor, crowded with numerous ocean liners, its vast dimensions almost lost to sight.

The city spreads up its gray-brown heights. The streets climb upwards as well, with small terrace-like interruptions. We see smoking factory chimneys, quays lined with corn warehouses crammed from top to bottom with thousands of sacks containing this same California alimentary gold, i.e. corn, and at last we tie up at the dock. The S.S. *G. W. Elder* has finally stopped rolling.

We disembark, have our luggage inspected and, surrounded by a noisy tumultuous crowd urging upon us their services, carriages and hotels, we arrive in San Francisco. Through the Golden Gate—that is what the harbor entrance is called—after a trip of 750 miles from Victoria, we have reached that soil which, according to the ideas of many Europeans, is strewn with gold.

> *[After having been "taken for a ride," in every sense of the expression, they arrive at the Palace Hotel.[147] Lewin writes that the hotel has six stories around a patio whose paved middle square is reserved for carriages. Uncle and Lewin have separate rooms, each with a wardrobe, bath and toilets. There is hot and cold running water, five elevators, electric light and gaslight. When they inquire, they find that mail is there waiting for them and they gratefully acknowledge its arrival. They send a telegram ahead to Washington informing them of Lewin's slightly delayed arrival.]*

On a walk through the city we saw many noteworthy sights. The pavement is so wretched throughout that one is in constant danger of breaking a leg. We see granite slabs only at street crossings, but it's unhewn and of incredibly poor quality. The smallest township in Germany has better pavement than this city in which millionaires many times over live.

We are amazed by the beauty of the fruit and its low cost. Passing the fruit market, we saw pears, apples, peaches, etc. of almost pathological size. How fertile this California must be! However, the intermediate trade raises the price of produce here more than perhaps in any other country, so that later I had to pay a quarter (1 mark) for two peaches, whereas Uncle was charged only 3 mark (75 cents) for a carton full of the finest fruit.

The merchandise in the stores is nothing out of the ordinary and comes either from Asia or from Europe, predominantly from Berlin. Its poor quality betrays it. The prices are exorbitant. A small felt hat was marked 16 Mark; men's boots, handsewn, 20 Mark; simple ties, 2 Mark; and so on. We live in a Promised Land! I don't understand how the common people here find the money to go about decently dressed! The milkman and the cabdriver dress like gentlemen!. The only explanation is that all these people overcharge their customers drastically in order to balance income and expenses. And what about the prices of the fur collars or fur-trimmed velvet coats that the ladies

75

wear, oddly enough, in the burning sunshine—which is, however, tempered by the sharp sea breeze that blows in from the ocean across the city.

There are many tram-lines throughout the city. We get on one such tram and ride along the wide and endlessly long Montgomery Street. There are interior and exterior seats—we choose to sit on the outdoor seats. We pass the strangest shops, doctors' houses with large advertising posters, second-hand shops, a "Naturalist" who displayed stuffed monkeys on the porch of his wood-frame house, a "Photographer's Studio" and other big advertisements.

Seeing a rather remarkable building, I asked the carriage to stop so that we could look at it more closely. It turned out to be the City Hall, still under construction but already partially in use.

Old City Hall, San Francisco
(contemporary photograph)

This building probably cost millions of dollars; some of those millions went into the construction of the building and the rest went into the pockets of the corrupt city officials overseeing the construction. We spoke later to a business associate of Uncle's, Mr. H., who said we shouldn't be surprised at the bad pavement, or at the shoddy construction of buildings such as the new City Hall. There was enough money for everything, but it had a way of disappearing into the pockets of people whom everyone knew but whom nobody would lift a finger against. In this connection, he told us that the city's tax assessor had called him into his office and told him, after first closing the door, "Either you send me 200 dollars today, or I will assess your property at two or three times the amount that you yourself assessed it at." Naturally, Mr. H. came up with the 800 Mark. America, the Land of the Free! Land of rascals and scalawags!

Back at the hotel we had our first decent meal in a long time,[148] and went to the theatre in the evening. I sent you the words of the songs which the principal actor sang with great virtuosity. It was amusing for both of us. There were many Irishmen in the audience and they applauded at every on-stage mention of the "poor Irish."

Wednesday, August 31

We went by electric tram to Golden Gate Park,[149] the drive of about one-and-a-half German miles costing 20 cents. It is worthwhile seeing how this tramway overcomes the difficulties of the terrain. The tram goes straight up so steeply that one falls backward, and then straight down again at such an angle that one fears being toppled overboard. But this tramway is actually as safe as if one were traveling at ground level. The conductor applies the brakes at the steepest points; it's really a remarkable piece of work!

Golden Gate Park is a garden which has been created by scrupulous care on arid sandy soil. Strong sea breezes carry dust with them so continuously that elsewhere there is not a leaf on a tree that isn't covered under a layer of dust and dirt. But here in this park there is no such problem. Beautiful green lawns and European and tropical plants delight the eye by the variety of their colors.

It was a pity that we could see only the front part of the garden, because a steam-tramway was already waiting nearby to take us on a trip to the coast. This drive is not worth recording, taking us through waste and desolate ground and over hilly and only partly cultivated land. A dirtyish yellow dust, the detritus of the stony masses that lie here, hangs in the air, replaced further down by the white sand of the dunes. As at Sylt, dune-grass has been planted in the relatively flat dunes as a means of stabilizing the sand.

We arrived, refreshed by "acid" drops which we had acquired on the way. With a lot of accompanying palaver, a man had tossed a tidily-wrapped bonbon to every passenger on the tram to Golden Gate Park. After a while he came back and placed next to every person a little box containing the same sweets, and then he came back a third time to see who would buy. Liking the originality of his approach, we did.

But we are not yet allowed to enjoy the sea. First, we must pass by a man who shows off the tricks of his trained canaries; then comes a huge billboard showing an old man in a long snow-white beard and a velvet cap, bent over a book while sitting at a table laden with alembics and retorts. This billboard bears the legend: "Dr. Liebig's wonderful German invigorator, the oldest, greatest and best remedy for . . ." Then, we pass those inscriptions which we see painted on every rock: "Drink Geyser Soda for Health!"

Only then can we behold the Pacific in all its beauty. How it surges against the flat shore and how the smell of the sea or the seaweed refreshes us! Below is a splendid beach for bathing. I would have loved doing it, but nowhere is there a bath-house to be seen. Many mothers come here with their children in order to enjoy the sea-breeze for a few hours. This is easy and cheap enough. The whole trip costs only 20 cents.

We inhale the sea air deeply—deeply—while the waves lap at our feet. Then, always staying near the sea, we ascend a slope to Cliff House,[150] a wooden house perched on a rock and with two porches open to the sea, one on each of its two stories. The view from Cliff House is fabulous. Out in the ocean, perhaps 50 meters from where we stand, there are three separate masses of rock outcroppings, almost all of them in full view, and they teem with barking bellowing seals who make themselves heard in every imaginable way. Some just bask in the sun; others roll their massive bodies down into the sea to catch some food; one barks loudly into the four winds while twisting his neck and head in every direction like a snake; many others can be seen in the water, swimming playfully among the rocks.

It is not that they are kept here, as I had thought at first; no, they are quite free and on their own. Formerly, people were allowed to shoot them, but that is no longer so, to the annoyance of the fishermen who scarcely find any fish here. One side of the rock is covered with guano and numerous birds are sitting there, often roused from their meditative posture by the clumsy seals.

The same conveyance brought us back to our starting point. Here we could observe the small wood-frame houses, built for one family each, which line both sides of the steeply rising streets. They are built along the same lines that I wrote about from New York, with pretty fretwork, and they are set off by pleasant street-front gardens.

Our main purpose in visiting San Francisco had been for me to see its "Chinatown,"[151] as the Chinese quarter is called, especially the smoking of opium. Back in our hotel we asked for a guide. It appeared that we could get one for 10 dollars (40 Mark)—an outrageous overcharge! At a ticket office, they wanted the same price, but with a reduction to half-price if the tour were in daytime. But in daytime there is nothing to see there and everyone can walk through the streets and the shops. I decided to prove to those swindling Yankees that we could find our way by ourselves. We asked a policeman how to go about finding a police officer as a guide. He directed us to the police station. There I explained my request after having sent my card in. When the police captain began long deliberations with someone else, I showed him the letter of introduction I had received from Washington. That did the trick. We were told to meet up with our police guide at 9 o'clock in the evening at the station. We told Mr. H. about this because he also wanted to see Chinatown at night. Strange to say, the better element of San Francisco society is not acquainted with Chinatown.

So we had time until the evening to stroll through the streets and look at people and things. I noticed a special fashion among the ladies: instead of putting their hat-feather in front of or at the side of the hat, they wear it in the back. In the window of a jewelry store I found silver pins, exactly the form and length of common dress pins, but with a flat instead of a rounded head.

Passing the stock exchange, we entered it. A large hall, shrouded in shadow, with a mob of people milling around, shouting and spitting. A man was standing on some kind of dais, striking a hammer against a steel plate. The noise was so ear-splitting that I couldn't wait to get out. This primitive means is used to signify that the exchange is closed for the day and all trading must stop. The moment that the hammering ceased, the shouting began again, then the hammering was repeated, until finally the hall was cleared.

In a dirty cellar-restaurant the exchange transactions continued. A man in shirtsleeves was writing stock prices on a blackboard and all around the room all kinds of people were sitting and standing who seemed to have lost a lot during the trading day and wanted to make good their losses. I would not have chosen to sit down at a table or take a walk in the mountains with any of them.

As we still had some time left, we took a cablecar to "Nob Hill," officially California Street, the street where the mining-Croesuses live. Again we traveled more and more steeply uphill without feeling any jerking and jolting in the smoothly-gliding car. The wood-frame palaces show off the wealth of their inhabitants even from the outside. The windowpanes are plate-glass, the houses are adorned with candelabra, bay-windows, turrets and conservatories, guarded by statues of reclining lions and surrounded by green lawns. Up here on the hills, the houses are not built of stone, but of wood, because of the danger of earthquakes. From here, we were treated to a beautiful view of the city and then returned to our hotel for dinner.

We set out for our evening at 8:30. From an open shop in a side street we heard people singing. We were told that this was the Salvation Army and we went in. There were rows of benches to the left and right, with an aisle down the middle, somewhat like a classroom. The men who were sitting on the benches looked at us in amazement. In front, on the dais, sat two young ladies, two youngish men and an older man in a red shirt. A lady with an enormous straight-peaked hat stood at a table with a trumpet on it. On a chair behind the table I saw a drum. To the accompaniment of the choir and with the vigorous assistance of her neighbors to the left and right, the prophetess sang one hymn after another in a piercing voice. Suddenly, she stopped singing and introduced a young man sitting in front of us. He got up and gave a speech, saying that he, a poor sinner, had come to know the truth of the Salvation Army, and had reformed, etc. etc. That was followed by more hymn-singing, and so ad infinitum. We left, not waiting for the meeting to end. Outside, in the street, children were imitating the singing.

After a few paces we met up with the strapping police officer who was to be our guide for this excursion, and soon we entered the Chinese quarter. How can I deal with the multitude of impressions that I took with me from this evening? From the moment that we entered the quarter, in which approximately 30,000 Chinese live, we encountered a most unpleasant odor, which stayed with us until we left it. It is impossible to describe it; it is so repugnant that even Uncle was, at the beginning, somewhat repelled and disgusted. The streets were repulsively dirty and filthy. People throw everything into the streets and leave it there to rot. It is impossible to use the so-called sidewalks, partly because they are taken up with baskets and boxes, and partly because everywhere there are open cellar-holes that one might fall down into. I had to turn up my trouser-cuffs to avoid the filth.

From the filth outside, we stepped into the first shop, a barbershop where two Chinese were sitting, being tended to by the barbers. They had just finished shaving their customers' heads, from the forehead to the base of the skull, and were now occupied in trimming the hair from their ears and noses, with very small knives, not wider than a straw, and very fine sponges with handles. After that, the barbers carefully removed the hair and other substances from the floor of the shop.

Across the street was a grocery store. I went in, but Uncle, being fastidious, stayed outside. I can't begin to describe the food that was available for sale here. Nauseating dried Chinese fish, dirty-brown pieces of chicken, swimming in dark-brown oil, evil-smelling cabbage, small dog's feet wrapped in dog's stomach or the stomach of other animals, pickled cuttlefish, etc. etc. Bravely, I endured the sight and smell of these foods and even ended up buying a dried cuttlefish.[152]

The streets are almost pitch-dark, lit only by the lights from the shops and by candles at the doors of the houses on the streets. Every few paces, 6-8 wax candles are stuck into the ground. They burn down very quickly, but their long tapers consist of incense, so that there are hundreds of these incense-burning candles glowing in the streets. China in America! What a contrast of customs and habits! But that was not the worst by far. We entered a pitch-dark house, or so it appeared to us as we went in, because we had to use matches to illuminate our way into the house. By and by we could make out some light in the passageway that we were standing in. We were in the only house built in Chinese fashion. I am not expert enough to describe it to you as it really is or to make a drawing of it. Perhaps you will get some idea of it if I sketch it for you as follows: as far as I could see there are 2-3 stories, a cellar-level, the ground floor and one above.

I could be mistaken as to the dimensions and numbers of rooms but the arrangement shown in the plan is correct (I sketched it from memory while traveling through Colorado). I must explain the broad dark areas. These are apartments leading into the cellars and corresponding apertures in the first story, I think for illumination. If I remember right, there is a banister on one side. Holding candles to light our way, we stepped carefully down the stairs leading to the courtyard and then to the cellar-story. Darkness enveloped us. Our guide opened a door with a glass window—all of the doors have this same kind of glass window—through which a faint light was glimmering. What we were about to see was interesting for me, but in general an unpleasant sight.[153] In a small room, less than two arms-lengths long and wide, we saw plank-beds lying all around, leaving only a very small space free in the middle of the room. On one of these beds I saw a man crouching, holding an opium pipe and inhaling deeply the pernicious fumes. A small oil lamp was burning in front of him, for the preparation of the opium pill. Such a pill, even a bigger one, is, as I saw it, enough only for two or three inhalations, seldom for four.

The opium extract has a honey-like consistency. With a fine metal spatula—I have a similar one—the man takes a small amount of the extract, slowly places it on the clay-top of his pipe, then takes the opium up again, this time with the needle-like other end of the spatula, passes it lightly through the flame to condense it and make it more malleable and tries, by turning the needle round and round, to give the opium pill a cylindrical form. After passing the material once or twice more through the flame, until the desired form is attained, he sticks the needle into the opening of the pipe-bowl and, while drawing it back, uses his index-finger to press the small plug of opium into the bowl.

Now, he puts the opening of the pipestem to his mouth and inhales deeply, deeply, while letting the opium plug evaporate near the lamps. He looks for all the world like a thirsty man putting his pint to his lips and emptying it in deep endless gulps. After a half minute or so he exhales the fumes which, in the meantime, have been partially absorbed by the mucous membranes of the linings of his lungs. He repeats this procedure six, eight or ten times and even more until the gratifications of his opium-visions compensate him for the effort expended in these bothersome preparations.

He sees himself transplanted from his wretched surroundings; he sees palaces, riches, opulent repasts, splendid garments, beautiful amorous women and perhaps offices, titles and decorations heaped upon him.[154] In the morning he awakes, on a straw mat or a heap of rags in a lightless hole filled with pestilential air. Again he toils in the light of day and then returns to his hole. Who can blame this man if he returns night after night to the pleasurable worlds of his opium vision?

In this house, in which more than 900 people live, we saw many more of these rooms, and in other houses even more wretched than this one. What a terrible sight met our eyes in a room in yet another such house! Not more than 2m high and 2m long, it was filled with double-tiered sleeping bunks. About 15 men were lying on these bunks—some smoking opium, others stupefied and brooding. You open the door and the characteristic sweetish odor betrays the presence of opium smokers.

In another street we walk along a dark passage and arrive again at another one of these caverns.

[Text missing]

[*Lewin and Warburg attend a theatrical performance in Chinatown.*] Even for a fairly strong man it is difficult to push forward. Moreover, all these passageways are crooked. Many of the jutting walls have been fitted with niches, lights burning in them, probably some feature of their Buddhist cult. There is another narrow staircase to be climbed, and now we find ourselves in the actors' dressing room, men and women of course together. An interesting sight, but fundamentally no different from our theatres back home. Made-up heroes, made-up kings, beggars, etc. A door leads us out onto the stage where the actors perform. There is no scenery, or any other visual representation of the locality where the action is to take place. Instead, where the scenery would otherwise be, is an orchestra, its most important instruments being two gigantic cymbals, which are beaten incessantly, so loudly that you can't hear your own words.

I am checking out the actors when whom do I see, sitting there full of self-importance:

(Mr.) Hirschberg   Berlin   Karlstrasse!

Of course, I had to recover first from the sight of so much greatness; and only then did I get my bearings. In the fairly large parterre level the Chinese were sitting in a dense mass, so closely packed as I have seldom seen persons sitting in one place. The first balcony held only women. On the stage a hero, dressed in black, performed even during the most terrific clanging of the cymbals. His costume was open about three hands' breadth from the neck to the navel, which was visible to all. He seemed to be a sort of Hercules who has to carry out the tasks set out for him by a strongly-rouged princess. Three times he bends his bow, and then he engages in a fight with the heroine herself. She will be defeated if he succeeds in touching both her breasts with the flat of the palms of his hands. She skips around him, turning and twisting, both her forearms outstretched, as his are, thereby pushing him away and trying to defeat him. Then comes the finale—his hands come to rest on her breasts, she leaves hastily through the door, then comes back with companions, the cymbals clash: like men possessed, one man each belabors the cymbal, the drum, and the fife, while the fourth wields his bow on a small instrument with one or two strings. It's an infernal noise, but all the actors speak and indeed seem to be understood. The hero screams and roars until he is blue in the face.

H. [*Hirschberg*] leaves, and so the great attraction for me leaves with him. A vigorous handshake says, more than any words can, how much we love each other. After some time we too leave, and—through a narrow passageway— come back into the open air. How can something like this be tolerated? If the gaslight which burns here and in these narrow corridors should set even a splinter of wood on fire, not a soul could be saved. What a dreadful prospect! This is what must and will happen one of these days.

We enter another house, proceeding along passageways that seem even narrower than those we had just left. You feel your heart pounding at the thought of a sudden conflagration! Not even the most precipitous point on the Canadian Pacific Railway gave me such a fright. The feeling of being shut in in these passages nearly choked me! Here the little rooms looked a little cleaner. But what was this house for? I had not yet guessed the truth, when the policeman led us into one of them. A young woman came in and negotiated with the man. I understood but a few words, and the next moment was outside shouting for Uncle. I could scarcely believe it, but Mr. H. tried to call me back inside and Uncle tarried within. Waiting for them, I stood by myself in this corridor, where several more of these whores had gathered. At last, my companions came out. It was horrible! Disgust, deep disgust gripped me there, deeper than at any other time in my life, and I was happy to breathe the air of the streets, pestilential as it was. After this experience, I had little interest in our subsequent visit to a big Chinese restaurant, sumptuously decorated with gold leaf and elaborate wood carvings.

I don't know how often I spat, in the American way. I felt as if I had been in an infectious diseases ward and had to get rid of contagion. Our route from there led through still another lane where whores of the Caucasian race plied their nauseating trade.

Only then did we reach a civilized neighborhood. In the printing office of the *Chronicle*,[155] the day's activities were still going on. We ask for permission and are allowed to enter. Oh, what a relief this spectacle is, after what I had seen of filth, misery and depravity! I breathe in afresh, watching three Herculean figures busy at the rumbling, rattling and clanking machines. This meant a partial purification for me. I still had need of a whisky, which we bought. Later, after midnight, at one o'clock, I took a cleansing bath.

How is it possible, I have been asking myself, that America puts up with this element of Asian culture? How can it happen that this state of things is allowed to exist, in a place where the word "hygiene" must have been heard by at least one or two medical men? Only big-time graft, trickery and dishonesty can account for it. They are indeed prevalent here in America, so grossly, so directly, so openly prevalent as nowhere else in the world, not even in Russia. There are six Chinese companies[156] that have some sort of jurisdiction [*i.e., a monopoly*] here. They cause—and this is a fact—any inconvenient Chinese citizen to be murdered, and nobody will be able to find and arrest the killer. I am convinced that our policeman guide was paid, that is, bribed, by the Chinese. How else could it be possible that he led us to a place where the lottery was played, that he placed his bet as we did, pocketed his ticket and, later, when we came back to see whether the hourly or two-hourly draw had brought us any winnings, placed his bet for the next day, right then and there! The answer can only be that he has been bribed!

By the way, you can easily understand how the lottery works. On the one ticket which I sent you, I have marked eight numbers with Chinese ink. The cashier has written his notes alongside. Now you compare the numbers on the official perforated list with the numbers on your ticket. If four numbers are the same, double winnings, 5 numbers=triple winnings, and so forth.

Thursday, September 11

We both slept badly last night. After a bath, early to town. I wanted to have a look at the California State Mining Bureau, Pioneer Hall.[157] This is a handsome collection of Californiana from the animal, vegetable and mineral kingdoms. Of course, special emphasis is placed on minerals, with veins of gold and models of the big nuggets that were found here. An irregular jagged piece [*of gold*] weighed 1,200 ounces; that is, 36,000 grams or 36 kilograms. Worth about 400,000 mark, by Uncle's calculation. There is a still larger nugget here, and also small ones, partly free, partly embedded in rocks, but all of them genuine gold.

Also to be found here are the originals of two extraordinary meteorites, the San Bernardino, 99.67 ounces, and the Chiliat, of the same size. Many

California stuffed birds, quadrupeds, etc. under glass, as well as what the sea yields of shells and suchlike. It is remarkable that a few betel-nuts are also to be seen here, some with their fibrous covering, some without it. They may have made their way by water, driven by wind and current, maybe from the not too far away Caroline Islands, across the ocean eastward to the California coast.

At the hotel, we settled down to a few hours' writing, having seen the sights and something of the people. As Homer writes [of *Ulysses*], I have "seen the cities of many nations and known their character." We ask for mail at the post office, though without success, buy some notepaper, and so—back East!

At 2:30 the ferry brought us to Oakland, across the bay from San Francisco, [*the bay*] impressing us more by its dimensions than by its beauty. After landing, we drive by railway more than a quarter of an hour over a jetty built stunningly out into the bay; water to the left and right, we enjoy the view of the rocky coast which edges the bay. Then we drive further along a wide inlet of the sea, lying to our left and penetrating deeply into the mainland, and straight on through the mountain ranges which cross the railroad [*right-of-way*] here, the sea inlet obstructing our further progress. Then the whole train, together with one already waiting there, is transferred onto a steam-ferry. We are ferried across and, leaving California more and more behind us, we head toward Nevada and—most important—the Sierra Nevada.

While in San Francisco, we had made inquiries at all sorts of offices, all sorts of shops, and at different merchants about the shortest route to Washington. We had been told that the shortest route was by way of the Union Pacific and Pennsylvania Railroad,[158] that is to say:

San Francisco to Ogden
Ogden to Denver
Denver to Kansas City
Kansas City to Chicago
Chicago via the Limited Express to Washington

In order to make quite sure, I had had the ticket-office make out a timetable for us. Let me say right away that the fellow cheated me out of 12 hours. That's nothing to an American!

While daylight lasted, we could see well-cultivated country, with grassy plains and much cattle; no mountains were to be seen. We had supper in Sacramento, or rather, paid a dollar each for eggs—not good ones—and a little bread and butter before continuing east to Nevada. The rascally German who served us such unsatisfactory food was only the first in a succession of his kind. I went to bed and for a long time heard the clatter of the wheels repeating "Sacce-ra-ment, Sacce-ra-ment."[159]

Friday, September 2

That kind of swearword—Saccrament, repeated over and over—finally lulled me to sleep, and I slept soundly until morning. The next day and the days following gave me many opportunities to repeat that swear-word, putting my heart more at ease.

	TRAINS WEST	Dist. fr San Fran	STATIONS	Population	Elevation	TRAINS EAST	
Day	No. 2 Exp					No. 1 Exp	Day
Th	A M					P M	Sun
"	11 10		Ar...**San Francisco**..Lv	233000	....	3 00	"
"	10 45	4	......Oakland Pier....	......	14	3 28	"
"	....	6	......West Oakland......	45,000	12	....	"
"		12	..........Highland........	......	....	3 50	"
"	10 03	24	..........Pinole..........	......	....	4 10	"
"	9 53	29	.....Vallejo Junction.....	......	....	4 18	"
"	9 45	32	.....**Port Costa**......	......	....	4 25	"
"	9 20	33	... .Benicia	2,000	....	4 50	"
"	8 42	49	... .Suisun......	1,600	....	5 22	"
"	8 20	60	;........ Elmira	250	....	5 47	"
"	8 10	65	..........Batavia	......	....	5 56	"
"	8 03	68	... .Dixon	1,500	....	6 05	"
"	7 45	77	..........Davis	700	....	6 25	"
"	†7 20	90	........**Sacramento**	27,000	30	†7 15	"
"	....	93	....American Riv Bdg....	......	52	7 23	"
"	6 20	108	..........Junction........	650	163	8 00	"
"	6 10	112	..........Rocklin	1,000	249	8 30	"
"	5 30	121	........Newcastle........	500	957	9 15	"
"	5 10	126	..........Auburn........	2,200	1360	9 40	"
"	4 44	133	........Clipper Gap......	......	1759	10 05	"
"	4 00	144	..........Colfax........	500	2422	11 20	"
"	3 06	157	..........Dutch Flat.......	1,000	3395	12 15	Sun
"	2 58	158	.... Alta	150	3607	12 30	Mo
"	2 15	168	.... Blue Cañon	250	4093	2 00	"
"	1 40	174	......Emigrant Gap........	250	5221	2 20	"
Th	12 10	195	.... Summit........	......	6749	3 50	"
We	11 35	203	.......Strong's Cañon......	......	6317	4 20	"
"	11 10	209	..........**Truckee**......	2,000	5819	4 50	"
"	9 15	234	..........Verdi, Cal.	......	4895	6 00	"
"	†8 40	214	........Reno, Nev......	4,000	4497	†7 00	"
"	6 50	279	..........Wadsworth......	400	3077	8 25	"
"	5 35	305	..........Mirage......	......	4247	9 22	"
"	4 50	325	...... Browns	......	4918	10 05	"
"	†3 10	374	...... Humboldt......	......	4236	†12 15	"
"	2 27	386	......Mill City......	......	4226	12 40	"
"	1 35	414	......**Winnemucca**	1,300	4332	1 45	"
"	11 58	455	...... Stone House	......	4422	3 11	"
"	11 17	474	......Battle Mountain	500	4511	3 50	"
"	10 08	507	...... Be-o-wa-we	......	4995	5 02	"
"	9 25	525	..........Palisade	109	4841	5 46	"
"	9 00	535	..........Carlin	500	4897	6 22	"
"	†7 50	558	..........Elko	1,000	5063	†7 40	"
"	6 35	581	..........Halleck........>	......	5230	8 38	"
"	5 20	614	..........**Wells**	128	5629	10 00	"
"	4 40	629	..........Independence...	......	6007	10 51	"
"	3 40	650	..........Toano	......	5873	11 45	Mo
"	2 00	676	....Tecoma, Nevada.....	......	4812	12 52	Tu
We	12 20	709	......Terrace, Utah... ...	258	4544	2 25	"
Tu	10 25	741	..........Kelton......	155	4223	3 55	"
"	8 35	780	......Promontory	......	4905	5 40	"
"	7 05	809	..........Corinne..........	500	4232	6 52	"
Tu	†6 00	833	Lv........**Ogden**...... Ar	8,000	4294	†7 55	T
	PM					A M	

Timetable, San Francisco to Ogden, Utah

Even Uncle, as patient as he is, was transformed into a roaring lion as the cheating, we believed, reached its high point. I put forth the not entirely unfounded conjecture that those who were in charge of providing meals to travelers had conspired among themselves always to serve travelers the same adulterated food. An American stomach can, perhaps, tolerate the kind of meat that we were offered, but not a German one. In fact, throughout our entire tour of America, there was no city where we could enjoy the meat that was put in front of us, and the rest of the food was so badly prepared and looked so unappetizing that we left it on our plates, untouched. The very word, "steak," was enough to give us both the creeps.

[Here part of the text is missing]

In comparison, Luneburg Heath[160] is a paradise. And when I think of the wonderful plant-carpeted surface of that moor, then in my opinion this stretch, hundreds of miles long, is like a desert. A terrible land without any welcoming features, unbearable by reason of its nature and made more so by the rascally caterers who compensate themselves for the arid sterile land by taking it out on their fat or half-fat customers. If there were at least a flower, or heather, to gladden the eye, but nothing! Nothing!

At Winnemucca [*Nevada*], we saw a family of Indians at the station. Several women and children were squatting around a telegraph pole. Their faces seemed to be unpainted. A young mother was particularly noticeable by her handsome face and by the way she had cradled her baby.

Imagine a narrow carrier which can be strapped to the back. It consists of a backboard wrapped in canvas; the canvas wrappings extend around to the front, where the left and right pieces meet. Both straps have holes for fastenings. At the top there is a shade made of canvas; at the bottom two pieces of wood permit the carrier to be set down on the ground. From under the shade, well laced-in, the little redskin looks out.

Not far from the station we could see the Indians' mudhuts. How much worse off these Indians are than the Canadian Indians whom we saw—at least the latter can find in the forests or on the prairie what they need for a living!

The desert-like panorama, sun-scorched soil, the plains interrupted here and there by rising ground, stayed the same until evening. The train stops everywhere, so that I would have lost patience if I hadn't been writing to you, my sweet Clara, all day long. Uncle was

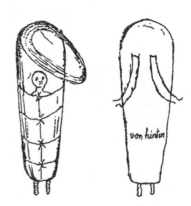

"From under the shade, well laced-in, the little redskin looks out."
(Louis Lewin drawing)

asked whether I was writing a "paper"—you would be pleased with my pronunciation of the word—about America. He answered in the affirmative, adding that my account was favorable.

Saturday, September 3

At 4:30 I was already up and dressed. Staying in the car when the other passengers get up is unpleasant. Not only must one take in their exhalations, but one cannot avoid the dust from their bodies and bedding which whirls about when blankets and pillows are shaken up. It is difficult to provide sufficient ventilation; that is why we are usually the first to get up, staying in the smoking room until the [*sleeping*] car was tidied up.

At this early hour the scenery is still the same: desolate. Of course, the train is behind schedule. As there is no need to be punctual, despite the timetable, one can assume from the outset that one will be adding one or two hours to the scheduled arrivals and departures.

The bleakness of the region and the conversation of some of the travelers about "lots," which even in the "Great American Desert" are of prime importance, cause Uncle to devise the plot of a comedy.

[Lewin describes the plot of the proposed comedy and his embroidering of it.]

We were interrupted in our conversation by a couple who smacked their lips, clicked their tongues, snapped their fingers, kissed, ate fruit with great relish and carried on like this all day.

Finally, the scenery improves. We begin to see grass, trees, and neat houses. We have arrived in the State of Utah. I had hoped that here we would get rid of the lady who had been traveling with us since yesterday. With a rare volubility, she kept on telling the men and women around her stories about her family, using the word "kill" at least once in every sentence. Like the figure of a Bavaria[161] she sat facing her fascinated audience, which changed but never diminished. I had thought she was a Mormon woman, but it turned out that she was not.

From the train we see the Great Salt Lake, which extends from northwest to southeast, its water a striking blue color. All the houses we pass look tidy. It is obvious that we have reached a region with an industrious population. The land that we have passed was probably once blessed with trees, but now it has been denuded by wholesale burning. As a result, the soil is arid, dry, lacking water—which can be blamed partly on the absence of trees. Horses and cattle can be seen grazing here, but I have seen no sheep here, grazing or otherwise.

Hungry and thirsty, we arrived in Ogden at nine o'clock. From here another line leads to Salt Lake City, the Mormon town. First we buy tickets and, having been identified by our accents as Germans, are cheated out of two dollars. When we protested, we were told that the next section would cost us that much less to make up for it. That was a brazen lie. I wrote this man to demand that he send the money immediately to my Washington address, but "Horse and rider were never seen again."

Made wiser by our past experiences, we do not partake of the "shoe-sole" [*steak*] dinner. Instead, we have a cup of bad coffee and bad bread while standing at a kiosk. At a bookstore in the station I saw photographs relating to Utah, especially to the Mormon city [*Salt Lake City*]. Some of them came close to obscenity. Among them is one of a Mormon man, with many little children playing on top of him and around him. Another photograph depicts a huge Mormon family on a bed on which the different wives roll about, quarreling and bickering, while the husband, squatting atop the stove, watches and grimaces.

From this point on, the country is getting more scenic. It is not mighty heights nor forest-worlds that impress you here, but rather the small-scale beauties of nature, a hilly range, a peculiar arrangement of rock-masses, such as granite rocks that assume the shape of a human head. Or of castles with battlements and towers, or of light-houses, and so on; or those two sharp rocky ridges which stretch from the middle of a hill down to the plain, parallel and very near to each other, thus forming a natural conduit for water.

At about two o'clock we see in the distance fairly large snowy surfaces on mountain ranges. The little illustration which I enclose shows that from Ogden to Cheyenne, or, as the Americans say, "chei-en," there is a considerable gradient.

"From Ogden to Cheyenne . . . there is a considerable gradient."
(Louis Lewin drawing)

Here we meet our old acquaintances—the Rocky Mountains that extend from Canada to Mexico. Nowhere do they disown their fierce character. The part through which we now proceed is, as far as I could make out, without any vegetation at all, save for a few shrubs here and there.

Except for the gradient, the railroad has only a few difficulties to overcome—from time to time a little rock-gate, a bridge, a snowmass—that is all. To the eye, the region we pass through seems to be a flat plateau. Later in the afternoon, we travel again through a hilly wilderness with stony ground; water is seldom to be seen, and then only in narrow ditches, its color mostly a reddish yellow.

In the evening, we check to see whether we are going to be able to be in Washington as scheduled, on September 7th. It appears that it will be practically impossible. As you can imagine, I was just a little worked up, and I asked everyone—or had Uncle ask—whether there was a shorter route than the one we had decided upon. Nobody had any information and I went to bed angry, or, rather, annoyed.

TRAINS WEST		Dist. fr San Fran	STATIONS	Popula-tion	Elevat'n	TRAINS EAST	
Day	No. 201 Exp & Emgt					No. 202 Exp & Emgt	Day
	P M					A M	
Tu	5 40	833	Ar .... Ogden Lv	8,000	4294	10 00	Tu
Mo	5 35	1349	Ar ...... Cheyenne Lv	6,000	6038	10 35	We
"	3 25	1403	..... Greeley	3,000	4670	1 00	"
Mo	†1 25	1455	Lv .... Denver .... Ar	55,000	5203	2 55	We
Mo	†7 15	1455	Ar ...... Denver Lv	55,000	5203	†8 05	We
"	......	1477	.... Watkins	100	5546	......	"
"	5 44	1499	.... Byers	63	5221	9 32	"
"	5 20	1512	.... Deer Trail	150	5203	9 57	"
"	......	1539	.... River Bend		5511	10 51	We
"	3 45	1561	.... Hugo	500	5068	11 38	We
"	2 05	1608	.... Kit Carson	50	4307	1 04	Th
"	1 35	1623	.... First View		4595	1 35	"
Mo	1 10	1634	..... Cheyenne Wells		5295	..	"
Su	11 40	1673	.... Wallace	100	3319	4 09	"
"	11 15	1717	.... Oakley			5 23	"
"	......	1730	.... Grinnell		2912	......	"
"	10 35	1739	.... Grainfield	100	2829	6 01	"
"	......	1744	..... Buffalo Park	50	2773	......	"
"	9 55	1759	.... Collyer		2608	......	"
"	9 28	1774	.... WaKeeney	550	2474	6 59	"
"	†8 50	1792	.... Ellis	500	2135	†7 50	"
"	8 05	1805	.... Hays	1,000	2009	8 13	"
"	......	1816	.... Victoria	1,500	1946	......	"
"	7 14	1832	.... Russell	1,000	1850	9 02	"
"	......	1842	.... Bunker Hill	200	1882	......	"
"	6 30	1855	.... Wilson	700	1702	9 45	"
"	5 58	1861	.... Ellsworth	1,100	1556	10 13	"
"	5 17	1894	.... Brookville	650	1366	11 00	"
"	......	1901	.... Bavaria	100	1289	......	"
"	4 40	1909	.... Salina	3,120	1243	11 24	"
"	4 12	1923	.... Solomon	725	1193	11 50	"
"	3 55	1931	.... Abilene	2,300	1173	†12 08	"
"	......	1936	.... Detroit	100	1153	......	"
"	3 08	1956	.... Junction City	3,260	1100	12 55	"
"	......	1960	.... Ft. Riley		1090	......	"
"	......	1965	.... Ogdensburg	225	1078	......	"
"	2 28	1976	.... Manhattan	2,400	1042	1 34	"
"	......	1984	.... St. George	400	1018	......	"
"	2 00	1991	.... Wamego	1,800	1018	2 03	"
"	......	1998	.... Belvue	300	983	......	"
"	1 31	2004	.... St. Marys	1,000	973	2 29	"
"	......	2011	.... Rossville	500	951	......	"
"	†12 40	2027	.... Topeka	23,000	904	3 35	"
"	12 19	2028	.... A. T. & S. F. Crossing		902	3 36	"
"	11 49	2043	.... Perryville	350	870	......	"
"	11 25	2056	.... Lawrence	10,800	846	4 25	"
"	......	2057	...... Bismark Grove		837	......	"
"	......	2058	..... Lawrence Junction		832	......	"
"	......	2093	.... Armstrong	1,000	773	......	"
Su	10 09	......	.... State Line		663	5 41	Th
Su	9 35	2090	.... Leavenworth	22,000	782	6 05	Th
Su	10 05	2094	Lv ...... Kansas City ...... Ar	125,000	763	5 45	Th
	A M					P M	

Trains between Denver and Wallace are run on Mountain time; between Wallace and Kansas City on Central time—one hour slower than Mountain time. †Meals. Time between noon and midnight indicated by **bold faced** figures.

Timetable, Ogden to Kansas City

Sunday, September 4

We proceed slowly. In the east the snow-covered mountains still accompany us. Until now, we have been in Wyoming, but now we approach the [*eastern*] border of this state and the edge of the mountain ranges that we have crossed. The sun was burning hot all day. Variety of scenery is non-existent; monotony prevails. Even here in this desert, however, advertising reigns. At about ten o'clock we crossed a deep gorge. Written across its bottom, so that one cannot escape it, one reads "Lehmann Wall Paper" in big letters.

Before reaching Cheyenne, we came to a stone-pyramid on a hill; I think it marks the highest point [*i.e., the western Continental Divide*]. The train made an unduly long stop here, even though there is but one house here. Some of the passengers got out, to look for rocks containing gold.

Further on we saw much cattle on the pasture and handsome farms lying amidst verdure. The train races along to make up for lost time, but it's *Love's Labor Lost*. It makes no difference, because at our next stop, Denver, there will be a six-hour layover! Uncle is singing along to the rattling of the train. I didn't catch the words, but it seems to be something heroic. Perhaps it was because we were now in Colorado, and he was reminded of "coloratura."[162]

At last we reach Denver! We have not eaten all day and it is already around five o'clock. We thought to find something in town and set out cheerfully in that direction. We asked many people for a good "Eating House"—or the best of them. At last one gentleman showed us the one where he himself had dined. Only a few minutes elapsed between our entry, full of confidence, and our exit, thoroughly disgusted by the dirt. As we were very thirsty, we had a bottle of beer at a dishonest German's establishment; he made us pay 1 mark 60 for a bottle of the commonest lager.

The dining room of the grandiose train station (three wings, and built throughout of stone), was due to open at five o'clock. At last it was time, we enter, settling down comfortably. Two soups? Don't have any. Corned beef? Don't have any. Beef tongue? Same. Uncle continued the examination, all the way down to the eggs, while I had a good laugh. No eggs either, but boiled pigs' feet and steak, oh yes! We left the dining room in a hurry and went back into town, where we managed to have some bread and butter and scrambled eggs.

What a state of affairs! How hard must a German worker who had hoped to find golden opportunities here, to earn one to two dollars, and how little he can get for those comparatively high wages! No, I wouldn't even want to be buried in this country, to say nothing of living here! What a fine country

Germany is! I have learned a lot on this journey, and that is perhaps the best lesson of all.

Back in the train station we had another argument with the man in the Pullman office. We wanted to get the two dollars back that the Yankee in Ogden had cheated us out of, but we got nowhere.

Monday, September 5

This was an unnerving day. Everything depended on our making the connection at Kansas City to Chicago. The train was stopping everywhere and we were seriously behind time. In Ellsworth [*Kansas*], where we arrived at 9:15, a musical band of blacks was marching past the train. They all wore long grayish-white smocks, white top hats, black trousers and the natural color of their skins. They marched along briskly, their white smocks fluttering in the wind. They made me think of the "Five Jolly Darkies."[163]

From morning to night we saw, to left and right, corn and nothing but corn. This area must produce huge quantities of this crop. The land is also densely populated. It can be said that the houses—at least along the railroad—form an unbroken line. I saw many huts with adjacent fields belonging to blacks. Fertility must be considerable—seldom have I found grass growing as it does here.

It is now noon. As fertile as Kansas is, it offers us nothing to eat. At Abilene, where a steak-eating was scheduled which I did not wish to participate in, there was not a drop of beer to be had. Oh, this sanctimonious nation! The women drink whisky and Eau de Cologne from so-called smelling bottles, the men get drunk on sparkling wine, but to sell beer publicly or drink it—Heaven forbid!

For just such an emergency as this one, we had bought a bottle of whisky in Denver. A young girl sat facing us in the car, overdressed and with an expression of blasé disgust on her face. I roused her from her *dolce far niente* of thought and action by raising the bottle to my lips and taking a hearty pull. She laughed out loud and couldn't stop when Uncle took a swig of it too. Oh, you miserable water-drinkers! Though in your country there can be no romance of drinking as there is in Germany, you should at least be shown that drinking is no disgrace or sin. I myself am not a passionate drinker, but the conditions here make drinking in Germany appear in a kind of halo, compared to this milk-, ice cream- and water-slurping people.

Everywhere on our way, men, women and children, dressed in their Sunday best, stood at the stations. They were all making *Blau Montag*—blue Monday[164]—but we also stopped everywhere. I was terribly worried. Suddenly the train stopped altogether in open country. All the passengers got out. What was amiss? Indeed, this sort of thing can only happen in America: completely at their ease, two trains stood facing each other at a distance of about fifty feet. Instead of stopping at the siding and waiting until our train had passed, a freight train had strolled onto the same line as our train was using, the engine had broken down and couldn't be rolled back. The maintenance men were busy trying to repair it as best they could.

There was another hour's delay, before we could proceed. Hurray for Freedom! Every train can move on any track—down with European regimentation and compulsion! There's no one to whom you can register a complaint, no train station inspector in sight and, when you finally find an official, he scarcely hears what you're saying or, at the most, utters a long-drawn-out "Well!" and then—silence.

Finally, we arrive in Kansas City, pay no attention to our hunger and thirst, unload our heavy hand-baggage and run the length of the platform. Where is the train to Chicago? Here? No, the conductor tells us, the train has already left! It had indeed left, after waiting for some time for our train to arrive. When can we get the next train to Chicago? Tomorrow morning at the same time! We went to the ticket office and to the Pullman office, always with the same answer. I was beside myself with anger, irritating Uncle by my insistence.[165] I made one more attempt, found a brakeman and asked him "Where is the train to Chicago? We have to be in Washington by Wednesday for the Congress." He pointed to those whom we had already asked and who had ignored us, then took me by the hand, so as to lead me to the right place. While we were walking, he told me a long story. Of course, I didn't understand a word of it, but he seemed to be talking with firm conviction.

I rushed to get Uncle, and together we ran back to get our luggage, which had been deposited on the platform, so as to be ready to get on the train. Then I remembered that we had no tickets for the Pullman sleeping-car. Uncle ran with the brakeman to the office while I ran to the waiting train, and at the office Uncle was dismissed just as he had been before. This train was heading for St. Louis. I ran back to the counter and asked the brakeman again. He stood firm. The three of us went back to that train. The brakeman explained everything to the conductor, who, with a snarling "All right," allowed us to come aboard. Because of our hunger and fatigue, we could scarcely stand up.

What we've learned is that this train, like the one that took off without us, must travel 2-1/2 hours through the Roodhouse[166] station, and that we had to meet the [*Chicago*] train at five o'clock in the morning. It seemed inconceivable to us that we could catch that train. Our tickets were made out for two upper berths. I haggled with the train conductor outside our car, making it clear to him that the "old man can't sleep in the upper berth." My pleas were met with a shrug of the shoulders. I found out that the train would not be leaving for another twenty minutes. I got hold of Uncle, and we went to the dining-car, where we were able to get a bite to eat, and then the train got underway. The conductor now took pity on us and gave us a lower berth where Uncle could lie down.

I didn't get undressed and didn't sleep at all. Uncle's repeater watch chimed every half-hour. Would we reach our destination in time or no? At about 3:30AM we got out of bed. At each little mail stop the train halted, and then raced through the night at redoubled speed, through regions which I recognized as partly mountainous. I go outside onto the platform in order to see daybreak. Suddenly, the train slows down. We cross over a mightily long and high bridge. Under me the river current breaks noisily against the piers of the bridge. Slowly, slowly, we pass over the Mississippi. Ahead of us lies the east.

I see the first light of day in the sky, which turns gradually into an indistinct yellowish-white, showing a violet tinge where the horizon meets the earth. The yellowish-white disappears and, more and more, the violet turns to red, covers a wider area, sends radiating beams across the sky, the red is intensified—the splendid spectacle drives away my fatigue—and now the glowing sun-ball rises blood-red over the horizon and shines on farms, forests, and cornfields, which we pass through rapidly.

Our tension grows. The train which we were supposed to meet in Roodhouse was to have left for Chicago at 4:30. It is now 4:45! At last we reach Roodhouse and find to our relief that the Chicago train was still standing there.

Tuesday, September 6

What a rush that was! I am glad that now there is a chance of our arriving in Washington on time. We occupy a "Reclining Chair Car," with seats recalling those in a dentist's office. Each passenger has his own chair, complete with high back and armrests. By pressing a spring you can place your back and legs—which of course are also supported—in any position you want, even the horizontal. So we enjoyed a good rest after our tribulations. There was also a dining car attached to the train and we went there in order to satisfy our animal needs. Food and drink are good. Traveling in this country, you never know when the next opportunity for having a meal will present itself, so it is wise to eat when you have the opportunity to do so.

On this day our route lacked special interest, but it was preferable at any rate to the journey through western America. This entire area is heavily populated. One sees much livestock, especially horses, in large pastures. More striking, though, are the numerous marble quarries which appear to the left and right during the last leg of this route. How admirably arranged are Nature's gifts to man! Layer upon layer is deposited here. Compact rock-masses without stratification do not exist. In thick and thin slabs the marble is deposited here as if predestined to be used for consoles and staircases, monuments, etc. The workmen cut out the slabs and think it is they who made them.

Marble walls and fences, stairs and thresholds, houses and towers lie hidden here, in overwhelming quantities. One day, however, all this plenty will come to an end, as everything in this world does. Marble is already being quarried from under the surface. More work, more sweat, is required to haul the material from the interior of the earth and it will get more expensive accordingly. What was valued but little at first because it was obtained in plenty and without toil is now highly appreciated. It is possible to extract from this fact a moral principle. One should learn from it. Happy the one who understands and has the willpower to draw the appropriate conclusions from this insight!

In the meantime, it had become almost unbearably hot:

> *Hunger quällte, Durst that weh,*
> *Und ein einziges Loth Kaffee . . .*[167]

was not to be had for any money.

> *Bier hier, Bier her,*
> *Oder ich verdurst!*[168]

Regardless—there wasn't a drop to be had!

To our right we could see a huge building—a prison—built, of course, of marble. On the broad, medievally-crenellated walls I saw soldiers, or guards, with their rifles, walking to and fro on patrol between every two watch-towers.

Our arrival at the Chicago train station was endlessly delayed. For about a half-hour we knocked about on the sidings. Finally, at two o'clock, we "landed," left our luggage in the cloakroom (it cost 1 mark 60—quite funny, isn't it?) and walked into the city. We asked about ten people for a restaurant, but only three bothered to answer. Finally, we took a cab for two Mark and were led to one of those miserable milk-water-and-ice-cream restaurants where we left the beef tongue we were served on our plates on account of its toughness and were soon off again.

The town seems unprepossessing. It made the most unpleasant impression of all the towns and cities I have seen thus far. It may be an excellent town for business, but for me there is nothing attractive there, neither its streets nor its houses. We soon headed back to the station to catch our train to Washington.

We got underway at five o'clock. The interior decoration of this Palace Car is a sight to behold. We again had a compartment to ourselves, with double seats and backs covered in light blue velvet. The wainscoting is highly polished, smooth as a mirror, all made of finely-veined light citrus wood. Illumination is by electricity; crystal mirrors throw back its light. In whatever direction you look, you see a reflection of yourself and other passengers. The lavatories are as I've come to expect them, but the washbasins are made of Napoléon rosé. The cars are connected with each other so that you can get from one to the other, as through an enclosed corridor, closed from all sides. Thick pleated rubber sheets protect you from the draft and prevent the cars from colliding. The two platforms join precisely. If you want to get in or out, there are beveled cut-glass doors leading to steps with elaborate wrought-iron handrails.

The smoking car

The sleeping car

The parlor car

The dining car

Uncle and I visit the dining car and find the same luxury here. Seats covered in tooled leather, electric lighting, handsome dinner-service; at the far end a sideboard. We walk in, passing on our way a barber shop with an elegant bathtub that can be closed off by a curtain.

Returning to our compartment after lunch, we passed a drawing room, which costs about 3-4 times as much as a compartment. Here young couples are able to travel by themselves in complete privacy. Every car has one such section. In one of them we saw a young man stretched out on a sofa, a guitar in his hands, singing out loud to the accompaniment of the guitar. His singing could be heard above the noise of the clanging cars.

> [*Here Lewin inserts, in its English original, a promotional brochure for the railroad line entitled, "What a Business Man Thinks of the Pennsylvania Limited."*]

Wednesday, September 7

Chicago, Washington, Baltimore, Philadelphia and New York.

EASTWARD

L've Cincinnati, Every Day, Central Time,	7.45 P. M.
L've Columbus, Every Day,	11.45 P. M.
L've Chicago, Every Day,	5.00 P. M.
L've Fort Wayne, Every Day,	9.00 P. M.
L've Crestline, Every Day,	12.15 N'HT
Arr Pittsburg, Every Day, Central Time,	6.00 A. M.
Arr Pittsburg, Every Day, Eastern Time,	7.00 A. M.
L've Pittsburg, Every Day, Eastern Time,	7.15 A. M.
L've Altoona, Every Day,	10.40 A. M.
Arr Harrisburg, Every Day,	1.55 P. M.
Arr Baltimore, Every Day,	4.40 P. M.
Arr Washington, Every Day,	5.50 P. M.
Arr Philadelphia, Every Day,	4.45 P. M.
Arr New York, Every Day,	7.00 P. M.
Arr Brooklyn, Every Day,	7.15 P. M.
Arr Boston, Every Day,	7.50 A. M.

Timetable, Chicago to Washington

This little timetable [*see above*] will give you, my dearest Clara, an idea of our route. Refreshed by an uninterrupted night's sleep, we were able to enjoy the glorious beauties of nature that could be seen from our car. We have seen nothing more beautiful on our entire return trip. None of the states that we passed through—California, Nevada, Utah, Wyoming, Colorado, Kansas, Missouri, Illinois, Indiana or Ohio—offer what Pennsylvania possesses (we entered this state early this morning). How unexpected are the changes from one extreme to another here in America! First, we passed through arid desert, and now fat, arable land follows, splendid cornfields, flowery pastures, fields that shimmer from afar with yellow sunflowers—here we encounter plains and now mountains, there a treeless region, and now, all of a sudden, wonderful forests which bring Canada to mind.

At about 8:00 we enter smoke-blackened Pittsburgh, where the Alleghany and Monongahela Rivers join to form the Ohio. Afterwards the real beauty of Pennsylvania begins, as far as I have seen it. The train takes us through hills covered with leafy forests, through long tunnels, over bridges, in bold curves on a road which dynamite and pickaxe have formed out of the rock. The road offers wonderful vistas far into this most-blessed of all the American lands. Wherever we look, we see forests that remind us of home, and, in the valleys and up on the mountain slopes, the results of human endeavor embodied in the beautiful fields, pastures, gardens and orchards. This region can compete with any Swiss landscape.

But there is a higher interest here that gives the region importance for the whole inhabited world: the treasures of its soil, which seem to be inexhaustible. California's gold and Africa's diamonds are nothing compared to the value of the coal, iron, oil and natural gas which man extracts from the ground here.

Again you can observe here the abrupt transitions characteristic of this country: you drive through woodland, thinking you are far away from human crowds, when unexpectedly smoke rises up; mighty chimneys emit gases glowing like embers or flaming in a bright blood-red; hammers pound; collieries appear where freight cars are being loaded with coal on the spot; workers' houses surround the industrial areas; then comes a town; then again a coke-plant where fierce flames burst forth from 20 or more ovens; then immense glass factories and so on throughout Pennsylvania. The dense population here is proof that this state can provide a living for many people.

This goes on for hours and hours, yet we are still in the Allegheny Mountains. The railroad follows the course of the rivers but, even so, there are many difficulties to overcome. For instance, the little picture I enclose shows a magnificent S-curve, boldly structured and running close to the edge of the rock.[170]

Altoona S-Curve (above); signal tower (below)

In most places here, the produce of the fields has been gathered in, and the foliage shows autumnal coloring. The yellow and red leaves tell us that we have been away from home for a long time! And, in spite of all the beauty I see here, the longing for my dear ones preys on my mind. I wish I were back with you, my darlings! Or that you might enjoy these pleasures with me without the hardships of traveling! Pictures cannot convey experiences; only the eye can absorb the colorful images in all their harmony and transmit them to feeling and comprehension for re-interpretation.

Nevertheless, during this entire trip I never had any unpleasant feeling of anxiety, and never on this route did even a part of the landscape seemed as rugged and wild as it did everywhere in British Columbia. In spite of the not-inconsiderable height, in spite of the widespread forests and the massive rocks, the scene is almost consistently beautiful.

The scene keeps its attractions as far as Harrisburg and even further. The

Limited brought us to this town, which lies on the Susquehanna [*River*], an hour behind schedule, despite its name, the Limited Express. The beauties of nature got the better of my impatience to reach my destination, all the more so since the Congress has been in progress for two days and the White House reception, which I would have liked to attend, has already taken place.

In Harrisburg, we had to change cars, and we were installed in a Parlor Car, where each passenger has his own comfortable upholstered chair and a foot-rest. These chairs are attached to the floor at the train-windows and you can swivel them. The region which we pass through now also has its beauties. The rich iron content of the mountains and the interior of the earth manifests itself in the rust-color of the rivers. These Yellow Rivers change their color to a bluish black, when materials containing tannic acid, like treebark, etc., fall into their waters, and indeed it makes them look inky. Everywhere on this fertile soil I see nice red-painted farmhouses, reminding me of the ones I see in Westphalia. A considerable portion of the population seems to be quite well-off.

It vexes me that we are traveling so slowly and stop at each whistle-stop, but it gives us time to look at details. From our side, we have to go through some very long tunnels before we get to Baltimore. Afterwards, the train begins to crawl more and more—every ten minutes another stop. I wanted very much to receive your letters today, my dear, but it is dark already. Despite my fretting over these delays and over the uninteresting parts of Maryland through which we traveled, it was 7:30 before we got to our hotel.

Now we are in Washington.[171] The rooms we had booked are ready—one room with a closet. This costs 36 Marks per day with full board, no matter whether we take the meals there or not. What to do? We stay! But the meals were so badly cooked that we could not eat them and during our entire stay we had to pay to eat somewhere else. Some German doctors whom I talked to on the street pointed us to some better food. These were cheerful fellows from Stuttgart, Potsdam and someplace else who certainly had come here for pleasure and not for the advancement of science or their own knowledge. In a pub kept by a German we had a glass of beer with some bread and cheese, and thence to bed.

Thursday, September 8

Where did I go first today, dear Clara?[172] Yes, I got all the letters. According to the dates, some were missing at first, but I found them among Uncle's letters. It was a great comfort—at last, after so long a time, a sign of life and love from you. How many times have I read them over! Thank God, you are all in good health! Oh, what happiness! I thank God for giving me a loving wife and sweet children! Were it possible, I would love you all now, after this long and cruel deprivation, more than ever before!

We had our luggage brought [*to the hotel*] and enjoyed the feeling, for a change, of being well-dressed. The streets were full of doctors with their medals on blue and red ribbons, the red ones denoting that the wearers were officers [*of the association*]. We went to the conference offices to register but were told that the office would not open until 10:30. Typically American! In general one does not hear much German spoken. But I studied the dignified physiognomies of the Yankee doctors, with and without whiskers. Most of them have studied for only two years. Some of them have not even finished a real high school [in German, *Gymnasium*]. With the exception of the University of Pennsylvania in Philadelphia, Harvard University in Boston and, I think, Johns Hopkins University in Baltimore, all the university medical schools accept even a farmer who wants to matriculate. Some require an entrance examination, but don't require much more than that. Because of their short period of study, their general medical knowledge can't be high, but they do get practical professional training and might be quite capable in everyday medical work. Here everyone seems to be looking not only for melons, steaks, etc. but also for a handshake with this or that famous personality.

We walk along the streets. What a beautiful city! Streets 60-150 feet wide everywhere. It's clear that these streets have been laid out by a planner's ruler. Everywhere there are park-like gardens with beautiful flowerbeds and large public buildings adorned with Ionic, Doric or Corinthian columns, sometimes occupying entire blocks. The dome of the Capitol[173]—the symbol of the Union—gleams from afar over the city, the connecting link with the heterogeneous states that stretch out from there in every direction of the compass.

We go back to our hotel. My preliminary impression is that this Congress does not promise much. I don't like occasional nibblers. In my opinion, meetings such as these should be restricted to scientists striving for the advancement of medical knowledge, and not open to holiday trippers. We answer all letters. I had learned that our section would be meeting at Columbian University[174] at three o'clock. When we get there we find ourselves in a beautiful lecture hall, with the chairman, the secretaries and an audience of nine. We sit down—two minutes later, Uncle is fast asleep. I have to wake him up and make him leave. I cannot decide if I should disclose my identity and give a lecture or not. The reasons for not doing so are stronger.

I decide to look first at the other sections. They are meeting in the Congregational Church.[175] I had thought to meet Unna[176] and a researcher in leprosy there. When I went in, there he was, in tails and white tie. I was flabbergasted to hear this man talk impudently and tritely about matters you can find in any textbook. In the neurological section, Hendel was putting on airs. I had met him in the street before going in, and he had asked me: "How do you come to be here?" and I had answered, "By ship and train, just like you." He told me proudly that he already given his lecture. I went back in to see Unna. He had just finished his lecture, to great applause, but there were only a few people present. I approached him and said, "How are you, Dr. Unna? I am Dr. Lewin." "So you are Dr. Lewin. Yes, you wanted to have a talk with me? I'm sorry, but I am very busy today, till two o'clock at night. But tomorrow morning we can have coffee together." At that moment I knew that I was finished with this gentleman and knew that I would not be having coffee with him.

We left the church. I sent Uncle back to the hotel because he was too tired and went on to my section. I intended to complete my undertaking. A young man, a certain Dr. Gnesda from Berlin whom I had not heard of, was lecturing about snake poison. Through an attendant I sent my card to the chairman. He and the secretary acknowledged my presence with a nod, a silent greeting.

The young man spoke deliberately and confidently about experiments he had done at DuBois.[177] When he had finished I began to speak, drawing his attention to some unclear statements and some omissions. The silly fellow got very impudent. Well, as you know, I don't stay cool very long. I let him have it, so well indeed that the Americans who were present and spoke no German understood nevertheless that something serious was going on, all the more so since I had the secretary, Mr. Woodbury, translate my explanations into English. He performed this task most satisfactorily. I had warmed to my subject. The young man was silent, so I explained to the audience what I wanted from him.

In the meantime the audience had grown considerably. Ladies were present; that is to say, ladies with an M.D. degree. My voice, resounding through the open doors. had attracted these new listeners. Since there was no blackboard, I chalked the formula on the doorpost. Having finished, I asked for permission to give my lecture directly, although there were other speakers on the agenda. This, too, went off well. Mr. Woodbury gave the audience a summary of what I had said, a short discussion followed, and, before seven o'clock, it was all over.[178]

I felt I had not done badly today. So I decided to go to the banquet in the Pension Building which the Washington authorities were giving for the visiting doctors, but I had no tickets. Back at the hotel, I managed to get tickets for myself and for Uncle, although we had not yet registered at the hotel.

We were both in excellent spirits. We slipped into our formal wear, our white ties looking quite solemn in contrast to the black coats. Uncle insisted on wearing awful black silk gloves, but I persuaded him once we arrived at the dinner to take them off.

Together with others we drove by bus to the building[179] (comparable to the Berlin *Invalidenhaus*) on the main floor of which the banquet was being held. On entering the hall, I was enormously impressed. Powerful columns, white in color, rise to an immense height from floor to ceiling. These spatial dimensions are typically American. Pillars and gallery, walls and windows, all richly decorated with flags, and all in good taste. Within a square space formed by the columns in the center of the hall, a military band played continuously behind a rippling fountain decorated with plants. Electric light illuminated the entire scene, shining on clever and stupid men alike, and on all the clever women in low-necked, lower-necked and lowest-necked evening gowns and decked out in jewels and gold, wearing velvets and silk of every hue. It was a rich and colorful scene, the likes of which I had never seen before.

Pension Building (now the National Building Museum)
(contemporary photograph)

We strolled about. A gentleman whom I had seen in my section today came up to me and gave me his visiting card. I did not understand him and went to fetch Uncle. He expressed to Uncle his great satisfaction with me, said that he had been pleased with what I had said, etc., etc. He invited me to stay with him in London. I understood him to be an examiner or curator at the University of Edinburgh. Unfortunately, he will not be leaving leave New York until [*October*] 5th, so I will not be able to meet him in London. He seemed to be very pleased to meet me, knew of course of the "*Untoward Effects . . .*" and wished to keep in touch with me. I was glad about this acquaintance. He makes a good impression, is perhaps 55-60 years old and very distinguished-looking.

This called for drinks. Earlier, I had said hello to *Regierungsmedizinalrath*[180] Wurmich, and we had expressed our disappointment at having no beer. He, too, had lectured at the Congress. He pointed out to me the naïveté with which the Americans had staged this thing— the naïveté of big children, he called it. I had had the same impression, although I am convinced that this conference will cause its organizers to make changes the next time. Americans who have been in Europe are refined and well-informed, and they understand what is lacking in their compatriots.

Next day I saw persons showing disgust for those medical practitioners who not only want to enjoy themselves, but try to play the role of scientists without being in any way qualified for it, thereby discrediting meetings of this sort. It seems to me that we have such people at home as well. All the same, I was in good spirits. It also helped that two more people came up to me, expressing—in broken German—their pleasure with my lecture. One of them made me laugh when he said, "It was so dull in our section until you came."

At the northern end of the hall a buffet was laid out. I went to get champagne for both of us and we drank—to our wives. Yes, dearest heart, I never forget you, and my only regret today was that you could not participate.

Among others, we also saw the "busy gentleman"[181] in animated conversation with a young lady. This *faiseur*[182] had gone to the banquet like everyone else tonight and, trying to give himself a special grandeur, had told me that he was tied up until two o'clock. We might have stayed that long if we had wanted to, but we preferred not to compete with the gentleman and we left after having stayed about an hour and a half. There is no warmth in American social functions; they are not formal and, notwithstanding that, not warm and congenial either. As before, we went first to a *Bierstube* and thence to bed.

Friday, September 9

We took a morning walk to the obelisk [*the Washington Monument*].[183] It appeared to be quite near, but it took us about a half-hour to get there. The obelisk is about 600' feet high, dedicated to the memory of Washington, the revered national hero par excellence. The ornamental landscaping at its base is not yet in its final stages, but the marble at the bottom of this colossal monument is already cracked and shows signs of fissure in many places. The height and the sheer mass of the material used are imposing, but the structure is not in good taste!

On our way back [*to the hotel*] we ran into Woodbury, had a cocktail with him, and he saw to the registration. Uncle also got in as "Dr. Warburg," and was given a badge to boot. He took this with characteristic calm and went home, while I, willy-nilly, got into the carriage of the venerable Joseph M. Tanner, M.D., Registrar of the Congress, in order to accompany him on his patient rounds. He speaks not a word of German, and I myself have no English, but it doesn't matter—I draw on my stock of superlatives, murmuring all the time "largest in the world"—"beautiful"—"indeed splendid"—"very beautiful"—"wonderful"—and he answers every time. What he says is lost to me.

Today our section was due to start its meeting at 11:30 and at long last we got there. I am immediately asked to preside, took the chair and give permission to Dr. Andeer[184] to deliver his lecture on resorcin.[185] It takes all kinds indeed to make a world. For ten years now this man has been mouthing the same platitudes over and over again, with the perseverance of a Niagara Falls, without offering anything new. Today's variation was that he inserted the phrase "my friend Unna" at every turn, his intention being to boast of the acquaintance of a man whom all the Americans knew. Unna had the nerve—though Waldyer, Gusserow and others were present—to take it upon himself to respond to all the official speeches as if he had been delegated to do so by the German government. When Andeer had finished his talk, I took the floor and elucidated upon Unna and Andeer in a talk of about a half-hour. From the further answers he gave me, I realized that this gentleman had so little knowledge of and such a lack of correct notions about elementary medical matters that I preferred to be silent. After two more lectures, the section was closed.

On my way back to the hotel I met Herter and invited him to lunch. We three then went on to see the world-famous Smithsonian Institution, a complex of buildings situated among magnificent gardens—or, rather, park-like grounds—which contain one of the best collections to be found anywhere in the world. The Institution is endowed with millions [*of dollars*] and, as usual in this country, most of it was raised through private initiative. A Mr. Smithson gave the millions. We looked only at the collection of birds and fish, and the anthropological exhibits. I found several items of special interest to me, but was unable to acquire them.

Then we drove to the Capitol. Americans think of this building as the most beautiful in the world. I must say that I have never seen anything to compare with it and that nothing comparable is likely to be built at home. Please don't make me describe this building, since I wouldn't be able to do it justice. At every turn you find marble and granite in every color, in every kind of surface treatment, and everything is in perfect harmony and serves its purpose (with the exception of the Senate-Chamber, which is low-ceilinged and oppressive). Statues of famous generals and statesmen, large murals representing the most important events in national history, are housed in gigantic rotundas. You wander from one hall to the next, through endless passageways, up and down stairs, and everywhere you turn is beauty. From whichever side you leave the building, you find yourself on a wide terrace, surrounded by lawns and flowerbeds. Descending the marble steps, you find yourself on asphalt-paved roadways, endlessly wide, edged in grassy plots and blooming round beds. No stinting of space or of money here. This building and its surroundings surely symbolize the national wealth of the United States.

We drive down the incongruously-wide Pennsylvania Avenue. It leads directly to the U.S. Treasury, an enormous building with countless Ionic columns, in imitation of the Temple of Minerva in Athens, in front a large area planted with grass and ornamental flowers. We pass through the garden, take a turn to the right and move on to the White House, the President's Mansion. More Ionic columns, more beautiful gardens, but much simpler in design than the neighboring State Buildings![186] We were unable to get inside the White House because visiting hours were over. After a refreshing meal, we strolled down the city streets. It is now evening. We went to the post office—twice, three times, four times—but no mail had come in.

From the busiest part of Pennsylvania Avenue, we hear music. We approach. Crowds surround a group of about 4-5 men and 3-4 women. One man is holding a flag and singing, two others blow on their trumpets, one plays a small harmonica. They are singing spiritual songs [*i.e. hymns*], the women, or rather, maidens, leading the choir. It is the Salvation Army. The rhythm is such that you could find yourself dancing to it. Suddenly they fall to their knees. One of the girls starts praying; one of the men utters a few words as if gripped by an inner urge. I am glad that in this way everyone [*in America*] is vouchsafed freedom of action and opinion. This is a kind of personal liberty well worth emulating in Europe—even so, this kind of Liberty will never prevail with us.

The German residents of Washington have invited the German physicians to a banquet tonight. But, although Uncle would like to go, I shall not participate, not wanting to have my good humor spoilt by the "eloquent and busy man" and his sort. Over a beer, we spoke—ah, that was better—of you, my dearly beloved ones—we drank to your healths and the thought of you was my last before slumber embraced me on my bed.

Saturday, September 10

I have Americanized myself a little, wearing a turned-down collar and a long tie, blue with white polka dots. My collars, soiled by spilled whisky, have not yet come back from the laundry. It's raining, but that doesn't stop us from walking. The [*Medical*] Congress has come to an end and the Congress-babblers are going in all directions on the special reduced-price add-on tours that have been arranged for them.

Seeing that my stock of visiting cards had given out, I had new ones printed without further delay. From there we took a cab and returned to the Smithsonian. My plan had been to see the materia medica [*botanicals*] collection. I find a wonderfully complete pharmacological collection. Catalogues hang from chains. I ask someone if I can get such a catalogue. No, the director is absent. I begin to copy the labels. Then I see a gentleman heading towards us from across the hall, a man who had been at the meeting of our section and who had invited me to visit with him at the country house of the general commanding the Medical Services. I followed him back to his office and, when I asked him whether he could help me get hold of a catalogue, he laughs and says that he, Dr. Beyer—he speaks German very well because he is of German extraction—is the director of the collection at the National Museum. He had already yesterday intended to invite me [*to the Museum*] but had not seen me at the excursion. He leads me into his office. Uncle pays the cabdriver. We smoke and exchange experiences. I ask him if he could give me a certain trifle which had attracted my attention. Not only that; he leads me into another room full of specimens in many boxes. "Take your time," he says. "Choose whatever and however much you like." You can imagine how I fell upon these things, some of them rarities. I brought Uncle in (he had been waiting outside), and took whatever I fancied from the shelves, wrote down the name of the preparations, and Uncle wrapped them up. Soon an assistant of Beyer's came in and we began to make excellent progress. I even got samples in glass jars from the collection itself. Since Beyer is a naval officer, he has friends on warships in Asian waters. With their help, he will try to get poisonous fishes for me. He gave me the published proceedings of the museum and suggested I mark everything that I wanted, and he would send me what I wished. Perhaps he will translate my book. I have found Dr. Beyer to be an excellent man, well-known and respected in America, as is the entire Smithsonian staff.

He invited us to a frugal lunch, along with Reynders of New York,[187] the world-renowned instrument-maker who had come [*to the Congress*] later. We drove with him to the Anatomical Museum, which houses quite a few objects of interest, and thence home.

Our things had been already packed [*in anticipation of departure*]. Quickly I extracted the *Toxicology*,[188] drove to Beyer's flat, from there to the printers who had printed my visiting cards, then I rejoined Uncle. Into the carriage and off! On the way there, Uncle asks after my umbrella. He had been carrying it all morning, and I knew nothing about its whereabouts. He swears that he had put it down in our room. So, we go back. We look, we ask, but to no avail, what's gone is gone. During the quarter of an hour that it had taken us to go downstairs and into the carriage, it had been stolen by the thievish chambermaid, who must have come quickly to our room as soon as we left. So it found its end in America. How bitter it will feel, loyal German that it was, to be squeezed by a light-fingered Yankee hand!

Eastern Seaboard

September 10	Baltimore
	Philadelphia
	Pittsburgh
	Cleveland
	Detroit
	Boston
September 20	New York

Saturday, September 10 (cont'd)

We race to the station for the "Limited Express to Philadelphia"! We got the tickets, reached the gate to the platform—only passengers with tickets are allowed through here, and only five minutes before the train is scheduled to leave—only to find out that the train had already left! Fortunately, there is another train leaving in ten minutes. It takes us, but not our luggage. Never mind. Hot, perspiring and exhausted, I sit back in my seat. It takes a long time to recover from this chase.

Soon we arrived at Baltimore. I wanted to have a look at the Johns Hopkins University, one of the most important and certainly the wealthiest university in America. We had about 2-1/2 hours until the next train left [*for Philadelphia*]. I persuaded Uncle to get off, and we went by tram to the University, but the Medical Department is not at that location. We drive on, with no end in sight and time getting shorter and shorter. At long last we arrive at the Clinical Institutes[189] which extend over a vast area the size of a small town. In front of us is a gigantic building crowned by a cupola made of brick and sandstone; further on and connected to that building by a maze of corridors and passages are many smaller buildings, the whole interspersed with lawns. The premises are still under construction. There is work being done in the Experimental Department; peering in from the outside, I could see the fungus cultures in the test tubes.

Johns Hopkins Hospital and Medical School, c. 1887
(contemporary photograph)

But evening shadows had begun to lengthen over the graceful town of Baltimore, and we had to get back to the station. On our way out to the university, I had already been struck by the extraordinary neatness of the town and the lovely one- and two-family houses, built of stone or—in the more outlying areas—of red brick. Pöseldorf[190] can't compare to it. It is a pleasure to see these simple, harmoniously fashioned marble slabs, sandstone and granite blocks. Of course, here too [*General*] Washington is enthroned on a high column in the middle of a park,[191] surrounded at a distance by the fine residences of rich Baltimore citizens.

At the station we refueled our bodies, and so on to Philadelphia. We arrived there at about 11 o'clock at night, got our luggage and drove down the streets until, at about midnight, we arrived at the Hotel Continental. We had scarcely settled ourselves in our room, when we were asked how long we intended to stay. Later, we were told that there was to be a huge celebration in Philadelphia the following week, marking the centennial of the adoption of the Constitution,[192] and that all the rooms in the hotel had been booked for the occasion. They told us that the city was expecting 300,000 visitors—a typical American exaggeration, of course.

Sunday, September 11

The weather was overcast and dead silence reigned in the streets of Philadelphia. We drove and strolled this way and that. There seems to be no end to this town. I saw only a few ugly and dirty streets; most of the houses that I saw resembled those in Baltimore, red brick with sandstone facings. Market Street and Chestnut Streets—the main business streets—are narrow, especially the latter. You can't apply the Washington standard here. Chestnut Street has all the banks, built throughout of marble and granite, in architectural styles that are just plain ugly or so ugly that they strike you as funny. For the most part they are artificially asymmetrical, and, although Herter sees in this lack of symmetry a higher level of artistic taste, I for one had rather stand on the lower level and declare these structures to be abominably ugly. Moreover, some of them have oppressive proportions; doors and windows are adorned with short, clumsily-proportioned columns, looking like morbid growths on otherwise healthy limbs. Never have I seen buildings more unsightly and more expensive.

But there are also splendid buildings to be found in this town. Professor Jaine, professor of biology, for instance, has built his residence of fine white marble. A wide portion of the same material forms the entrance, and there are gardens all around.

Philadelphia, this rival to New York, can also boast of ancient buildings, among them the one in which the Constitution was adopted; these will, of course, be the center of the celebration during the next few days. Triumphal arches are being erected, spanning the streets and bedecked with all kinds of emblems. Houses are beginning to show flags, and in the streets we are already encountering members of the Jubilee crowd.

We stroll down Chestnut Street to the Delaware [*River*], to a dock where ferryboats are moored one next to the other. Boarding one such boat, we cross over to New Jersey and back. The river is very wide and very busy. Everywhere you can see ocean-liners moving from here directly out to Delaware Bay and then out to sea.

Like all such streets near docks and shipping centers, this one is dirty, ill-paved and lined with innumerable taverns. It would be quite possible to cite these local taverns to the Messieurs the Anti-Semites of Europe as proof that honorable thoroughly-baptized Christians, too, can, entirely on their own, "poison the people with alcohol." It's not the Jews who own these bars—but, regardless, it's the Jew who is burned at the stake.

Our quiet Sunday was to end with a drive through the town. We took the first of many available cable cars. These cars are propelled by a cable sunk into an iron groove in the street, which is then connected to the car's underside and pulled by steampower from a central steam station. Everywhere in America, wherever we went, the rule is: one trip by omnibus or cable car or elevated railroad: 5 cents (20 *Pfennige*). Never less, never more! For this fare, you can make the entire trip and—an advantage in my opinion—without being checked. Today's five-cent drive lasted 45-60 minutes. We had plenty of time to marvel at the vast expanse of this town, which covers more ground than New York.

A sore throat, and a cough which had troubled me since yesterday, made me seek out a pharmacy, where I bought Salmiak pastilles.[193] These pharmacies—and this goes for all the pharmacies I have seen in America and Canada—are remarkable establishments. They all sell soda-water, and many of them also sell towels, fancy-goods, plenty of toiletry items like sponges, brushes, soap, eau de cologne, and so on. Here in Philadelphia, I even saw one selling cigars. In general, they do not inspire the confidence in me to trust my prescriptions to them, but I may be mistaken as to their reliability.

In our hotel we were now given another room with only one bed, and this only after lengthy negotiations. The weather was still unpleasant. We sat in the unprepossessing backroom, where, in addition to a fire-alarm bell, there was a life-saving apparatus near the window with precise instructions on its use in case of fire. I didn't feel well and lay down on the bed for an hour while Uncle stayed up and wrote. The evening was utterly boring[194] and we went to bed early.

Monday, September 12

I didn't get much sleep last night. It was raining cats and dogs, the rain beating down on the zinc or glass roof under our window, keeping me awake. Moreover, Uncle not only coughed loudly but snored in such a fearful way that by comparison ten Canadian sawmills would have seemed like symphonies in a minor key. The morning broke as wet as the night had fallen, the massed clouds pouring down their floods. What could we do? We had no umbrella. Uncle had only his finest black coat, and I had nothing with me. My things were already in New York, but, since I looked like a tramp anyway, getting wet wouldn't have changed my appearance much. We decided to buy an umbrella and we did, paying a lot of money for one of less-than-average quality. You can't imagine how expensive everything is here, and not of good quality in the bargain.

We decided to part company, Uncle to see business acquaintances, I to the University of Pennsylvania. I had to drive a long way by trolley. Finally, I stood in front of a group of buildings erected of splendid green sandstone, with turrets, columns and other adornments. Certainly, this was not what I had expected here. I found my way on my own by bravely asking questions and finally I came to the Medical School, surrounded, as the others were, by garden grounds.

I entered, at first just wandering around. Then I saw two gentlemen entering a room; I followed them and gave them my card, stating my request. "From the University of Berlin" makes a favorable impression around here. One of the gentlemen, a dignified gray-bearded man—neither of them spoke German—asked whether I knew Miller, whom he had trained. Of course I said yes. I was shown around very amiably, saw the pharmaceutical collection, which is quite good, and finally the gentlemen brought me to the lecturer in medical chemistry, Dr. Marshall, who has studied in Germany. We soon warmed to each other. He showed me some of his experiments, including a new reaction to lead—which I had published five years ago[195] —and then he wanted to show me the town. But I had a special idea that morning: I knew that I was in the vicinity of the largest petroleum refinery in the world and wanted to turn my journey to scientific account by studying the effects of petroleum on humans, a subject about which little or nothing was known at that time. I told Marshall of my idea and asked for his help. Yes, he said, here in America the Standard Oil Company is sovereign. Let's try to look them up and to interest its president in the matter.

Soon we were on our way. First I had to have lunch with him. The oyster-lunch dispatched, he led me to what is perhaps the largest store in the world, Wanamaker's (I'll tell you more about it later), then on to the hotel, where Uncle was waiting for me outside. There wasn't much time, so we hurried on. We got the necessary information from two big stores where Marshall has connections or relatives.

Now we are in the headquarters of the Standard Oil Company. Over here an army of clerks sits behind their desks, and over here are the telegraph clerks of the company, with its own wires to the oil-producing districts. Over there are other desks where the stenographers sit, transcribing their dictation; over there the letter is immediately printed, rush and haste everywhere, and all of it very impressive. It is, as they say here in America, worth 400million dollars, or 2,000 million Mark!

Marshall sends his name in to the president. We are led into a large outer-room. Soon the president, Mr. Davis,[196] appears, still young, very good-looking. Marshall had not previously been acquainted with him. He submits my request. The answer comes cautiously: no diseases have been observed. I ask Marshall to tell him that I was interested in the general effects of petroleum on the workers in the oil tanks and, specifically, the effects on the skin. He saw that I knew what I was talking about and that I would not be put off.

I ask Marshall to tell Mr. Davis that the world of science, and not only German science, would be grateful to him if he, the only man who could do it, would help me. This impressed him! Yes, he would telephone the superintendent of their refinery, three miles away, to which the greater part of Standard Oil's production was conveyed, advise the man of our impending visit and give us his permission to tour the refinery. Moreover he would give me letters to the oil-producing area in Washington, Pennsylvania, and to the company offices in Cleveland. This man impressed me by his circumspection. On the other hand, I again saw that knowledge and the quest for knowledge are still valued in the world, and especially here. That is a good and cheering thought! This man didn't look at my shabby coat, my stained light trousers which I wear day after day as I have no others—the words, the language, make him overlook that! How grateful I am to God that He has given me this gift in so full a measure!

But now we had to hurry, because the refinery closes down at six o'clock. We rush back to the hotel. I don't find Uncle there, so I leave a note for him. Hot all over, I sit down in the carriage for our drive across country. At 4·30, we arrive at Point Breeze.

We find ourselves in an atmosphere of oil fumes. The superintendent, Mr. Livingstone, is waiting for us—and he speaks German! In order not to waste time in small talk, I ask him if he would answer my questions. I ask, and he and the other gentleman in the office answer. The answers in English are at once translated and I write and write until my fingers ache. Among other useful things, I find out what I had only floated as a kind of trial balloon: that the workers do indeed suffer from skin diseases.

In the meantime, Mr. Livingston takes us around the facility, "the Atlantic Refining Co.," a division of Standard Oil. This alone would have been worth the trip. Gigantic tanks—large iron containers partly sunk into the ground, and enormous towers standing in great numbers here and there on the widespread refinery grounds. All of these are connected by a system of pipes to the refinery itself, where the crude oil is resolved into its component elements, but the enormous contents of these tanks can also be piped to the ships which are anchored here and bring the oil to Europe. The petroleum can also be piped directly into barrels, to light up the world, living room and study alike. I imagine the two of us in the dark of winter, sitting—God willing—hand in hand by the light of our lamp while I tell of my journey. Then my thoughts wander back to those places where man garners Nature's bounty and refines it for the use of others.

The refining that is done here is no simple matter with a product so easily flammable, and the distillation process that is conducted here on such a gigantic scale is a dangerous operation, so dangerous that from what I have seen here I wouldn't want to the chief inspector or the division superintendent.

When we returned to the office, the three workers who had been summoned were already there. They all spoke German, so that mutual understanding was not a problem. I verified that all three of them showed the same abnormal skin condition.[197] One of them showed it to such a degree that I had the idea of having this man's arms photographed. I suggested that he receive pay for the day and come down to the hotel the next morning to have his picture taken. I also requested that a sample of the petroleum product that these men were working with should also be sent there. I noticed that the gentlemen in the office were standing about nervously while this was going on; it turned out that both Mr. Marshall and Mr. Livingston were expected for dinner by their wives, so I released them from any further obligations. I had accomplished what I had set out to do—without much effort—and I had "News"; on the trains in this country there is always a man who sells fresh fruit, matches, and so on, and, in addition, the latest reading material; the badge on his cap announcing that he is a "News Agent"—that's what I felt like now.

I had had the carriage wait for us. We got in and raced Livingston's buggy, which he drove himself, back into town, passing by the crowds of workers who were on their way home after a hard day's work in this refinery. I kept my notes safely stowed away. What I achieved today gives me the greatest satisfaction; these bits of paper are more valuable to me than many hundred-dollar bills.

On our way back to the hotel we passed endlessly long reviewing stands, still under construction.[198] Marshall had booked two seats at 12 Mark each. At regular intervals rough-hewn seats had been fastened to each of the bulky telegraph poles at about a one-story height. From these seats, telegraph clerks are supposed to relay the commands of the leader of the parade (or rather festive procession) along the whole line of march to every point along the way. At a certain spot on the parade route, a special reviewing stand had been set up for the President[199] near one of the most beautiful city halls to be found anywhere in the world, built entirely out of marble in the French chateau style, graced in front by an enormous portal.

Marshall dropped me off at the hotel. I paid the carriage driver his fare and this unendingly kind fellow pointed out a photographer's studio to me to spare me the trouble of looking for one the next morning, for my appointment with the refinery workers.[200]

Isn't it nice after all to reap the fruits of one's labor? Many times I have worked through the night, have often suffered from cold and want, slept on the floor, and been hungry and thirsty, but I have learned something and have been able to create something that did not exist before! Here in this distant continent I have found respect and appreciation, perhaps more than at home; if I were to go to India, I would find people there, too, who knew my name and would show their regard for what I have accomplished by obliging helpfulness. I had experienced that in Washington, where the treasures of the largest pharmaceutical collection were placed at my disposal, and here in Philadelphia as well.

The next morning, back at the University, Marshall took me to meet Mr. Wormsley, the toxicologist who has written an extensive treatise on that subject. He is an old, sour-looking gentleman who was sitting in his splendidly-furnished study. Although he might have seen in me a toxicological rival (still in the dim and distant future, to be sure, but I spoke of that possibility), we were soon on friendly terms, and I left with a good new acquaintance and with a gift. That pleased me and spurred me to further professional work!

My next task was to look for Uncle. Our hotel room was locked and I couldn't find him.[201] It was endearing of Uncle indeed that he didn't want to hear my apology, being only glad for me that I had accomplished what I had set out to do. We had dinner together, and then went to see a Sardou[202] play which had been produced to meet the American taste (you know that Uncle likes to go to the theatre in every town). The actors were quite good, the play has skillful dialogue, but it all amounts to nothing.

Tuesday, September 13

I waited and waited for the [*refinery*] worker, but he did not show up, so I went with Uncle to Wanamaker's,[203] a department store whose dimensions you will not find equaled anywhere in the world, even the Bon Marché [*in Paris*].

In this store, where 12 elevators[204] take care of the customers, you can get anything that a man, a woman or their family need for their bodies and their homes. To commemorate the Centennial, the storeowner has erected on the premises an old English home, exactly as it would have stood here in Philadelphia 100 years ago, with a shop inside that carried goods copied from the original antiques—a sort of general store with red calico handkerchiefs, lanterns, snuff-boxes, ladies' headgear, needles and so on. Behind the counter stood be-wigged salesmen in period costumes. An enormous crowd pushed through this shop. Opposite the house, an old wooden fence had been erected, covered with reprints of old advertisements.

The assortment of goods available for sale here is amazing. How can they keep track of so many things? No furniture store in Berlin has such a large stock of furniture or as many furnished rooms, each in its own distinctive style, as may be found here. The same goes for carpets, jewelry, ladies' French hats, children's toys, luggage and silk, men's wear and wallpaper, etc. etc.

On our way back to the hotel Uncle and I entered a large bookstore and asked for German or French books—neither were to be had. What isolationists these Americans are! No foreign books in a store with windows on two street-fronts, and in none of the many hotels that we stayed at was there a German- or French-speaking clerk!

Without my having photographed that refinery worker, we took a train to Pittsburgh at 11:20, after having bought direct tickets to Cleveland. Our final destination was Detroit and these two cities lay on the shortest route to Detroit.

We again had a Palace Car and the train led us through pleasant country which made me think of Switzerland. As soon as we passed Harrisburg and entered the Alleghenies—a route we had already passed over—the scenery was splendid. The sun shone on the wooded mountain ranges. Green, red and yellow foliage as far as the eye can see, rock and stone where the railroad passes. In the distance, delightful vistas open up across forest and field. And such a variety of scenery! After dense forests we see fiery chimneys and ironworks, and here is the wide Susquehanna River, whose course the railroad follows faithfully, making use of the gap which the river has broken through the rocks. Whenever I saw the Alleghenies, they were lovely, never wild!

Every inch of ground is utilized, perhaps even more so than in the most populous districts of Germany. I should have to repeat everything I wrote to you about this marvelous part of the country in order to do justice to its effect on me: the twisting of the railroad around rocky heights; the viaducts over the gorges; the train running across what appears to be virgin soil, even as, underground, thousands of workers toil by the light of lamps, digging coal, picking at ore to sustain their families; the travel through long tunnels, the electric light flaring up when we enter and fading the moment we exit the tunnel; the sight of twenty chimneys and more, belching fire, which we pass so closely that we feel the heat that they generate; the palatial Parlor Car; the over-familiarity and insolence of the railway personnel, who, for example, loll on the upholstered seats instead of seeing to the brake, and who don't get up even when a passenger is looking for a seat—all these are observations which I have had occasion to make before at some length and which struck me again on this leg of our trip.

Although this train was called a "Limited Express," we had an unanticipated stop of an hour-and-a–half in Pittsburgh, when we were already in sight of the station. It was 10:30 at night before we finally arrived at our hotel, the Hotel Duquesne.

Wednesday, September 14

We had two adjoining rooms, both very comfortable, both lit by electricity. But when we saw each other the next morning, we both groaned at the sight of each other. Without hearing anything of the other, we had both passed the night with a minimum of sleep. I had gotten up several times, turned on the light, paced to and fro, tried to write, gone back to bed, stripped, wrapped only in a sheet, all in vain! My body, especially my hands and feet, were stung everywhere by mosquitoes. The backs of my hands were covered with the bumps from their bites. Moreover, the heat in my room was stifling; I had found it hard to breathe.

At breakfast the German innkeeper asked how we had slept. I put on my most innocent face and assured him that we had passed an excellent night, and Uncle agreed. From his own room on an upper floor of the hotel, the innkeeper showed us the panorama of the town. Then he led us to a dealer in spirits—perhaps the largest dealer in the United States—his specialty being Monongahela whisky. The storeowner himself conducted us through all the floors of his store, showed us the enormous number of casks, cognac of which one bottle must cost 25 Mark, and at the end offered us a drink of excellent cognac. That drove away the weariness of the night and revived in us a spirit of enterprise.

First we went to one of the stations near the river, from which one can get up to that part of the town that lies atop the rocky promontory. This is indeed quite extraordinary and worth seeing. When we first came to this town, I had seen a conveyance moving down on rails in such a way that I was prompted to remark, "Look, people are flying down the mountain there."

Soon, we, too, were flying up the mountain and back down again. You see, it is a cable-car like others; that is to say, at the top a steam engine winds up on one large wheel the cable that is attached to the car, thereby pulling the car up or, by letting the cable out, letting the car back down. But, ordinarily, a cable car is suspended according to the angle of inclination. That's not how it works here. Underneath the body of the car are two long and two short legs, adjusted in such a way that at the top station one stands at a horizontal platform provided with one or two little shelters for the passengers.

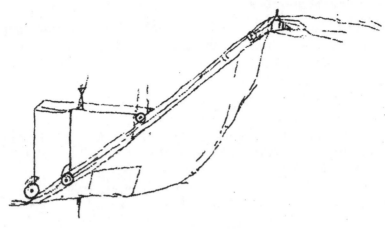

Penn Incline.[205] Pittsburgh PA
(Lewin drawing)

This "Penn Incline" ascent was very satisfactory, as was the view from the top of the twin towns, Pittsburgh and Allegheny, which are divided by the river but connected by numerous bridges. The latter town looks neat and presentable, but Pittsburgh presents itself as blackened by smoke and very grimy. There are gigantic iron- and glass-works here, whose hammering and pounding goes on day and night and whose chimneys are transformed at night into fiery abysses. The continuous roar of the furnaces is deafening.

We went to see the gentleman to whom my letter of recommendation [*from Mr. Davis at Standard Oil Co.*] had been addressed. He brought us to another man, and this one gave us a letter of introduction to the refinery in Washington, Pa. We drove there that afternoon. This is one of the most interesting trips I have made thus far. Almost everywhere along the rail line the railroad has forced its way through rocks, either through open clefts or through long tunnels. The landscape is fine, resembling a large park, but, compared to what I have seen elsewhere, nothing to shout about, although the rocky section is interesting. At the base of the rock so much of it has been blasted away that the overhanging mass forms a continuous balcony of sorts at a height of about one story. I should also mention the intensive cultivation and the dense build-up, which doesn't permit the eye to wander very far without encountering a house!

What really amazes me is that in the midst of a broad swath of grassland, of well-cultivated soil, suddenly 22 giant oil tanks appear, soon followed by 50 more, and so on. The air reeks of petroleum, with primitive pumps working everywhere to bring the immeasurable riches of the earth into those tanks. And that isn't all: suddenly you see at the mouth of a shaft a veritable geyser of flame burning fiercely. It has been burning like that all day and will go on burning for years and years until this easily-won treasure, too, has been exhausted by mankind. No need to go to Baku to see the Holy Fires![206]

What we heard and read about in our youth about these fabulous earth-borne gases, combustible and giving the power to illuminate as well, is realized here! It isn't only the blazing surface fires that show it to you; there is also that structure where, in broad daylight, a fiery shaft, thick as a man's arm, blazes forth from a pipe buried under it. The same can be seen here and there at many points along the way.

This product is "Natural Gas," the gas that accumulates in the earth and burns off without profit to anyone, when it is not piped by companies into towns as far away as Pittsburgh, and sold like artificial gas, or used on the spot to create labor. How many people at home might heat up their houses during a cold winter with a substance that does nothing else except to raise the temperature of the ambient air hereabouts!

Another manifestation of God's mighty creation having had its powerful effect on us, we arrived at "Little Washington." This is a wealthy town; there is even a university here.[207] Everyone here seems to be well-to-do or rich. The inhabitants are well-dressed; you don't see them working, many of them are seen resting in hammocks on the porches of their little houses.

We had learned at the station that the gentleman whom we had come to see was away on a trip, and his next-in-line, the superintendent, was not there either. I didn't want our tour to be for naught. In passing, I had observed what appeared to be oil pumps operating at full tilt. We walked over there, and encountered a worker sitting in front of one of them. Uncle explained what we wanted and mentioned that I had a letter to the representative of the Standard Oil Co. After reading the letter, the worker said he had been working at the refinery for more than 20 years, and that he knew as much about the oil business as the Standard Oil representative would.

I had my questionnaire ready. Uncle asked my questions, the worker answered and Uncle translated. The worker was very familiar with the skin eruption that I asked him about; he himself had suffered from it. We went into the engine room, where he undressed without further ado and I ascertained that his skin condition was identical to the one I had seen on the other employee [*at Point Breeze*].

The worker went on to explain the oil production process. He showed us how the steam boiler that moves the pump was heated by the natural gas which, spouting from the soil, is conducted to the furnace. When he opened the furnace door we saw a sea of flame. How extravagantly Mankind deals with this wealth of gas! They do not use the smallest bit of wood or coal. One match, and the furnace is ablaze!

I shall never forget the drive back [*to Pittsburgh*]. To the left and right, far and near, the glow of burning gas, streaming into the air in broad jets. All about us is the jet-black night, and out of this darkness gleams the fiery breath of the burning gas, interspersed with pillars of flame from the immense industrial plants which are to be found everywhere. It's an overwhelming sight; the blast-furnaces and coke pits in the iron-mining districts of Westphalia, when I saw them, were insignificant by comparison.

Mankind here is living as the beneficiary of Nature's riches. These beneficiaries appear to me to be like people who always eat in the finest restaurants, having everything served and ready-to-eat, needing only to add the proper seasoning—spices, salt, pepper—to suit their own and their guests' tastes. But woe betide them if Earth's prodigal hand closes—then they, like everyone at home, will have to work for a day's pay. Even so, this nation is inventive! They will always make more out of barren soil and rock than the Germans and, likewise, they use their natural riches in a grander manner than we would have done.

However, in the final analysis it comes to the same thing: where so much is squandered, exhaustion sets in before long. If at present the simple worker must work as hard as his counterpart in Europe, the time will come for America, too, when work-performance and profit are so abnormally disproportionate that, on account of the higher prices for commodities, social misery here will be greater than at home.

In the evening we chatted with our landlord and his sister. He showed me that all he needed to light the oven in his kitchen, ignite the baker's oven where he bakes his own bread, for his steam-powered laundry, and for the engine that generates the power for his electric light, was a match to perform what elsewhere would require hundreds of tons of coke. One match—and a comfortable flame leaps up inside the fireplace; one small move and the fire is extinguished. No smell betrays the fuel used, no grain of soot sullies the carpet! One match to the oven and a fiery blaze fills it. It is a wonderful sight!

Our bags packed, we head for Cleveland. We pass through the platform-gate, pass the guard standing at our car, take our seats and have our tickets checked a third time—everything is all right. Just before our departure, another train employee comes in to check our tickets, and tells us that they are invalid. I said I didn't care and refused to leave the compartment. The man, a fellow from South Germany, threatens to call the police. I told him I would take that risk and that he should stop bothering us, that our tickets are in good order. He maintains that we should not have interrupted our trip here [*in Pittsburgh*].

[They get out and negotiate in vain with the stationmaster. They are not allowed to re-board the train, even to remove their carry-on luggage. The train leaves without them, with their hand-luggage on board, leaving them with only their nightshirts and shaving gear. They return to their hotel and have a passable night. They get up at 5:00AM, return to the train station, pay for new tickets—under protest—and entrain for Cleveland.]

Thursday, September 15

We were glad to travel in bright sunshine through a veritable garden-landscape, along the Ohio River. Had we traveled at night, we would have seen nothing of these lovely regions, the mere sight of which is refreshing. The Ohio River itself is not impressive but for the remarkable phenomenon which we suddenly became aware of: an extensive bright fire breaking out in the middle of the river! It looks fabulous. Here, natural gas is erupting from the riverbed and—piped and lit—makes a natural beacon by night and a superfluous one by day.

The fine woodland, the neat gardens and meadows come to an end after two hours. Now we travel through an area that is absolutely flat, looks arid and is altogether unattractive. On the outskirts of Cleveland, oil pumps and giant manufacturing plants re-appear. Our annoyance had vanished. We arrived in Cleveland with our souls cleansed and at ease, but our exteriors terribly dusty. We had our luggage brought to the steamer pier because we intended to go to Detroit by way of Lake Erie. We ourselves went to a barbershop. Uncle had himself shaved, I washed, soaped my cuffs clean *coram publico*,[208] brushed my clothes, had Uncle cleaned up and then we went into town.

Wonderfully wide and tidy streets, tall buildings of 6-7 stories, set up in straight lines as if for a parade along endless streets. We drove down an imposing avenue to call on Mr. Rockefeller, vice-president of the Standard Oil Company, but did not find him at his residence, so we just resigned ourselves to not seeing him. We weren't going to wait for him, as both of us had caught the return fever and wanted to get the trip behind us. But we did walk and drive through the town in every direction. On one of our drives I saw very little; my eyes closed and I nodded off.

On our way back I was awake again and noticed that we were traveling through a thoroughly German neighborhood. Just as in New York,[209] here, too, the Germans stick together and—as I heard later—keep more to themselves than may be politically or socially desirable in terms of their relations with Americans.

In this city I was especially pleased with the straight clean streets. I am certain that these towns, which are so regularly laid out and let plenty of sunshine and air in will, in the event of an epidemic, respond much better to sanitary measures than the old European crooked and dark alleys, even if the interior of those [*European*] houses are completely up to sanitary requirements. In these modern towns, they can comply with hygienic standards from the start and I think that, as far as technical knowledge is concerned, very good work has already been done.

Again the weather was splendid, with fresh air and sunshine. We felt fine, and the thought that we would soon be heading home made us both cheerful, although we didn't say so. While we were strolling, I discovered a German bookshop and, better still, one that dealt in pirated editions of German authors. We were not punctilious enough to turn our backs on them for that reason alone, and Uncle very generously bought for me the ones that I had chosen. Mostly, I had you in mind with my selection, dearest heart; I chose the books that you had always intended to read, but I am not going to tell you which ones!

As evening approached, we sauntered down to our boat. We had a nice cabin. The boat is not nearly as large or as well-appointed as the Hudson River boats, but it reminded us of them by its cleanliness and the elegance of all that it offers.

The "City of Detroit"[210] got underway after we were already asleep. I woke up repeatedly during the night, because the ship's rolling caused the window blinds to rattle and caused the glass globes of the lamps in the parlor to come crashing down with a hell of a noise.

Detroit waterfront

Very early the next morning, we arrived in Detroit. It took Uncle a long time to get dressed, while I paced around on the quay, freezing and reading. At long last he appeared from the cabin, very elegantly dressed, and we drove to Russell House.[211]

Russell House, Detroit, Michigan, 1887
(contemporary photograph)

My first errand was, of course, a visit to Parke Davis & Co.[212] We drove down a splendid avenue bordered by residences with beautiful gardens. Soon we were marveling at a very large building adorned with limestone. This building, headquarters for Parke Davis, is not yet fully completed. We entered the offices, where well over 50 bookkeepers, male and female, cashiers, clerks, stenographers, etc, were busy working, and asked for Mr. Wetzell. He had just been dictating to his secretary,[213] and was pleased to show us around the office and the print-shop. Even with the favorable impression I had had of these people over the years, I still had not expected such grandeur and such skilled precision in workmanship. It is impossible to enumerate all the particulars.

Summing up, I can only say that the various departments were exemplary, from the preparation of juices and extracts, the extraction of drugs, bottling, labeling, the grinding and compression of the plant material to the manufacture of the pillular paste, sugaring and coating of pills, etc, etc. In short, the manufacture of pharmaceutical preparations is worthy of the American genius for machinery and of yours for exactitude and cleanliness of use.

Mr. Wetzell brought us to meet the co-founder, Mr. Davis, a real gentleman in outward appearance and in his way of speaking. He made an extraordinary impression on Uncle as well. Before entering, I had asked Mr. Wetzell what the price of their *Index Medicus* would be for me. This is a huge compendium of medical papers from all over the world, published by Parke Davis and subscribed to only by librarians and very wealthy people. About 100 dollars—400 Mark—for others, 90 dollars for me. He added that only a few complete copies remained, the value of which would of course go up from year to year, as no reprints would be published because of the enormous costs involved. At ninety dollars, it was, of course, too expensive for me. Well, Mr. Davis made me a present of this precious work! This is really a princely gift, which is of a piece with the generosity and refinement that I had already observed here. Then he excused himself for the day and asked us to content ourselves with Mr. Wetzell's company; Mr. Davis prefers to be at his country estate and I can't fault him for that. Everything else that I received in the course of this trip, the preparations, drugs, and so on, you will see for yourself when it all arrives in Berlin.

We returned to our hotel, and then Mr. Wetzell took us by carriage for a sightseeing tour of the town. I complained to Mr. Wetzell about the railway and the rude German-American railroad official, as well as the unused tickets from Pittsburgh. He thought he could take care of the matter for us.

From our sightseeing trip, we were able to get a much better idea of the city. You will see from the map what an extraordinarily favorable site it occupies, between two of the Great Lakes and close to Canada, no further than a rifle-shot away. It is likely that this city will achieve even greater importance in the course of time.

Today we saw fine streets everywhere, handsome villas or, rather, single-family homes, built of every conceivable stone, all in good architectural taste and surrounded by lawns and gardens. The surrounding countryside is beautiful, too. We drove to Fort Wayne,[214] originally built to protect the settlers against the Indians and today directed against Canada, which lies across the Detroit River from the city. The fortress seemed so small that it hardly deserves the name, "fort." Here I saw American soldiers for the first time, watching them parade on the drill grounds. What a mess they made of it! A Prussian sergeant would have torn his hair out in despair at the sight.

As it was getting dark, we drove with Mr. Wetzell to the Clubhouse, where a *jolie petit diner* awaited us. It tasted very good. Wetzell, Uncle and I walked up and down the street in front of our hotel, observing the animated scene. Trumpet music drew us, and hundreds of other people, to a store which had closed for the day but was still advertising its wares. The trumpets that we had heard were being played by store employees who were organized into a band, standing on the other side of the street. Stretched three or four stories high against the front of the store was a huge translucent screen, actually a piece of canvas. A camera projected pictures on this screen. After about five images, depicting classical art, American personalities or genre art, the sixth image always advertised this store and the merchandise that it sold.[215] Tired, we at last said goodbye to our guide, because we knew we had to get up early the next morning to get to the train station.

Central Standard Time.	Day Express	Limited N. Y. & Bos. Ex.	Atlantic Express.
Lv. DETROIT, via Mich. Cent.	7.15 PM	*10.55 PM	* 6.10 AM
" St. Thomas.	11.10 PM	2.05 AM	9.50 LM
Ar. Falls View.		4.54 "	1.12 PM
" Niagara Falls, Ont.	2.21 AM	5.03 "	1.22 "
" Suspension Bridge.	2.36 "	5.17 "	1.36 "
" Niagara Falls, N. Y.	2.51 "	5.30 "	1.55 "
Ar. BUFFALO (Exchange St.)	3.35 AM	6.15 AM	2.40 PM
Eastern Standard Time.			
Lv. BUFFALO, N. Y. C. & H. R. R. R.	† 4.50 AM	* 7.25 AM	* 4.15 PM
Ar. Batavia.	5.55 "	8.20 "	5.20 "
" Rochester (Central Ave.).	6.50 AM	9.10 AM	6.15 PM
" Canandaigua.	8.45 AM	† 1.10 PM	† 7.57 PM
" Clifton Springs	9.08 "	1.26 "	10.00 "
" Geneva.	9.40 "	2.10 "	10.35 "
" Seneca Falls.	10.02 "	2.32 "	10.57 "
" Auburn.	10.40 AM	3.15 PM	11.35 PM
" Lyons.	8.05 AM	*10.20 AM	* 7.25 PM
" Clyde.	8.17 "		7.37 "
" Syracuse (Railroad St.).	9.30 "	11.35 AM	8.40 "
" Canastota.		12.25 PM	
" Oneida.	10.37 "	12.34 "	
" Rome.	10.58 "	12.53 "	10.15 "
" Utica (Genesee St.).	11.30 AM	1.17 "	10.41 "
" Palatine Bridge.	12.38 PM		11.53 PM
" Fonda.	12.58 "		12.12 AM
" Amsterdam.	1.17 "		12.31 "
" Schenectady.	1.45 PM	3.20 PM	1.00 AM
" Saratoga, D. & H. C. Co.	† 2.50 PM	† 6.20 PM	
" Rutland.	5.15 PM	9.00 PM	
" ALBANY (Maiden Lane)	2.20 PM	* 8.50 PM	1.80 AM
" Troy.	2.35 "		
" Hudson.	3.35 "	5.04 "	2.58 "
" Poughkeepsie.	4.40 "	6.05 "	4.15 "
" Fishkill (Newburgh).	5.15 "		
" Garrison's (West Point).	5.30 "		
" Mott Haven (138th St.).		8.05 "	
Ar. NEW YORK (42d St. and 4th Ave.)	7.00 PM	8.15 PM	6.45 AM
Lv. ALBANY, Boston & Albany R. R.	† 2.30 PM	† 4.05 PM	* 1.50 AM
Ar. Chatham.	3.25 "		2.40 "
" Pittsfield.	4.32 "	5.35 "	3.40 "
" North Adams.	6.15 "	9.25 "	8.20 "
" Westfield.	6.09 "		5.07 "
" Springfield.	6.30 PM	2.12 PM	5.25 AM
" Hartford (via N. Y., N. H. & H.)	* 7.40 PM	* 9.05 PM	† 8.05 AM
" Chicopee Falls, via Conn. Riv.	6.50 "	9.05 "	7.00 "
" Holyoke.	7.32 "	8.31 "	7.00 "
" Greenfield. "	8.40 "	9.25 "	9.35 "
" Bellows Falls. "	10.57 PM	10.57 PM	11.25 AM
" Palmer.	* 8.24 PM	† 7.41 PM	* 6.06 AM
" West Brookfield.		8.05 "	6.35 "
" East Brookfield.			6.47 "
" Worcester.	9.23 "	8.51 "	7.25 "
" Providence (via P. & W.)			11.30 "
" Ayer Junction, via B. & M.			9.06 "
" Nashua.			9.34 "
" South Framingham.	9.58 "	9.32 "	
" BOSTON (Kneeland St.).	10.30 PM	10.10 PM	8.55 "

Timetable, Detroit to Boston

Saturday, September 17

As always when I have something to do in the early morning and know that I have to get up at a definite hour, I woke up at 2:30, at 3:30, and at 4 o'clock. Shortly after 4:00 we dressed, and had another rather long wait until the hotel car came and drove us to the station to catch the train to New England, the cradle of American liberty, and particularly to Boston.

The maps which I sent you and the enclosed timetable [*see p. 131*] may give you an idea of our route. As you see, part of it goes through Canada. The train crossed the Detroit River on a stern-wheel ferry. On this ferry the English [i.e. *Canadian*] custom-house is on one side, the American on the other. Our luggage went through customs and got a passing grade. Presently, the train rolled off the ferry and onto dry land, and we raced through the country we both love, southern Canada.

What a change from the country we have just left! While in America every stretch of land is fully cultivated and utilized, we now drive through a region where mile after mile is just beginning to be cultivated. Large sections are partitioned off by wooden planks, laid one on top of the other to form a fence-like pattern. Here we see again the omnipresent charred or cut-off tree stumps sticking up from the soil, and only at a great distance are farms or small towns to be seen. No factory smokestacks, no coal mines. But nonetheless this region is a match for the neighboring one in the United States. The future is here. When America becomes overpopulated and exhausted, then it will be Canada's turn to produce what until now still lies unused in its virgin soil!

At 1:30 we arrive at Falls View Station [*at Niagara Falls*], where the train stops for five minutes to give the passengers an opportunity to look at this marvel of nature.[216] We got a second chance to see the Falls from the Canadian side. Our weather-luck held: we saw the Falls in bright sunshine. A mighty rainbow spanned the Falls just as, on Raphael's frescoes, mighty arches span his representations of life.

Powerful clouds of spray tumble down the deep precipice in a furious turmoil that can be heard far and wide, and, at the bottom, the misty spray turns into foam which soon takes its previous form and races, whirling, as greenish water into the distance.

Rapt in thought, I absorbed this fascinating spectacle, this symbol of human life. Matter and its essence are imperishable. Whether it tarries, like the Niagara River, on the heights, running its smooth undisturbed course, or whether it crashes into the depths, into apparent nothingness, it stays what it is, eternally matter with all its attributes. It is immortal. Its form may change, but its essence remains.[217] You understand me, don't you, my dearest and best?

Presently, we crossed over into the United States on the Suspension Bridge. Once again, a part of Lake Erie came into view, an immense surface of water; we entered Buffalo and left it again, quickly and hungry.

It is impossible to get fat on a journey such as the one we have experienced. I had taken that for granted beforehand, but that one has to go hungry so often and for such a long time, living like a badger in winter on one's own slender store of fat—that is more than I would have believed possible. But both of us detest American food, so we would rather go without than to partake of this so-called "meal" at the "bar." Oh, these loathsome steaks and the warm bread! And to see a line of people drinking milk with their meal makes me sick!

Late that night, we entered classical soil, in Syracuse, where we ate for 6 Mark. If the tyrant Dionysius[218] were alive today and came here, there would be no need for the Syracusans to drive him away! He would have gone of his own accord if he had had to eat at that station.

We went to bed, on what I hope is our last night in a sleeping car in this country. Funny: we made our first trip in a Palace Car, and today the last. This car was every bit as bad as the first one, but we have become hardened. A little more or less discomfort doesn't matter—we are on our way home, into the arms of our loved ones.

Sunday, September 18

We awoke in New England, a populous and prosperous region. With beautiful landscape, soft undulating hills, dense woods, swiftly-running rivers, and, here and there, rock which is crushed and used in manufacturing. These features followed one upon the other without a break until we arrived in Boston at about 10:00 AM.

We registered at the United States Hotel, near the train station. We quickly encountered Puritanism and the strict observance of Sunday [*Blue Laws*]. We had asked at the desk to have our luggage brought to our room; we waited for it for some time, but in vain. We rang for one of those lazy blacks,[219] putting the same request to him, with no response. Finally, we gave up and got our bags upstairs by ourselves.

The streets were deserted, the shops all closed, and not a sheet of notepaper was to be had, although that was what I needed most to get a letter to my dearest. We decided that we were staying in the ugliest part of the town. A carriage drive brought us to another ugly neighborhood to see Mr. Heberlein, who lives in a narrow little house somewhat like Klausner's. We chatted for a while with him and his wife, but avoided a possible invitation by firmly taking our leave. Then we drove past innumerable churches and festive crowds in their light-colored Sunday best—a long way out of town for five cents—to Bunker Hill.

Everywhere in Boston you hear talk of Bunker Hill. You feel, if you haven't been there, that it must be something extraordinary! Not so! What we found was a small square adorned with lawns, and on it the usual obelisk, but here a low one, made of granite, with the words "In Memory of . . ."[220] That was enough for us; we ambled back to our hotel, rested, and wrote.

Today was Erev Rosh HaShanah [*the Jewish New Year*]. My heart was unusually moved. I was far from my loved ones and have been for so long without any word from them. In the synagogue I prayed quietly for you, and to find enlightenment for myself. I pray that God heard my wishes!

Monday, September 19

Today I went to the synagogue to celebrate the new year. L'Shana Tovah [*"Happy New Year"*]! Good fortune in the new year! Thousands of hearts beat as one today, expressing this fervent wish to the One who mysteriously and eternally guides the destinies of mankind. Good [*people*] and bad pray for the same! Yes, I know that such praying from the depths of the heart finds its intended place. I pray, as only a man can, for the happiness of my loved ones, and I thank God for the contentment which He has sent me. Am I good? Am I bad? I strive to be good—maybe that's even better than being good![221]

We spent the day seeing the sights of Boston. I need not make a list of them for you, because you can find them in any travel guide. Of the monuments, the Franklin statue[222] was the most noteworthy. What a sly face that short rotund Bostonian had! With all his humanitarian endeavors and furtherance of enlightenment, he doesn't seem to have forgotten his round little belly, if I am allowed to use *pars pro toto*.[223]

From the State House we enjoyed a fine view across the intricate topography of Boston, seeing all those arms and inlets of the Charles River, the innumerable islands which the sea has formed, and the sea itself extending to the distant horizon—all in all, a splendid and colorful picture, not easily forgotten.

More than anything else, I wanted to visit the most famous of American universities, Harvard University. Its Medical College is situated in the best part of town. Churches built of the finest marble and sandstone, in authentic styles: Gothic, Romanesque, Norman, they can all be found here. I am convinced that they are all copies, but no matter, they are beautifully executed. Here again are wide city avenues, handsome private homes and landscaped grounds. Part of the park has delightful flower beds, such as only the highest horticultural art can produce.

Broad steps lead to the lobby of the College. The janitor was ready to show us around. I must say that it is a splendid institute, from top to bottom. The lecture halls, the examination rooms, the floors and windows are of the most excellent workmanship, and their contents—that is to say, the equipment and apparatus, the samples in the anatomical collection, and the gas and water fittings—are all absolutely up to date.

I went to see Professor Wood, who knew of me. The other professors were not there, because classes were not to begin for another week. But you will be glad to hear that my *Nebenwirkungen* [*Side-Effects*] in the English edition was part of the reference library of Professor Williams, the pharmacologist. The janitor was mightily impressed![224]

Although the planning is unexceptionable, nearly everything follows European—and especially German—models. In this respect the Americans are still learning, but no doubt they will grow up quickly. Who knows? Europe may be senile when America reaches its prime!

Tuesday, September 20

Yesterday, we saw some very handsome lamps in a show window, especially one representing the Statue of Liberty, about three-fourths of a meter high, made of fine bronze. I would have bought it as a wedding present for R. if it had been inexpensive. I asked the price: 45 dollars, or 180 Mark, and the Liberty, which carried a lamp instead of the torch, cost 75 dollars, or 300 Mark. Of course I did without.

At 11:50 we departed for New York. I was looking forward to it. During the trip I literally counted the hours that passed, but I didn't shut my eyes to the fine views which Connecticut offered.

BOSTON	9.00	11.00	4.30	10.30
So. Framingham	....	....	....	11.11
Worcester	10.13	12.20	5.38	12.00
E. Brookfield...........	....	12.58	....	....
W. Brookfield...........	....	....	....	12.53½
Palmer	....	1.29	....	1.19
Springfield .... { Arr.	11.41	1.54	6.58	1.47
Springfield .... { Lve.	11.45	1.58	7.03	1.51
Hartford	12.24½	2.40	7.40	2.41
Meriden	12.56	3.12	8.08	3.19
New Haven	1.24	3.42	8.33	3.53
Bridgeport.............	1.57	4.17	9.06	4.30
So. Norwalk...........	....	....	....	4.56
Stamford...............	....	....	....	5.15
NEW YORK...........	3.30	5.50	10.90	6.20
(Grand Central Stat'n.)	P.M.	P.M.	P.M.	A.M.

Train schedule, Boston to New York

The scenery is not overwhelming: the train races through leafy forests and, suddenly, one gets a glimpse of the ocean. From Springfield on,[225] our train follows the seashore; we see wide fields, ranges of hills, farmhouses surrounded by lovely gardens—it is this charming variety that attracts and refreshes. Unfortunately, in the midst of this pleasant journey, we had to move to another car, because we were so sickened by the spitting in ours.

Now we were approaching New York: another hour, then another half hour, and finally—we arrived! I don't know why, but I breathed more freely. Above all, I could expect to find letters from you—at long last!—because I had taken care (through a letter from Uncle) to have Mr. Schlesinger deposit all the accumulated mail at our hotel, where we found them. I glanced through them and absorbed every word of love and longing from you, my dearest. Thank heaven that you are all well. True, I would have liked to have heard more about you, how you feel, whether you have gained strength—but I was content.

When I return home, I will tell you about the days we are now spending in New York. No more for the moment. My ability to take in impressions has shrunk to a minimum. I have seen so many things, so many magnificent things, have learned so much, that nothing more will find its way into my senses. It is now my heart's turn. I want your love and want to embrace my children. May God grant that I shall soon be with you. Goodbye, my beloved wife!

END

STEAMSHIP WIELAND.

A ALBERS, COMMANDER.

SALOON PASSENGER LIST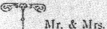

From New York, Sept. 29, 1887.

Mr. John R. Warburg.

Dr. Louis Lewin.

Mrs. Mathilde Begerow.

Miss Begerow.

Miss L. Homer.

Mrs. H. F. Rice.

Miss M. Chapman.

Mr. F. Cranz.

Miss M. Lucy.

Mr. Herman Marcus.

Mr. Emil Silverstein.

Mrs. Kenneth McKenzie.

Miss Bella McKenzie.

Mrs. Emilie Klode.

Miss Julie Gesswein.

Dr. Carl Thieme.

Dr. Herman Rathgen.

Dr. & Mrs.

    Joseph Heckscher.

Mr. & Mrs.

    Emil Schmid.

Miss Dorothea Schmid.

Mr. Wm. Goodenough.

Mr. Gottfried Graf.

Miss Margarethe Kreusler.

Mrs. Beatrice Hee.

Mr. August Finnen.

Miss F. H. M. Patterson.

Mrs. Friederike Bachmann.

Miss Gretchen Bachmann.

Miss Johanna Kakerbeck.

Mr. Mor. Roth.

Mr. J. E. Dorrinck.

Mr. T. H. Vallentin.

Mr. I. Haines.

Miss Josephine White.

Dr. Robert Goehring.

First-class and cabin-class passengers on the S.S. Wieland, New York to Hamburg, Sept. 29, 1887. Lewin and Warburg head the list.

137

OFFICERS OF THE S. S. "WIELAND."
A. ALBERS, Commander.

H. Martens,	- - Chief Officer		L. Jonas,	- - - Chief Engineer
W. Kühlewein,	- - 2d "		H. Nagel,	- - 2d "
A. Bardsch,	- - 3d "		J. Pete,	- - - 3d "
C. Wahlert,	- - 4th "		W. Hottorp,	- - 4th "

Dr. Otto Ziegenhorn, Physician.   H. Goedeke, Purser.

H. Steffens, Chief Steward.

Officers of the S.S. Wieland

Poems of Louis Lewin, Composed on the Voyage

Ausreise (Outward Bound)

Sonnenglanz liegt auf dem Meere,
Dessen Fläche, leichtbewegt
Von des Westwinds Flügelschlage,
Mich geduldig zielwärts trägt.
Abseits von dem Menschenstrome,
An die Schiffswand angelehnt
Denke ich, erfüllt von Liebe
Derer, die mein Herz ersehnt.
Denke an die liebe Kleinen
Und mein Weib, die weit zurück —
Meergetrennt von mir nun leben —
Fern dem Blick, mein fernes Glück!
Meine Lippen sprechen leise
Was mein ganzes Ich bewegt,
Senden Worte auf zu Jenem,
Der das Menschenschicksal trägt.
Halt, O Gott, mir meine Lieben
Immerfort in guter Hut,
Niemals lasse sie entbehren
Der Gesundheit höchstes Gut!
Schütze Du auch meine Pfade
Leite mich zum Heimatherd.
Daß gesund ich wiederfinde
Alle, die mein Herz begehrt!

Ausreise (Outward Bound)
(English Translation)

The sun's reflection dapples the sea
Whose surface, moving gently
On the Westwind's beating winds,
Carries me patiently toward my destination.
Remote from the currents of humanity,
Leaning on the bulkhead and
Filled with love, I think
Of those for whom my heart yearns.
Thinking of my little dear ones.
And of my wife, who now live,
Far from me, by ocean separated—
Distant the sight, distant my happiness!
My lips speak softly
That which moves my entire Self,
Sending words to that One
Who alone carries Man's fate.
Keep, O God, my dear ones,
Ever in your sheltering care.
Never let them go without
The highest good of health!
Protect me also on my path,
Lead me back to hearth and home,
So that, healthy, I may find again
All those whom my heart desires.

25 August 1887

Mein theures Weib, ihr süßen Kinder,
    An wen als Euch hab' ich gedacht,
Als jähes Unglück mich bedrohte
    In der vergangenen finstern Nacht!
Ihr wart die Engel, die mich schützten
    Und Euer Beten war mein Hort—
"Den Vater gieb gesund uns wieder!"
    So tönt zu Gott auf dieses Wort.
Erhörung fand der Liebe Flehen,
    Das Fallen aus dem Kindermund—
Für sie, die meiner noch bedürfen
    Erhielt der Höchste mich gesund.

English Translation

My dear wife, you sweet children,
    Who else but you came to mind
When misfortune menaced me,
    In the dark nights of the recent past!
You were the angels who protected me
     and your prayers were my refuge.
"Give us back our father, healthy,"
    So it sounded to God in these words.
The request was heard, that fell from the
    children's mouths.
It was for them, who still need me,
    that the Almighty kept me healthy.

Heimkehr (Homeward Bound)

Zur Heimath! Welch' wonniger Klang!
Nie ahnte ich, was die Heimath ist!
Jetzt weiß ich's, wo ich so lang
Kinder, Weib und heimische Sitte vermißt.
Großes sah ich im Ost und West—
Gewaltige Ströme, üppigsten Wald,
Himmelstrebende Felsen mit dem Adlernest
Und Flächen schier endlos im Gestalt!
Staunen ergriff mich allüberall,
Sinn und Geist war gefangen—
Doch das Herz im nachtönenden Wiederhall
Nach der Heimat trägt es Verlangen.
Sei ruhig Meer, sei günstig Winde
Führt schnelle mich den langen Pfad
Daß in der Heimath die Lieben ich finde
Und auf die Ruhe folgt die That.

English translation

To the homeland! How sweet the sound!
I had no idea what "homeland" meant!
Now I know, where I for so long
Children, wife and our domestic customs missed.
In East and West I saw great things,
Wild streams, luxuriant forests,
Cliffs, with their eagles' aeries, reaching for the heavens,
And vistas seemingly endless in their layout.
Wonders seized me everywhere,
Capturing both intellect and spirit,
But in its nocturnal throbbing,
The heart for the homeland
Still expresses its longing.

Be still, O sea, O favoring winds,
Drive me quickly forward on the lengthy path,
So that, in the homeland,
 I'll find my loved ones once again,
And so that peace and quiet follow
    my weeks of activity.

Endnotes

1. Verein Stiftung Scheunenviertel, ed. *Das Scheunenviertel*. Berlin: Haude & Spener. 1994. ISBN 3-7759-0377-1.

2. Among other illustrious graduates of this Gymnasium were the two sons of Otto von Bismarck, the 19th-century German chancellor, and Victor Klemperer, whose World War II diaries as a Jew in hiding were later published as *I Will Bear Witness*. New York: Random House, 1999. See http://de.wikipedia.org/wiki/Friedrichswerdersches Gymnasium (January 15, 2011). For a description of the Prussian educational system in which Lewin was schooled, see http://en.wikipedia.org/wiki/Education_in_Germany (January 15, 2011).

3. See en.wikipedia.org/wiki/Paul_de_Lagarde (January 15, 2011).

4. Renamed in 1949 the Humboldt University of Berlin.

5. Aconite is the dried tuberous root of *Aconitum napellus*. In appropriate doses, aconite is used as an ointment in the treatment of neuralgia, sciatica, and rheumatism. It is also used as a cardiac depressant and as a component in cough mixtures.

6. Max von Pettenkofer (1818-1901); see ocp.hul.harvard.edu/contagion/vonpettenkofer.html (January 15, 2011).

7. Carl von Voit (1831-1908); see jn.nutrition.org/cgi/reprint/13/1/2 (January 15, 2011)

8. Oskar Liebreich (1839-1908); en.wikipedia.org/wiki/Oskar_Liebreich (January 15, 2011).

9. The habilitation was the additional coursework that was required of those with doctorates who desired to go on to become professors at higher-level German universities.

10. Richard Koch specialized in the history of science and medicine at the University of Frankfurt. In 1936, when other German Jews were fleeing to the United States or to Palestine, Koch emigrated to the Soviet Union and settled in Essentuki in the

Caucasus, living there in desperate financial circumstances. After World War II, he declined the opportunity to return to Germany and died in Essentuki in 1949.

11. Walter Siegfried Loewe (1884-1963) left Germany in 1935 and taught as Professor of Pharmacology, first at Princeton University and then at the University of Utah.

12. Defined in the Merriam-Webster Dictionary as "a volume of writings by different authors presented as a tribute or memorial, especially to a scholar."

13. (1860-1933). See en.wikipedia.org/wiki/Otto_Lubarsch (January 15, 2011).

14. (1840-1913); see www.workersliberty.org/node/5764 (January 15, 2011)

15. (1871-1919); a leading opponent of the Kaiser and of German participation in World War I, it is thought that he and Rosa Luxembourg (q.v.) were murdered together. See www.historylearningsite.co.uk/karl_liebknecht.htm (January 15, 2011).

16. (1871-1919); see en.wikipedia.org/wiki/Rosa_Luxemburg (January 15, 2011).

17. Lewin, L. *Die Gifte in der Weltgeschichte. Toxikologische, allgemeinverständliche Untersuchungen der historischen Quellen.* Berlin, 1920.

18. See www.wilpf.org (January 15, 2011).

19. See http://www.theinfidels.org/zunb-sugmundfreud.htm (January 15, 2011).

20. Published in an English translation as *Phantastica: Narcotic and Stimulating Drugs, Their Use and Abuse.* New York: E. P. Dutton. 1931.

21. See www.biopark.org/peru/schultes-obit.html (January 15, 2011).

22. Today, Lewin is remembered by a street name and U-Bahn station in what had been East Berlin. After the City was reunited, East and West, the city government renamed many of the streets in the former East Berlin, which had been named after Karl Marx, Friedrich Engels, Vladimir Lenin and other members of the Communist pantheon. A street in Hellersdorf,

an outlying area of the city, formerly named for Paul Verner, a high ranking Communist Party functionary, was renamed in 1992 the Louis Lewinstrasse, and the nearby U-Bahn station named for him as well.

23. For a partial family tree, see www.loebtree.com/warburg.html. For an interesting description of an apartment building funded by J. R. Warburg, perhaps the earliest example of privately-financed affordable housing in Germany, see www.rrz.uni-hamburg.de/rz3a035bundesstrasse2.html (January 15, 2011). The full history of the Warburg clan, with a comprehensive genealogy, appears in Chernow, Ron. *The Warburgs: The Twentieth-Century Odyssey of a Remarkable Jewish Family*. New York: Random House, 1993.

24. Because Germany was at that time the foremost center for medical research, and English was not yet the international language of science that it is today, it was to be expected that many of the papers presented at the conference would be read in German. Lewin could not speak or read English, and would have read his paper in German, had he been invited to do so. The paper would have been translated into English for the English-speaking physicians in the audience, and that would have been no hindrance either.

25. See D. L. Ashliman, ed. *Germany Discovers America: An Annotated Bibliography of German-American Travel Narratives*, 1800-1918. Univ. of Pittsburgh, 1997.

26. For other notable examples of travel journals, see http://en.wikipedia.org/wiki/Travel_blog (January 15, 2011).

27. Eli Nathans, review of Schmidt, Alexander. *Reisen in die Moderne: Der Amerika-Diskurs des deutschen Bürgertums vor dem Ersten Weltkrieg im europäischen Vergleich*. Berlin: Akademie Verlag, 1997. ISBN 3-05-002859-9, in http://hsozkult.geschichte.hu-berlin.de/rezensio/buecher/nael0598.htm (January 15, 2011).

28. See Ashliman, ed., *supra*, note 25.

29. *Ibid.*

30. *Ibid.*

31. *Ibid.*

32. *Ibid.*

33. The President at the time of Lewin's travels across America, Grover Cleveland, had in common with the other presidents of that time his bushy mustache, but was unique in two respects: he was the only Democrat to serve in a 43-year span of otherwise Republican presidents, and the only man to have been elected to the Presidency in two non-consecutive terms, in 1884 and again in 1892.

34. For a general outline of the events of this decade, see http://kclibrary.lonestar.edu/19thcentury1880.htm (January 15, 2011).

35. Kate Richards O'Hare (1876-1948), quoted in http://www.spartacus.schoolnet.co.uk/USAohare.htm(January 15, 2011).

36. Vose, George L. *Bridge Disasters in America: the Cause and the Remedy.* Boston: Lee & Shepard, 1887.

37. *Heidereutergasse* was a street in Berlin *Mitte* (its "downtown"), today renamed *Almstadtstrasse*. The Heidereutergasse Synagogue was the oldest in Berlin, built in 1714 and known as *"Die alte Sinagoge"* ("the Old Synagogue"). For the history of the Jews in Berlin, see www.jewishencyclopedia.com/view.jsp?artid=849&letter=B (January 15, 2011).

38. At the time of his travels in Canada and the U.S., only the two older daughters, Gertrud and Herta, had been born; the youngest, Irene, was born August 31, 1888, the year after the journey.

39. In his striving to remain modest, Lewin was fighting a losing battle, as is evidenced throughout this travel diary.

40. An island in the North Sea, off the coast of Schleswig-Holstein in Germany. Its beaches drew many summertime visitors. Because Lewin's wife, Clara, had grown up in Hamburg, near the North Sea coast, she must have been familiar with the island, and Lewin and his family had evidently vacationed there.

41. This was the third of five vessels of this name, named for the patron goddess of Hamburg. Launched on September 13, 1881, she carried a crew of 125 and accommodated 150 passengers in first class, 100 in second class and 700 in steerage.

42. The town at the mouth of the Elbe River, the last town that Lewin would encounter before the ship entered the open sea.

43. Clara Lewin's brother.

44. Her other brother.

45. Cocaine was first used successful as an anesthetic in 1884, to anaesthetize the surface of the human eye in preparation for surgery, to relieve earaches, and to lessen the pain of childbirth. Soon cocaine was seen as a 'miracle cure', one that could change the world, and was prescribed for drug addiction, alcoholism, depression and fatigue. Endless cocaine syrups, pastilles, wines, tonics, and elixirs appeared, alongside toothache drops, hemorrhoid creams, balms, ointments and cordials. These products usually contained huge amounts of cocaine. Rayno's Hay Fever remedy, for example, was basically a pure cocaine solution. The bottle recommended that you take it "two to ten times a day." Coca-Cola had been invented in 1886, the year before Lewin's journey. Its original "secret" formula included a hefty dose of cocaine. It wasn't called *Coca*-Cola for nothing! By 1900, cocaine was in the top five pharmaceutical products in the US and was selling for around $2.50 per gram.

46. In the days before the unitary shirt and collar, the collar was attached by buttons to the shirt after the shirt was put on. The Phillips-Jones Co., makers of Van Heusen shirts, marketed the first men's shirt with unitary collar in 1920.

47. Warburg was at that time 77 years old.

48. *Mauscheln* is a verb with anti-Semitic overtones that was not spoken in polite company. It means to "carry out a con or a fiddle" and had its origin in the name "Moses."

49. Here Lewin is echoing, if only to his wife, the canard that Jews are interested only in trade and money. It appears that Lewin believed this to be true, except for the thoughtful minority, of which he was one.

50. In German, "*zwischendecken*" (between the decks). At the end of the 19th century, a place could be had in steerage on most of the trans-Atlantic lines for $20.00, while cabin class passengers (first- and second-class) paid from $75.00 to $100.00.

51. Talmi is fake-gold—a zinc and copper alloy plated over in gold leaf; by extension anything false or phony.

52. "Poland is not lost" the German translation of the Polish national anthem.

53. We see here an expression of Lewin's natural sympathy with authentic, however downtrodden, ragged and emaciated, men and women, as against the poseur, the inauthentic man, the self-hating Jew. In this revealing paragraph, Lewin has by implication contrasted that would-be "cosmopolitan" with himself. Lewin did indeed cast aside the bonds that tied him culturally to the *Scheunenviertel,* the ghetto, but never cut his ties to his Jewish faith, never sought to join that "Christian mob," and never came to despise his Jewish co-religionists.

54. Reseda perfume, named after *reseda odorata* (white mignonette) is still made today, as White Reseda, by Roger & Gaillet.

55. A peninsula of Cornwall; its tip is the southernmost point of the island shared by England, Wales and Scotland. Lizard Point has two light-houses, the seas off the point having been the graveyard of many ships over the centuries.

56. Still another example of the contrast that Lewin notices, and draws for his wife, between the slothful and inauthentic upperclass women who laze on their deckchairs and the energetic steerage passengers, expressing their emotions in uninhibited music and dance.

57. "The truest words are often spoke in jest."

58. Mr. P. Toots, a schoolmate of the eponymous Paul Dombey, owner of the firm Dombey & Son in Charles Dickens's novel of that name (serialized 1846-1848). He appears in the novel as a dandy who seeks the hand of Dombey's daughter, Florence.

59. Orange-flavored bitters still being sold under the same trade-name today.

60. Founded in 1881 in Berlin by Xaver Scharwenka (1850-1924), called "one of the great composer-pianists of the second half of the 19th century." See http://naxos.com/composerinfo/xaver_scharwenka_23030/23030.htm (January 15, 2011). In 1891, Scharwenka established a branch of the conservatory in New York.

61. René Antoine Ferchault de Réaumur (1683-1757) in 1731 invented the scale of temperature measurement named after him, in which water freezes at 0° and boils at 80°.

62. The Fifth Avenue Hotel, built in 1858, stood at the corner of 24th Street and Fifth Avenue, now the site of the New York Toy

Center. In its heyday the most exclusive hotel in NYC; presidents Grant and Arthur stayed there, as did the Prince of Wales. It was a watering hole for politicians and corporate entrepreneurs like Boss Tweed, Jay Gould, Jim Fisk and Commodore Vanderbilt, and a hangout for cultural figures like Mark Twain, O. Henry, William Cullen Bryant and Stanford White. It was demolished in 1908.

63. Bedloe's Island was named originally for its Dutch owner, Isaack Bedloo, and renamed Liberty Island in 1960. In the 1760's, it was operated by the State of New York as a quarantine station. In 1800 the island was ceded to the federal government, which built on the island a five-pointed fort, Fort Wood, guarding the approaches to New York harbor. During the Civil War, it was an infirmary for Confederate soldiers. In 1877 it was designated as the site for the proposed Statute of Liberty Enlightening the World.

64. For the history of the Statue, see http://www.nps.gov/archive/ stli/prod02.htm#Statue of (January 15, 2011).

65. A residential area in Hamburg near the Alster River, where Clara Lewin grew up and where her relatives still lived.

66. What we now call "fire escapes." It is noteworthy that the way to safety was seen as leading upward.

67. The S.S. *Eider* was a four-masted, two-funnel screw steamer, gross weight 4,700 tons and over 430' long. Five years later, on January 10, 1892, she ran aground about half a mile from shore in a dense fog at Atherfield Ledge off the Isle of Wight. In a landmark rescue-and-salvage operation, her entire crew, passengers and cargo, as well as 500 sacks of mail and 10 tons of gold and silver, were saved.

68. The city's first regular elevated railway service began on February 14, 1870, on a line running along Greenwich Street and Ninth Avenue in Manhattan. In September, 1883, a cable-powered railway across the Brooklyn Bridge opened between Park Row in Manhattan and Sands Street in Brooklyn. For further information: http://www.nycsubway.org/lines/9thave-el.html (January 15, 2011).

69. Central Park, the largest urban park in the country, was laid out by Frederick Law Olmstead The idea of a large park, to preserve

open space in the rapidly urbanizing island of Manhattan, was first publicly proposed by *Evening Post* editor William Cullen Bryant in 1844. Between 1853 and 1856, the city commissioners paid more than $5 million for land from 59th Street to 106th Street, between Fifth and Eighth Avenues. In 1857, a public competition was held to choose the design team for the new park. Out of 33 entries, the commissioners chose the Greensward plan by Frederick Law Olmsted, superintendent of the Park work crews, and Calvert Vaux, the British architect who had convinced the commissioners to hold a design competition. Most of the landscaping of Central Park as we know it today was completed 20 years after the design competition was announced. See http://www.centralpark.com/guide/history. html (January 15, 2011).

70. The large park in the center of Berlin, akin to New York's Central Park, Chicago's Lincoln Park and Paris's Bois de Boulogne. In addition to its forests and gardens, it includes Berlin's zoo and many of its most important public buildings. Its origins date back to the 1830's.

71. This obelisk, originally erected around 1500 B.C. as a tribute to Pharaoh Tutmose III, was donated by Ismail Pasha, khedive of Egypt, in 1869. The obelisk arrived in New York City on July 20,1880, and was finally installed at its present site on February 22, 1881.

72. Lewin is evidently referring here to the Suez Canal, which was opened to shipping on November 17, 1869, making possible the new trade route between Europe and the Far East that had been sought over millennia.

73. The Metropolitan Museum of Art, chartered by the New York State Legislature in 1870, opened in its present location in Central Park in 1874.

74. Rosa Bonheur (1822-1899) was perhaps the most noted woman painter of the 19th century, specializing in the painting of farm animals and domestic scenes. Perhaps it was her "Horse Fair" (1852-1855) that Lewin saw hanging in the Metropolitan Museum of Art.

75. Vàclav Brozik (1851-1901), a Czech artist who made his reputation in Paris as one of the leading painters of the Beaux Arts Realist School.

76. The Madison Square Theater was located on 24th Street near Broadway, next door to the Fifth Avenue Hotel where Warburg and Lewin were staying. The theatre had opened February 4, 1880, with a seating capacity of 500. Its greatest innovation was a double stage. As one act was going on, the lower stage was set for the next act, and during intermission was raised to its proper place by four men, two on each side, working pulley cables by hand. The theater was kept open all summer and advertised as "Cooled by Iced Air." A blower blew air over cakes of ice, the chilled air emerging onto the stage and through the same floor gratings used to convey heat in the winter. See http://www.wayneturney.20m/madisonsquare theatre.htm (January 15, 2011).

77. Castle Garden, at the southern tip of Manhattan Island, was the immigrant processing station for entry into America from 1855 until 1890. Until 1882, the processing of immigrants was solely under the jurisdiction of the State of New York. In 1875, the Supreme Court affirmed Congressional supremacy over immigration (under the commerce clause), but it was seven years later that Congress enacted the Immigration Act of 1882, which authorized the Treasury Secretary to contract with the states for enforcement of that law. From 1882 to 1890, the reception of immigrants was handled as a joint state/federal system. On April 18, 1890, the Treasury Department assumed total control of immigration at the Port of New York. The New York State authorities refused to allow the federal government to use the Castle Garden facilities. Ellis Island opened on January 1, 1892 and the Castle Garden structure burned down in 1897.

78. The reference is to Antonio Allegri da Correggio (1489–1534), the foremost painter of the Parma school of the Italian Renaissance.

79. One of the Bacchae, women who participated in the orgiastic rituals worshipping the Greek god Dionysius. They and their rites were the subject of classical drama, epic poetry, ceramics and sculpture. For more on the Dionysian cult, see http://home.earthlink.net/~delia5/pagan/dio/tp99s-dnys-donnr.htm (January 15, 2011).

80. The reference is to the Brooklyn Bridge, one of the first suspension bridges in the United States, stretching 6,016 feet over the East

River to connect Manhattan and Brooklyn. Designed by the German-born engineer John Augustus Roebling, the bridge was, on its completion, the largest suspension bridge in the world and the first steel-wire suspension bridge. Opened for use on May 24, 1883, it was the first permanent connection between Brooklyn and Manhattan.

81. Lewin had good cause for concern. A ship similar to the one on which he and Uncle took their day trip to Long Branch, the S.S. *General Slocum*, caught on fire in the East River on June 15, 1904 and burned to the water line, with the loss of 1,021 people. It was the worst loss of life in a single event in New York until the destruction of the twin towers of the World Trade Center on September 11, 2001.

82. The major beach resort on the Belgian coast, favorite vacation destination of the Belgian kings Leopold I and Leopold II.

83. Sylt is an island in the North Sea, part of the German state of Nord Friesland. Its main importance today is as a tourist destination for its beaches. Evidently Louis and Clara Lewin spent their summer holidays there.

84. The S. S. *Wieland* was built in the Glasgow shipyards in 1874, sold to HAPAG in 1875, and for the next twenty years was used in the Hamburg to New York run. She was scrapped in 1896.

85. Saratoga Springs had been a Mecca for vacationers since the middle of the 19th century. Its race course opened in 1863. The Grand Union Hotel on Broadway in Saratoga Springs, New York was built in 1802 by Gideon Putnam. A luxury hotel that catered to the wealthy elite, it eventually grew to 824 rooms and was in its time the largest hotel in the world.

86. A suburb of Hamburg, on the Elbe River, now the site of the Hamburg Airport.

87. According to German legend, a beautiful young maiden named Lorelei,in despair over a faithless lover. threw herself headlong into the Rhine River. In death she was transformed into a siren who could be heard singing on a rock along the river's edge, near St. Goar, luring sailors to their death. Heinrich Heine wrote the words, Friedrich Silcher the music to the song, *Die Lorelei*, familiar to all Germans and to countless others around the world.

88. The reference is to the great capitalist entrepreneurs of the second half of the nineteenth century, many of whom erected palatial castles for themselves on the cliffs overlooking the Hudson River. These included men such as Jay Gould, E. H. Harriman, John D. Rockefeller Sr., Cornelius Vanderbilt and J. P. Morgan. The term was first applied to medieval lords who demanded the payment of tolls from ships sailing up and down the Rhine River.

89. The region between the west bank of the Rhine and the French border, noted for its scenery and much of it preserved as an undeveloped national forest.

90. For the history of the ceiling fan, see http://en.wikipedia.org/ wiki/Ceiling_fan (January 15, 2011).

91. In Germany, the term "brothers-in-color" was used by university men to refer to fraternity brothers, because each fraternity man sported colors different from those of men in other fraternities.

92. "The name signifies the thing"; in other words, he would be worried that the assets of the Cataract Bank would fall precipitously like a waterfall.

93. Phineas T. (P.T.) Barnum. For an Internet biography, see http:// en.wikipedia.org/wiki/P._T._Barnum (January 15, 2011); for a Barnum bibliography, see http://www.barnum-museum.org/ pdf/BOOKSTORECATALOG.pdf (January 15, 2011)

94. Niagara Falls—the oldest state park in the United States, created by act of the New York State Legislature two years before Lewin's visit, in 1885.

95. For an explanation of the hydrology of the whirlpool, see http:// www.niagaraparks.com/nfgg/geology.php (January 15, 2011).

96. In German, *Völkerwanderung*, the name given by historians to the mass migration which occurred within the period of roughly 300–700 C.E. in Europe, marking the transition from Late Antiquity to the Early Middle Ages.

97. The first bridge across the Falls, a 770-foot suspension footbridge, opened on August 1, 1848. The second bridge, a double-decker designed by John A. Roebling with rail on the upper level, opened to trains on March 18, 1855. When the bridge opened, the railroads feeding into it operated on three different gauges,

and the track on the bridge had four rails to allow for all three. A renovation was completed in 1886, completely replacing the bridge in sections.

98. Songs written by Jean-Pierre de Béranger (1780-1857), a popular French songwriter. From *Wikipedia*: "He had a strong sense of political responsibility. Public interest took a far higher place in his estimation than any private passion or favor. He had little toleration for those erotic poets who sing their own loves and not the common sorrows of mankind, who forget, to quote his own words, 'those who labor before the Lord.' Consequently, many of his pieces are political, and so many, in the later times at least, are inspired with a socialist spirit of indignation and revolt."

99. Off the coast of North Friesland in the North Sea.

100. Again, Lewin and Uncle are staying in the leading hotel of every city that they visit. The Windsor Hotel, which had opened 1878, was considered to be the first grand hotel constructed in Canada, and for decades billed itself as "the best in all the Dominion." The opening gala in 1878 was the largest social gathering in Montreal history. Soon the hotel was the center of Montreal's social and business world, attracting business leaders, politicians, socialites, artists and even royalty. Sarah Bernhardt, Mark Twain, Rudyard Kipling and Lillie Langtry were among its famous guests in its early years. After several disastrous fires and restorations, the hotel finally closed in 1981.

101. The Foresters Lodge was a fraternal order related to the Independent Order of Odd Fellows, one of the large number of such lodges that sprang up in the second half of the nineteenth century for social and mutual benefit purposes.

102. English sailors were given lemons, rich in Vitamin C, to counteract scurvy, a condition characterized by general weakness, anemia, gum disease (gingivitis), and skin hemorrhages. Scurvy was a serious problem in the days when fresh fruits and vegetables were not available during the winter in many parts of the world and only nonperishable foods could be stocked aboard ship. In 1747 the Scottish naval surgeon James Lind treated scurvy-ridden sailors with lemons and oranges and obtained dramatic cures. Scurvy was probably the first disease to be definitely associated with a dietary deficiency.

103. Dedicated in 1860, the Victoria Bridge in Montreal was the first bridge to span the St. Lawrence River. Two miles in length, it was, when it opened, the longest bridge in the world, and remains in use to this day, carrying both road and rail traffic.

104. McGill College (today McGill University) was chartered in 1821, but did not open for classes until 1829. That same year, the Montreal Medical Institution became the college's Faculty of Medicine and its first academic unit. The Faculty of Medicine remained the school's only functioning faculty until 1843.

105. See note 212.

106. See http://www.psych.utoronto.ca/museum/verticalkym.htm (January 15, 2011).

107. Lewin finds it amusing because that was one of his specialties as well. Indeed, he had written a book with that title, *Die Nebenwirkungen der Arzneimittel* (translated as *The Untoward Effects of Drugs: a Pharmacological and Clinical Manual*). The English translation had been published in 1883 by George S. Davis, the "Davis" of Parke Davis & Co. He is obviously pleased that his fame has preceded him to this side of the Atlantic Ocean.

108. The original parish church of Notre Dame was built on the site in 1672. By 1824 the congregation had completely outgrown the church. The new church was finished in 1830, and the first tower in 1843. On its completion, the church was the largest in North America. The interior was not completed until 1879.

109. This was Uncle's firm; the "W" stands for Warburg.

110. For a gripping account of the construction of the line, see www.electricscotland.com/History/canada/steel10.htm (January 15, 2011).

111. The *Starnberger See* is Germany's fourth largest lake and a popular recreation area for residents of the nearby city of Munich. Lewin may have visited it often when he spent his year of postgraduate study at the University of Munich.

112. Lake Nipissing is the fifth-largest lake in Ontario. The lake's name means "big water" in the Algonquian language. The French fur trader Étienne Brûlé was the first European to visit the lake in 1610. The first permanent European settlement on the lake dates from around 1874.

113. He was at the time of their trip only three years from his death.

114. Port Arthur, on the northwestern shore of Lake Superior in Ontario, was originally a military outpost; it became a town when the railroad reached it in 1884. Port Arthur and Port William, the next stop on the line, were originally separate towns, but were consolidated in 1970 with two other townships and are now named the City of Thunder Bay.

115. In the original, *"Geheimräte,"* a title given originally to the highest officials of a German royal or princely court, and also to very eminent professors in some German universities.

116. Not the religious cross is meant here, but the badges of certain lodges, such as those of the Foresters, which incorporated a depiction of such a cross.

117. Literally, "by right of conquest," in other words, a trophy of battle.

118. This may have been *Mentha arvensis*, the wild mint, which grows everywhere on the North American continent except the extreme southeastern United States and the northernmost parts of Canada.

119. John Warburg's wife, Bernhardine Warburg (née Wolff), Clara's aunt.

120. List is the northernmost municipality in Germany, located on the North Sea island of Sylt, close to Denmark in Nordfriesland in the state of Schleswig-Holstein.

121. Posen at the time was a province in northeast Germany. The capital of the province was the city of Posen. Now it is renamed Poznan, in Poland.

122. A German physicist, contemporary of Lewin's.

123. A genus of plants that includes turmeric and ginger. www.alohatropicals.com/curcuma.html (January 15, 2011).

124. The Cree Indians are the predominant tribe of Canada's Plains provinces, being related linguistically and by custom to the Chippewa and Algonquin. It has been estimated that, at the time of their first contact with English and French fur traders in the 17th century, the Crees and related peoples numbered about 200,000. Today, they number all told about 10,000.

125. A town of 60,000, halfway between Winnipeg and Vancouver. The town was founded in 1883, when the Canadian Pacific Railway (CPR) reached that location and crossed the river on its way west. The name for the town has come down from Indian legends. As the west developed, Medicine Hat was the site of the first hospital west of Winnipeg in 1889 and also a CPR divisional point.

126. The reference is to the cog railway which ascends Rigi Mountain outside of Zurich, Switzerland. This was the first cog railway in Europe, opening in 18/1.

127. Mount Stephen, 10,495 feet in elevation, is located in the Kicking Horse River Valley of Yoho National Park. It was named in 1886 for George Stephen, the first president of the Canadian Pacific Railway, and it was first ascended in September 1887, one month after Lewin and Warburg passed through.

128. The Selkirk Mountain range begins at Mica Peak near Coeur d'Alene, Idaho and extends approximately 200 miles northward from the border and into Canada. The Selkirks presented a formidable barrier to the construction of the Canadian Pacific Railway, until A.B. Rogers in 1881-1882 discovered the mountain pass through the range that bears his name. He had negotiated with the officials of the CPR and the Canadian government that, if he were successful in finding a way through the range, that pass would bear his name.

129. Donald was once a divisional point on the CPR. When the railroad moved its divisional base to Revelstoke, Donald lapsed into obscurity and is now only a small saw-milling community.

130. See cdnrail.railfan.net/RogersPass/RogersPasstext.htm (January 15, 2011), www.islandnet.com/~see/weather/events/1910avalanche.htm (January 15, 2011).

131. Now a year-round resort near Revelstoke, B.C. About 27 miles west of Revelstoke, at Lake Griffin, the final spike was driven on November 11, 1885, which enabled the Canadian Pacific Railroad to span the continent across Canada.

132. For a contemporary description of the construction of the CPR line in this region, see http://www.electricscotland.com/History/canada/steel10.htm (January 15, 2011).

133. Kamloops, situated at the confluence of the north and south forks of the Thompson River, was originally settled by English traders as a fur trading post in 1812. At the time of Lewin's visit, its population was still less than 500. See http://www.tourismkamloops.com/home_showSection_ID_22.html (January 15, 2011).

134. Lewin's older daughter, born 1884.

135. Vancouver had been incorporated as a city a year earlier, in 1886. For more, see http://www.vancouverhistory.ca (January 15, 2011).

136. Cleveland, Ohio was the first American city to use electric street lighting, in 1879. Montreal was the first Canadian city to do so, using arc lamps first, in 1886, and then, in 1888, incandescent lamps.

137. Lewin's prediction proved accurate. In 2005, the Port of Vancouver traded $43 billion in goods (82.7 million tons of cargo) with more than 90 trading economies. It is the busiest seaport in Canada, and exports more cargo than any other port in North America.

138. A mild expletive, literally Sky-Thunder-Weather, akin to "Gosh darn it!"

139. Aconite is also known as wolf's bane and monkshood. Lewin had written his Ph.D. dissertation on the effects of aconite on the heart. For more on the medical and toxic effects of aconite, see http://www.a1b2c3.com/drugs/var001.htm (January 15, 2011).

140. In 1887, the year of Lewin's visit, there were fewer than 100 Jews in the city of Vancouver. The pioneering Jewish settlers, the Oppenheimer brothers, were born in Bavaria, Germany, came to British Columbia in 1858 following the gold rush in that region, and settled in Vancouver in 1885, a year before the city was founded. In 1888, David Oppenheimer was elected the city's second mayor. The family business, Oppenheimer Bros. & Co., Ltd., was Vancouver's oldest business. The brick building in which it was housed still stands in the city's Gastown district.

141. An equestrian maneuver.

142. Willy-nilly, in spite of one's best intentions.

143. King Jerome Bonaparte (1784-1860) was the youngest brother of Napoleon, who made him king of Westphalia (1807-1813). Apparently, he led a profligate life during his short reign.

144. *"Allerhöchste Zufriedenheit,"* a German term used by the Kaiser and other men of the highest rank, to express satisfaction with goods or services provided by vendors and tradesmen.

145. The following year, on July 19, 1888, the S.S. *George W. Elder* ran aground on its approach to Port Townsend, Washington. The ship was returned to service and, eleven years later, in 1899, outfitted for use as the flagship of the E. H. Harriman expedition through Alaska's Inland Passage.

146. Pacific means "tranquil." The German name for the Pacific Ocean is *"der Stille Ozean,"* the quiet ocean. Lewin is saying that, rather than merely quiet, the Ocean should be called the "quietest," *der Stillste.*

147. The original Palace Hotel, at 2 New Montgomery Street just off Union Square, opened in 1875. It was intended by its developers to be the American counterpart to the grand hotels of Europe. Built at a cost of $5,000,000, it was said when it opened to be the largest, most luxurious and costliest hotel in the world. Gutted by the fires that broke out after the great earthquake of 1906, it was demolished that same year. The New Palace Hotel opened at the same location in 1909 and is still operating today.

148. The sea-trip on the S.S. *George W. Elder* must have been so unsettling that Lewin forgets that he had had excellent French food in Vancouver only three days earlier.

149. Golden Gate Park is a 1,017-acre park, roughly rectangular in shape, the third most visited city park in the United States (after Central Park in New York and Chicago's Lincoln Park). In 1886, the year before Lewin's and Uncle's visit, streetcars brought over 47,000 people to Golden Gate Park on a weekend afternoon, when the city's entire population at the time was about 250,000.

150. Cliff House, which still exists today, had humble beginnings. It was built in 1858, using lumber salvaged from the wreck of a ship that had foundered on the rocks below. Success came when a toll road, later Geary Boulevard, was built to facilitate access

to the restaurant from the city. In 1883, the Cliff House was bought by Adolph Sutro, the multimillion-dollar silver mining magnate. Cliff House has gone through several fires and re-incarnations in its 150-year existence. In 1977, it was acquired by the National Park Service and incorporated into the Golden Gate National Recreation Area.

151. San Francisco was the port of entry for Chinese immigrants from the southern Guangdong province of China from the 1850's to the early 1900's. Many of these immigrants found jobs working for large companies seeking a source of cheap labor, most famously the Central Pacific on the Transcontinental Railroad. Other early immigrants worked as mine workers or as independent prospectors hoping to strike it rich in panning for gold in California's rivers.

152. Evidently Lewin did not observe the requirements of *kashruth*, at least not on this trip. On his visit to Long Branch, the New Jersey beach resort, he had eaten, or ordered, lobster; in Philadelphia, he had had an oyster lunch; now he buys cuttlefish here in San Francisco. These shellfish are taboo for observant Jews.

153. For depictions of San Francisco opium dens in the period of Lewin's visit, see www.sfmuseum.org/hist6/den.html (January 15, 2011) , and en.wikipedia.org/wiki/Opium_den (January 15, 2011).

154. In the United States, opium-smoking was called "the Chinese vice." For the full history of the use of opiates, going back to pre-history, see http://opioids.com/red.html (January 15, 2011). For a detailed description of gambling in Chinatown in the late 1880's, see http://www.sfmuseum.org/hist9/cook.html (January 15, 2011).

155. The San Francisco *Chronicle* was founded in 1865 as *The Daily Dramatic Chronicle* by teenage brothers Charles de Young and Michael H. de Young. By 1880 it was the largest circulation newspaper on the West Coast of the United States. Today it is still Northern California's largest newspaper and second only to the Los Angeles *Times* in circulation on the West Coast, ranking 12th in circulation nationally.

156. In the wake of the Panic of 1873, racial tensions in the city boiled over into full blown race riots. The Consolidated Chinese

Benevolent Association or the Chinese Six Companies, was created as a means of self-defense and to provide the community with a unified voice. The heads of these companies were the leaders among the Chinese merchants, who represented the Chinese community to the larger San Francisco business community and to the city government. In time, turf conflicts broke out among the Six Companies, leading to waves of homicides and other crimes.

157. Pioneer Hall, near the Civic Center in San Francisco, houses the museum and library of the Society of Californian Pioneers, devoted chiefly to the early (pre-1869) history of California.

158. In 1861, President Abraham Lincoln signed the Pacific Railroad Act, directing the Union Pacific and the Central Pacific Railroads to construct a transcontinental railroad. In 1863, ground was broken at Omaha for the Union Pacific, while the Central Pacific began construction east from Sacramento, California. On May 10, 1869, the famous golden spike was driven at Promontory Summit, Utah by officials of the Union Pacific and Central Pacific, marking the inauguration of the transcontinental railroad.

159. A pun on a mild oath in German, akin to English "darn" or "damn," or the French "sacre bleu."

160. The desolate region in Lower Saxony, Germany, between Hamburg, Hanover, and Bremen. Its heath-like landscape originated in medieval times when forests were cleared for firewood for the production of salt in Lüneburg.

161. The reference is obscure.

162. A play on words: "Colorado" and the operatic "coloratura (soprano)."

163. The stereotype of African-American men, appearing in children's toys and books, popular songs and theatrical entertainments. Such items still appear for sale today in antique shops, dealers specializing in ephemera, and on Internet auction sites.

164. The reference is obscure.

165. In Vancouver, Warburg had irritated Lewin by his stubborn insistence on sleeping on a bench in the train station; now, the tables are turned: Lewin irritates Warburg by his badgering of railroad officials for information.

166. Roodhouse, Illinois was laid out and named in 1866, for John Roodhouse. In 1871, when the Louisiana branch of the Chicago & Alton Railroad was planned, a group of entrepreneurs promoted the town as a railroad junction. It became a major railroad center, its depot described as the "handsomest depot between Chicago and Kansas City."

167. "Hunger wells up in us, we're dying of thirst, and a single cup of coffee."

168. "Beer here, beer there, or I'll die of thirst."

169. Portieres are the hanging curtains, usually of velvet or other heavy material, that once graced the entries to salons, sitting rooms and dining rooms in hotels and residences.

170. A possible reference to the famous "Horseshoe Curve," five miles west of Altoona, Pennsylvania, built by the Pennsylvania Railroad and opened for use in 1854.

171. For the Ninth International Medical Congress. The Tenth International Medical Congress, was held three years later, in 1890, in Berlin.

172. To the post office, evidently.

173. The Architect for the Capitol, Thomas U. Walter, commenced the design for a new cast-iron dome for the United States Capitol in 1854. Over the next 11 years, the dome was under construction over the nation's capitol. On December 2, 1863, the Statue of Freedom was set atop the dome.

174. Chartered by Act of Congress in 1821, the University was originally situated in one building on what is now called Meridian Hill, at 16th Street N.W. north of Florida Avenue. After the Civil War, in 1873, it relocated to its present campus in Foggy Bottom.

175. This may have been the church at the corner of 20th and G Streets N.W., near the present George Washington University campus.

176. Dr. Paul Gerson Unna (1850-1929), called the father of modern dermatology. For further information, see http://en.wikipedia.org/wiki/Paul_Gerson_Unna (January 15, 2011).

177. The reference is apparently to the DuBois Institute of Physiology, named for pioneer German physiologist Emil duBois-Reymond

(1818-1896). See Dierig, Sven. *Wissenschaft in der Machinenstadt: Emil Du Bois-Reymond und seine Laboratorien in Berlin.* Göttingen: Wallstein Verlag, 2006.

178. Apparently, he later wrote an article based on his impromptu remarks, published as *Über Maximale Dosen der Arzneimittel* ("Concerning Maximum Dosages of Medications") in "Transactions of the International Medical Congress, ninth session, Washington, 1887."

179. The Pension Building, in the block bounded by F, G, 4th and 5th Streets, N.W. was completed in 1887, just before Lewin's visit, to house the workers who were needed to process the pension claims of Civil War veterans. The building was designed by Gen. Montgomery C. Meigs, the U.S. Army quartermaster general, based on Italian Renaissance precedents. Its interior Corinthian columns are among the largest in the world, measuring 75 ft. tall and 8 ft. in diameter.

180. A governmental health official.

181. Evidently referring to Dr. Unna.

182. A man who puts on airs and puffs himself up.

183. The reference is to the Washington Monument, standing 555 feet 5⅛ inches (169.294 m) in height. Its cornerstone was laid on July 4, 1848; the capstone was set on December 6, 1884, and the completed monument was dedicated on February 21, 1885. It opened officially on October 9, 1888. Upon its completion, it became the world's tallest structure, a title it held until 1889, when the Eiffel Tower was finished in Paris, France. By 1888, a year after Lewin's visit, 55,000 visitors per month were going to the top of the monument.

184. Dr. Justus Andeer, of Munich. For an illuminating report on the exchange between Drs. Lewin and Andeer, see the *Therapeutic Gazette* for 1887, available on Googlebooks.com. Dr. Andeer had been promoting the virtues of resorcin since at least as far back as 1880, and it appears that he was right to do so, since it is still used as an ingredient in many preparations today (see note 185, below).

185. Used externally it is an antiseptic and disinfectant, and is used in ointments in the treatment of chronic skin diseases such as psoriasis and eczema of a sub-acute character. It is also present in

over-the-counter topical acne treatments at 2% concentration, and in prescription treatments at higher concentrations. Weak, watery solutions of resorcinol are useful in allaying the itching in erythematous eczema. A 2% solution used as a spray has been used with marked effect in hay fever and in whooping cough. It can be included as an anti-dandruff agent in shampoo or in sunscreen cosmetics. It has also been employed in the treatment of gastric ulcers in doses of 125 to 250 mg in pills, and is said to be analgesic and haemostatic in its action. In large doses it is a poison causing giddiness, convulsions, deafness, salivation, and sweating. It is also worked up in certain medicated soaps. Resorcinol is one of the main active ingredients in products like Resinol and Vagisil.

186. Now called the Eisenhower Executive Office Building, it is located at the corner of 17th Street and Pennsylvania Avenue, N.W., just to the west of the White House. It was built in stages between 1871 and 1888, to house the Departments of State, War, and Navy. Now a National Historic Landmark, Mark Twain called it "the ugliest building in America."

187. John Reynders, president of the renowned surgical instrument firm J. Reynders & Co., an important supplier of surgical instruments to the Union Army in the Civil War.

188. The reference is to Lewin's *Textbook of Toxicology*, published two years earlier.

189. From http://en.wikipedia.org/wiki/Johns_Hopkins_Medical_ School (January 15, 2011): "Toward the end of the 19th century, American medical education was in chaos; most medical schools were little more than trade schools. Often, it was easier to gain admission to one of these than to a liberal arts college. With the opening of The Johns Hopkins Hospital in 1889, followed four years later by The Johns Hopkins University School of Medicine, Johns Hopkins ushered in a new era marked by rigid entrance requirements for medical students, a vastly upgraded medical school curriculum with emphasis on the scientific method, the incorporation of bedside teaching and laboratory research as part of the instruction, and integration of the School of Medicine with the Hospital through joint appointments." The dates given here would seem to contradict the testimony

of Lewin, who refers to ongoing experimental work already in progress at the time of his visit.

190. For the second time (see note 65), he compares an American residential neighborhood favorably to Pöseldorf, the neighborhood in Hamburg where his wife had grown up.

191. The Washington Monument in Baltimore's Mount Vernon Square neighborhood was the first monument in General Washington's honor planned after his death. This one was designed by Robert Mills, the same man who designed the Washington Monument in Washington, D.C. Construction began in 1815 and was completed in 1829. Constructed of local white marble, it rises 178 feet from its base.

192. The Centennial was to be celebrated on September 15, 16 and 17 of that year.

193. Diamond shaped licorice-flavored pastilles from Holland, still being sold and consumed today.

194. This should not have been surprising, in view of Pennsylvania's strict Sunday blue laws.

195. Still another example of Lewin's one-upmanship; when it comes to advances in his field, he is reluctant to give pride of place to the contributions of others, and especially not to an American!

196. This may have been Henry L. Davis, who 24 years later was one of the named defendants in the landmark trust-busting case under the Sherman Act, *Standard Oil Co. of New Jersey v. U.S.,* 221 U.S. 1 (1911).

197. Lewin was later to write an article about this skin condition and had it published when he returned to Germany.

198. For the grand parade that was to be held that week to commemorate the Centennial of the adoption of the Constitution.

199. The President at that time was Grover Cleveland (1837-1908), then in the third year of his first term in office. After his defeat in 1888 by Benjamin Harrison, he ran for office again in 1892 and was again elected, the only president to serve two non-consecutive terms in office.

200. Evidently the worker did not show up for the scheduled meeting and the photograph was never taken.

201. What had happened was that Lewin had inadvertently taken the room key with him, causing Uncle some uncomfortable hours.

202. See en.wikipedia.org/wiki/Victorien_Sardou (January 15, 2011).

203. The first department store in Philadelphia and one of the first in the United States. The store's origins go back to 1861, but the department store concept had its beginnings in 1876 when Wanamaker purchased what had been Philadelphia's Pennsylvania Railroad train station. Innovation and "firsts" marked Wanamaker's history: it was the first department store with electric lighting (1878), the first with a telephone (1879), the first store to install pneumatic tubes to transport cash and documents (1880), and the first store with an elevator (1884).

204. The safety elevator was invented by Elisha Otis in 1852; by 1872 over 2,000 elevators were in use in office buildings and department stores throughout America. See http://www.ideafinder.com/history/inventions/elevator.htm (January 15, 2011).

205. Lewin and Warburg were riding the Duquesne Inclined Plane, which had opened in 1877 and is still in operation. See http://incline.pghfree.net (January 15, 2011).

206. The college Lewin refers to is Washington and Jefferson College, founded by Presbyterian ministers in 1787 and still thriving today.

207. These are the eternal fires maintained by the priests at the Zoroastrian temples at Baku, on the Caspian Sea.

208. Latin for "in open view."

209. The reference is to New York's Yorkville area, centered on East 86th Street and Lexington Avenue, once an overwhelmingly German neighborhood.

210. For the hazards involved in transportation on the Great Lakes, see http://www.maritimehistoryofthegreatlakes.ca (January 15, 2011).

211. Again, they stay at one of the best hotels in the city. Rates in that era were $3.00-$4.50 day on the American plan (meals included).

212. Parke-Davis had been founded a year earlier, in 1886, by Harvey Parke and George Davis. At one time the world's largest pharmaceutical company, it is credited with building the first modern pharmaceutical laboratory and with developing the first systematic clinical trials of new medications.

213. Perhaps Mr. Wetzell and his secretary were using the Dictaphone, invented six years earlier by Alexander Graham Bell, his cousin Chichester Bell, and the scientist/instrument maker Charles Sumner Tainter. If the secretary was taking dictation, she was probably using the Pitman method, invented by Sir Isaac Pitman in 1837; the Gregg system, which largely superseded Pitman, was introduced the year after Lewin's trip, in 1888.

214. Montgomery Meigs, as a young lieutenant, supervised the reconstruction of the fort, the same Montgomery Meigs who, as a general, built the Pension Building and the aqueduct that, even today, brings drinking water to Washington, D.C.

215. This may be a reference to the magic lantern, a forerunner of the slide projector and the motion picture projector.

216. The Falls View Station was an observation area along the top of the moraine which provided the best view of the Falls. Passenger trains would stop or proceed slowly as they passed through this area to enable passengers to disembark and gaze at the Falls before continuing on their journey. It remains today a favorite place from which to see the Falls but the train tracks have been relocated and the overlook is now lined by large tourist hotels.

217. Lewin here is espousing a fundamental principle at the intersection of physics, chemistry and theology that goes back to the Neo-Platonists and St. Thomas Aquinas: that, as God is unchanging, so His creation, i.e. matter, is likewise unchanging. This fixed view of creation was demolished in the early 20th century by Einstein and other physicists, who showed that matter is indeed transformed through irradiation, laying the groundwork for atomic fission and nuclear power. One wonders if Lewin, confronted with this evidence but always reluctant to concede error, changed his position on this subject after Einstein's discoveries proved it incorrect. See, e.g., http://www.fordham.edu/halsall/mod/1855buchner.html (January 15, 2011).

218. Dionysius the Elder, ca. 432–367 BC, known as the tyrant of Syracuse. See http://en.wikipedia.org/wiki/Dionysius_I_of_Syracuse (January 15, 2011).

219. Lewin in his letter uses the now-offensive term, "N----r," and not "black" as in the text.

220. See en.wikipedia.org/wiki/Bunker_Hill_Monument (January 15, 2011).

221. Here, on one of the last days of his trip, he echoes the sentiment that he expressed on the first day of his trip: "Yet I am not self-satisfied and strive to be modest."

222. The statue, dedicated in 1856, is located in front of Old City Hall on School Street, on the site of the first public school in America.

223. "The part for the whole." The technical term in prose is synecdoche.

224. Lewin so hungers for approval that, even if it is not a fellow scientist but only the janitor who is impressed, Lewin proudly points it out to his wife.

225. He is evidently confused in his geography or place names. Springfield, Massachusetts is inland, 77 miles from the shoreline.